CIMA

OPERATIONAL

PAPER F1

FINANCIAL OPERATIONS

P
R
A
C
T
I
C
E
&
R
E
V
I
S
I
O
N
K
I
T

This Kit is for CIMA's exams in 2011.

In this edition we:

- Discuss the **best strategies** for revising and taking your F1 exam
- Show you how to be well prepared for the **2011 exams**
- Give you **lots of great guidance** on tackling questions
- Show you how you can **build your own exams**
- Provide you with **three** mock exams

BPP's **i-Pass** product also supports this paper.

FOR EXAMS IN 2011

BPP LEARNING MEDIA

First edition January 2010
Second edition January 2011

ISBN 9780 7517 9456 4
eISBN 9780 7517 8711 5
(previous ISBN 9780 7517 7521 1)

British Library Cataloguing-in-Publication Data
A catalogue record for this book
is available from the British Library

Published by

BPP Learning Media Ltd
BPP House, Aldine Place
London W12 8AA

www.bpp.com/learningmedia

Printed in the United Kingdom

Your learning materials, published by BPP
Learning Media Ltd, are printed on paper sourced
from sustainable, managed forests.

We are grateful to the Chartered Institute of
Management Accountants for permission to
reproduce past examination questions. The
answers to past examination questions have been
prepared by BPP Learning Media Ltd.

©
BPP Learning Media Ltd
2011

Contents

Question index

Questions set under the old syllabus's P7 *Financial Accounting and Tax Principles* (FATP) exam are included because their style and content are similar to those that appear in the Paper F1 exam.

Mock exam 1

Questions 52 to 55

Mock exam 2

Questions 56 to 59

Mock exam 3 (November 2010 exam)

Questions 60 to 63

Planning your question practice

Our guidance from page xiii shows you how to organise your question practice, either by attempting questions from each syllabus area or by **building your own exams** – tackling questions as a series of practice exams.

Topic index

Listed below are the key Paper F1 syllabus topics and the numbers of the questions in this Kit covering those topics.

If you need to concentrate your practice and revision on certain topics or if you want to attempt all available questions that refer to a particular subject you will find this index useful.

Using your BPP Learning Media Practice and Revision Kit

Tackling revision and the exam

You can significantly improve your chances of passing by tackling revision and the exam in the right ways. Our advice is based on feedback from CIMA. We focus on Paper F1; we discuss revising the syllabus, what to do (and what not to do) in the exam, how to approach different types of question and ways of obtaining easy marks.

Selecting questions

We provide signposts to help you plan your revision.

- A full **question index**
- A **topic index**, listing all the questions that cover key topics, so that you can locate the questions that provide practice on these topics, and see the different ways in which they might be examined
- **BPP's question plan**, highlighting the most important questions
- **Build your own exams**, showing you how you can practise questions in a series of exams

Making the most of question practice

We realise that you need more than questions and model answers to get the most from your question practice.

- Our **Top tips** provide essential advice on tackling questions and presenting answers
- We show you how you can pick up **Easy marks** on questions, as picking up all readily available marks can make the difference between passing and failing
- We include **marking guides** to show you what the examiner rewards
- We summarise **Examiner's comments** to show you how students coped with the questions
- We refer to the **BPP 2010 Study Text** for detailed coverage of the topics covered in each question

Attempting mock exams

There are three mock exams that provide practice at coping with the pressures of the exam day. We strongly recommend that you attempt them under exam conditions as they reflect the question styles and syllabus coverage of the exam. To help you get the most out of doing these exams, we provide guidance on how you should have approached the whole exam.

Our other products

BPP Learning Media also offers these products for practising and revising for the F1 exam:

Passcards	Summarising what you should know in visual, easy to remember, form
Success CDs	Covering the vital elements of the F1 syllabus in less than 90 minutes and also containing exam hints to help you fine tune your strategy
i-Pass	Providing computer-based testing in a variety of formats, ideal for self-assessment
Interactive Passcards	Allowing you to learn actively with a clear visual format summarising what you must know

You can purchase these products by visiting www.bpp.com/lm

Revising F1

This is a very wide-ranging syllabus, but with not a great deal of depth in some areas. The format of the paper allows the examiner to cover a large part of the syllabus, so you cannot afford to neglect any area.

The syllabus is made up as follows:

Principles of business tax	25%
Regulation and ethics of financial reporting	15%
Financial accounting and reporting	60%

Areas to concentrate your revision on are:

- Statements of cash flows. This topic not always examined in each paper, but as seen in the November 2010 exam, could form the basis of a 25 mark question, so you really need to know how to assemble a statement of cash flows.

- Leases and construction contracts. These are tricky subjects. However the questions you get on them are likely to be of a standard format. So if you practice the questions in this Kit and learn how to do the basics, you should be able to pick up at least some of the marks for questions on these topics in the exam.

- Non-current assets. You will almost always have to calculate depreciation on property, plant and equipment, and probably also deal with a revaluation. This is not a difficult topic. Make sure you practice plenty of questions so you can gain as many of the easy marks as possible in the exam.

- Taxation and deferred tax – remember that tax makes up 25% of the syllabus. Do not neglect this area. International tax and VAT appear to be favourite subjects for the examiner to test.

- The IASB *Framework*. Defining the qualitative characteristics contained in the *Framework* is a popular question. This is just rote learning so make sure you take the time to learn here.

- Single company statement of comprehensive income and statement of financial position. You must know the correct IAS 1 formats. This topic is highly examinable and has formed the basis of a Section C question in all the new syllabus exam papers. Make sure you can draw up the proformas from memory very quickly, this will help you to tackle these questions.

- Consolidated financial statements. You need to be able to calculate goodwill and put together consolidated statements of comprehensive income and consolidated statements of financial position, including equity accounting for an associate. Unrealised profit on intra-group trading is also likely to feature in consolidation questions, learn how to deal with this adjustment. You also need to understand how to classify investments, whether as subsidiaries, associates or trade investments.

Question practice

You should use the Passcards and any brief notes you have to revise these topics, but you mustn't spend all your revision time passively reading. **Question practice is vital**. Doing as many questions as you can in full will help develop your ability to analyse scenarios and produce relevant discussion and recommendations. The question plan on page xiv tells you what questions cover so that you can choose questions covering a variety of topics.

Passing the F1 exam

Displaying the right qualities

The examiners will expect you to display the following qualities.

Qualities required	
Produce neat workings and readable answers	If you produce no workings, the marker can give you no credit for using the right method. If the marker cannot read what you have written they can give you no marks at all.
Carry out standard calculations	You must be able to deal with simple tax and financial instrument calculations.
Demonstrate understanding of the basics	Deferred tax and construction contracts can be complex, but you will only get fairly simple questions, so make sure you understand the principles.

Avoiding weaknesses

The examiners have identified weaknesses that occur in many students' answers at every sitting. You will enhance your chances significantly if you ensure you avoid these mistakes:

- Failing to provide what the question verbs require (discussion, evaluation, recommendations) or to write about the topics specified in the question requirements
- Inability to carry out calculations
- Not showing workings in 3-4 mark questions
- Repeating the same material in different parts of answers
- Regurgitation of definitions and lists with no application to the question
- Brain dumping all that is known about a topic (no credit is given for this)
- Failing to answer sufficient questions because of poor time management
- Not answering all parts of questions
- Not using the information provided in the question accurately
- Attempting to question spot

Using the reading time

Use the reading time to analyse the adjustments needed in the Section C questions and go over the requirements of the Section B questions deciding which parts to answer first.

Tackling questions

Numerical questions

Expect to see numbers throughout the paper. Approach them methodically and show all workings clearly.

Discussion questions

Remember that **depth of discussion** is also important. Discussions will often consist of paragraphs containing 2-3 sentences. Each paragraph should:

- **Make a point**
- **Explain the point** (you must demonstrate **why** the point is important)
- **Illustrate the point** (with material or analysis from the scenario, perhaps an example from real-life)

Gaining the easy marks

The first few marks are always the easiest to gain in any question. This applies particularly to Section B. Spend the same amount of time on each Section B question. This will give you a good chance of scoring marks on each question. Your Section C questions carry a lot of marks. Make sure you begin by getting down the format and filling in any numbers which don't require calculation.

The exam paper

Format of the paper

		Number of marks
Section A:	Around 7-10 multiple choice and other objective test questions, 2-4 marks each	20
Section B:	6 compulsory questions, 5 marks each	30
Section C:	2 compulsory questions, totalling 50 marks	50
		100

Time allowed: 3 hours plus 20 minutes reading time.

Section A will always contain some multiple choice questions but will not consist solely of multiple choice questions. For 3 or 4-mark questions, marks are given for correct workings.

Section B questions will be mainly written discussion, although some calculations may be included. This section will require breadth of syllabus knowledge and also good time management skills.

The **Section C** questions will cover statements of comprehensive income, statements of financial position, statements of cash flows for a single company and simple consolidated statement of comprehensive income and statement of financial position.

November 2010 (Mock exam 3)

Section A

1   Interaction of corporate and personal tax, employee tax, formal incidence of VAT, administration of tax, calculating VAT, audit opinions, treasury shares, IASB's *Framework*, related parties, IFRS 8 *Operating segments.*

Section B

2a   Relieving trading losses (company income tax)
2b   Withholding tax, including calculation of double tax relief
2c   *Framework*: qualitative characteristics
2d   Group accounts: calculation of goodwill and IFRS 3
2e   Group accounts: classification of investments
2f   Provisions, events after the reporting period

Section C

3   Financial statements preparation for a single entity, including an income tax computation and deferred tax.
4   Preparation of a statement of cash flows for a single company, ethical considerations.

May 2010

Section A

1   Ideal tax principles, tax rate structures, deferred tax, IASB's *Framework*, qualitative characteristics, revenue recognition, development expenditure, finance leases, discontinued operations, cash flows.

Section B

2a	Tax evasion and tax avoidance
2b	Indirect taxes
2c	International tax
2d	External audit and audit reports
2e	Construction contracts
2f	Discontinued operations, restructuring provisions, CIMA's Code of Ethics

Section C

3   Financial statements preparation for a single entity, including a share issue, operating lease and revaluation of property, plant and equipment.

4   Preparation of consolidated statement of financial position and consolidated statement of comprehensive income, calculation of income tax and deferred tax for the group.

Specimen exam paper

Section A

1   Tax avoidance and evasion, calculating income tax, VAT, systems of taxing corporate income, IASB Framework, CIMA Code of Ethics, external audit, IFRS 3, inventories, related parties.

Section B

2a	Tax residency
2b	VAT explanation and calculation
2c	Principles vs. rules based accounting standards
2d	Discontinued operations
2e	Accounting treatment of leases
2f	Accounting treatment of preference shares

Section C

3   Financial statements preparation for a single entity, including deferred tax calculation.

4   Preparation of consolidated statement of financial position, including the treatment of an associate in group accounts.

What the examiner means

The table below has been prepared by CIMA to help you interpret exam questions.

Learning objective	Verbs used	Definition
1 Knowledge		
What you are expected to know	• List	• Make a list of
	• State	• Express, fully or clearly, the details of/facts of
	• Define	• Give the exact meaning of
2 Comprehension		
What you are expected to understand	• Describe	• Communicate the key features of
	• Distinguish	• Highlight the differences between
	• Explain	• Make clear or intelligible/state the meaning or purpose of
	• Identify	• Recognise, establish or select after consideration
	• Illustrate	• Use an example to describe or explain something
3 Application		
How you are expected to apply your knowledge	• Apply	• Put to practical use
	• Calculate/compute	• Ascertain or reckon mathematically
	• Demonstrate	• Prove the certainty or exhibit by practical means
	• Prepare	• Make or get ready for use
	• Reconcile	• Make or prove consistent/compatible
	• Solve	• Find an answer to
	• Tabulate	• Arrange in a table
4 Analysis		
How you are expected to analyse the detail of what you have learned	• Analyse	• Examine in detail the structure of
	• Categorise	• Place into a defined class or division
	• Compare and contrast	• Show the similarities and/or differences between
	• Construct	• Build up or complete
	• Discuss	• Examine in detail by argument
	• Interpret	• Translate into intelligible or familiar terms
	• Prioritise	• Place in order of priority or sequence for action
	• Produce	• Create or bring into existence
5 Evaluation		
How you are expected to use your learning to evaluate, make decisions or recommendations	• Advise	• Counsel, inform or notify
	• Evaluate	• Appraise or assess the value of
	• Recommend	• Propose a course of action

Planning your question practice

We have already stressed that question practice should be right at the centre of your revision. Whilst you will spend some time looking at your notes and the Paper F1 Passcards, you should spend the majority of your revision time practising questions.

We recommend two ways in which you can practise questions.

- Use **BPP Learning Media's question plan** to work systematically through the syllabus and attempt key and other questions on a section-by-section basis

- **Build your own exams** – attempt the questions as a series of practice exams

These ways are suggestions and simply following them is no guarantee of success. You or your college may prefer an alternative but equally valid approach.

BPP's question plan

The plan below requires you to devote a **minimum of 40 hours** to revision of Paper F1. Any time you can spend over and above this should only increase your chances of success.

 Review your notes and the chapter summaries in the Paper F1 **Passcards** for each section of the syllabus.

 Answer the key questions for that section. These questions have boxes round the question number in the table below and you should answer them in full. Even if you are short of time you must attempt these questions if you want to pass the exam. You should complete your answers without referring to our solutions.

 Attempt the other questions in that section. For some questions we have suggested that you prepare **answer plans or do the calculations** rather than full solutions. Planning an answer means that you should spend about 40% of the time allowance for the questions brainstorming the question and drawing up a list of points to be included in the answer.

 Attempt Mock exams 1, 2 and 3 under strict exam conditions.

Syllabus section	2010 Passcards chapters	Questions in this Kit	Comments	Done ☑
The regulatory framework	1	1, 4	The MCQs are fairly simple here. The Section B questions invite you to spend a lot of time, so *don't do it* – practise answering these question with notes and bullet points.	☐
External audit and ethics	2, 3	2, 3 5, 6	Make sure you know the different types of audit report qualification and be very strict and to the point on the Section B questions.	☐
Financial accounts – presentation	4,5	7-8	This area is very important – IAS 1 and IAS 8. Do all of the MCQs. Make sure you can write out the formats.	☐
Statements of cash flows	9	9, 10	These are good revision for the various components of the statement, so do them before attempting the longer questions.	☐
Statements of cash flows	9	11-16	These are Section C questions on statements of cash flows. This is not a difficult topic. Do all of these questions and make sure you can produce *net cash flow from operating activities* using both methods.	☐
Non-current assets, inventories and construction contracts	6, 7, 11	17–20	These are fairly complex topics. If you have trouble with the MCQs, go back to the Study Text and revise the area.	☐
Capital transactions and financial instruments	12	21	These MCQs cover most of the important issues in this area. Make sure you understand how to deal with redemption of capital and purchase of own shares.	☐
Accounting standards	8, 10	22-25	These questions cover IAS 10, IAS 24, IAS 37 and IAS 17. These are all important because they are relatively *easy* to learn and apply, so if they come up they will be easy marks. Make sure you can calculate finance lease interest payments using both methods.	☐
Financial statements	4, 5	26-34	Section C will have an accounts preparation question, so practice on these. Make sure you can do all of them.	☐
Group financial statements	13, 14, 15, 16	34-40	This is a new topic at this level so it needs a lot of practice. Do all of these questions.	
General principles of taxation	17, 18	41-43	Answer all of these MCQs. There will be more than one question on each topic, so you will get lots of practice.	☐
		45, 46	These are Section B-type questions. Make sure you do not spend more than 9 minutes on each.	☐
Company taxation	19	43-44	Answer all of these MCQs. Make sure you really understand the adjustments necessary to get from accounting profit to taxable profit and can do it easily.	☐
		47	These are Section B questions on company tax. Deferred tax is the most difficult aspect. Just make sure you understand the basics.	☐

Build your own exams

Having revised your notes and the BPP Passcards, you can attempt the questions in the Kit as a series of practice exams. You can organise the questions in the following way:

	Marks
7-10 objective test questions	20
6 Section B questions	30
2 Section C questions	50
	100

The easiest way to do this is to do one of the two mixed banks of Section A questions (either question 48 or 49) plus one of the mixed banks of Section B questions (either question 50 or 51) and then for Section C, do one of the following: 12, 13, 14, 15, 16, 26, 27, 28, 29, 30, 31, 32, 33, 34 and one of 35, 36, 37, 38, 39, 40.

Once you have completed the mixed banks you can make your own Section A and Section B as follows.

For Section A of your exam, select from each of these banks to a total of 20 marks. If you do a 3 or 4-mark question, reduce the number of questions accordingly.

For Section B, do 6 sub-questions from the following questions – 4, 5, 6, 8, 10, 19, 24, 25, 45, 46, 47. Make sure you do at least one question from Part A, one from Part B, one from Part C and one from Part D – see the Question and Answer Checklist.

Also make sure you do the three mock exams.

QUESTIONS

2

Part A: Regulation and Ethics of Financial Reporting

Questions 1 to 6 cover Regulation and Ethics of Financial Reporting, the subject of Part A of the BPP Study Text for F1.

1 Objective test questions: The regulatory framework   70 mins

1 Guidance on the application and interpretation of International Financial Reporting Standards is provided by:

A The IASB
B The IASC Foundation
C The IFRIC
D The Standards Advisory Council   **(2 marks)**

2 Which of the following is *not* an advantage of global harmonisation of accounting standards?

A Priority given to different user groups in different countries
B Easier transfer of accounting staff across national borders
C Ability to comply with the requirements of overseas stock exchanges
D Better access to foreign investor funds   **(2 marks)**

3 The IASB has recently revised and improved a number of standards. One of the major purposes of these revisions has been:

A To make the standards more relevant to developing countries
B To eliminate alternative treatments of items in accounts
C To give preparers of accounts more choice
D To comply with the demands of pressure groups   **(2 marks)**

4 The International Accounting Standards Board's *Framework for the Preparation and Presentation of Financial Statements* defines five elements of financial statements. Three of the elements are asset, liability and income.

List the other TWO elements.   **(2 marks)**

5 Which two of the following, per the *Framework*, are *underlying assumptions* relating to financial statements?

1 The accounts have been prepared on an accruals basis
2 Users are assumed to have sufficient knowledge to be able to understand the financial statements
3 The accounting policies used have been disclosed
4 The business is expected to continue in operation for the foreseeable future
5 The information is free from material error or bias

A 1 and 3
B 2 and 3
C 1 and 4
D 3 and 5   **(2 marks)**

6 Which two of the following are not elements of financial statements per the *Framework*?

1 Profits
2 Assets
3 Income
4 Equity
5 Losses
6 Expenses

A	2 and 4	
B	1 and 5	
C	3 and 4	
D	5 and 6	**(2 marks)**

7   According to the *Framework*, the income statement measures:

A	Financial position
B	Performance
C	Profitability
D	Financial adaptability

(2 marks)

8   Which two of the following are underlying assumptions in the International Accounting Standards Board's *Framework for the Preparation and Presentation of Financial Statements*?

1   Accruals
2   Relevance
3   Comparability
4   Going concern
5   Reliability

A	1 and 5
B	2 and 5
C	3 and 4
D	1 and 4

(2 marks)

9   The International Accounting Standards Board's *Framework for the Preparation and Presentation of Financial Statements* defines elements of financial statements. In no more than 30 words define an asset.

(2 marks)

10   The term GAAP is used to mean

A	Generally accepted accounting procedures
B	General accounting and audit practice
C	Generally agreed accounting practice
D	Generally accepted accounting practice

(2 marks)

11   Which one of the following is responsible for governance and fundraising in relation to the development of International Accounting Standards?

A	International Accounting Standards Board
B	International Financial Reporting Interpretations Committee
C	International Accounting Standards Committee Foundation Trustees
D	Standards Advisory Council

(2 marks)

12   The setting of International Accounting Standards is carried out by co-operation between a number of committees and boards, which include:

1   International Accounting Standards Committee Foundation (IASC Foundation)
2   Standards Advisory Council (SAC)
3   International Financial Reporting Interpretations Committee (IFRIC)

Which of the above reports to, or advises, the International Accounting Standards Board (IASB)?

	Reports to:	Advises:
A	1 and 3	2
B	1 and 2	3
C	3	2
D	2	1

(2 marks)

13   The IASB's Framework for the Preparation and Presentation of Financial Statements provides definitions of the elements of financial statements. One of the elements defined by the Framework is 'expenses'.

In no more than **35** words, give the IASB Framework's definition of expenses.

(2 marks)

14   According to the International Accounting Standards Board's (IASB) *Framework for the Preparation and Presentation of Financial Statements* (Framework), what is the objective of financial statements?

Write your answer in nor more than **35** words.   **(2 marks)**

15   Financial statements prepared using International Standards and the International Accounting Standards Board's (IASB *Framework for the Preparation and Presentation of Financial Statements* (Framework) are presumed to apply two of the following four underlying assumptions

1   Relevance
2   Going concern
3   Prudence
4   Accruals

Which two of the above are underlying assumptions according to the IASB's *Framework*?

A   1 and 2 only
B   2 and 3 only
C   3 and 4 only
D   2 and 4 only   **(2 marks)**

16   Which of the following are functions of the International Accounting Standards Committee Foundation?

1   Issuing International Accounting Standards

2   Approving the annual budget of the International Accounting Standards Committee (IASC) and its committees

3   Enforcing International Accounting Standards

4   Reviewing the strategy of the IASC

5   Publishing an annual report on the activities of the IASC and IASB

A   1, 2 and 5
B   2 and 4
C   1, 3 and 5
D   2, 4 and 5   **(2 marks)**

17   The International Accounting Standards Board's (IASB) *Framework for the Preparation and Presentation of Financial Statements* (Framework), sets out four qualitative characteristics of financial information.

Two of the characteristics are relevance and comparability. List the other TWO characteristics. **(2 marks)**

18   State the TWO underlying assumptions outlined in the International Accounting Standard Board's (IASB) *Framework for the Preparation and Presentation of Financial Statements*.   **(2 marks)**

19   The process leading to the publication of an International Financial Reporting Standard (IFRS) has a number of stages.

List the FOUR stages normally involved in developing an IFRS.   **(3 marks)**

(Total = 39 marks)

2   Objective test questions: External audit   52 mins

1   An external audit:

A   Guarantees that the financial statements are free from misstatements.
B   Provides reasonable assurance that the financial statements are free from misstatements.
C   Guarantees that the financial statements are free from material misstatements.
D   Provides reasonable assurance that the financial statements are free from material misstatements.

(2 marks)

2   An external auditor gives a qualified audit report that is a 'disclaimer of opinion'.

This means that the auditor

A   Has been unable to agree with an accounting treatment used by the directors in relation to a material item.

B   Has been prevented from obtaining sufficient appropriate audit evidence.

C   Has found extensive errors in the financial statements and concludes that they do not show a true and fair view.

D   Has discovered a few immaterial differences that do not affect the auditor's opinion.   **(2 marks)**

3   There is a major uncertainty facing Z, a limited liability company. Actions are pending against the company for allegedly supplying faulty goods, causing widespread damage.

The directors have fully described the circumstances of the case in a note to the financial statements.

What form of audit report is appropriate in this case?

A   Qualified opinion – limitation on auditors' work
B   Disclaimer of opinion
C   Unqualified report with an additional explanatory paragraph
D   Qualified opinion – disagreement   **(2 marks)**

4   Which of the following matters are normally covered by the auditors' report?

1   Whether the company has kept proper accounting records

2   Whether the accounts are in agreement with the accounting records

3   Whether the accounts have been prepared in accordance with the relevant legislation and accounting standards

4   Whether other information presented with the financial statements is consistent with them

A   1 and 2 only
B   1, 2 and 3 only
C   3 and 4 only
D   All four matters are normally covered   **(2 marks)**

5   A company's auditors find insufficient evidence to substantiate the company's cash sales, which are material in amount.

What form of qualification of the audit report would normally be appropriate in this situation?

A   Qualified opinion – disagreement
B   Qualified opinion – limitation on auditors' work
C   Disclaimer of opinion
D   Qualified opinion – adverse opinion   **(2 marks)**

6   A company's accounting records were largely destroyed by fire shortly after the year end. As a result, the financial statements contain a number of figures based on estimates.

What form of qualification of the audit report would be appropriate in this situation?

A   Qualified opinion – disagreement
B   Qualified opinion – limitations on auditors' work
C   Disclaimer of opinion
D   Qualified opinion – adverse opinion   **(2 marks)**

7   Who is responsible for the preparation and fair presentation of financial statements of a company?

A   External auditors of the company
B   The finance department of the company
C   Management of the company
D   External auditors and Management are jointly responsible   **(2 marks)**

8   When carrying out an audit an external auditor must satisfy himself of a number of matters. Which of the following are not one of those matters?

      A   The accounts have been prepared by a qualified accountant

      B   Proper accounting records have been kept

      C   The accounts have been prepared in accordance with local legislation and relevant accounting standards

      D   The accounts are in agreement with accounting records   **(2 marks)**

---

9   If an external auditor does not agree with the directors' treatment of a material item in the accounts, the first action they should take is to:

      A   Give a qualified opinion of the financial statements

      B   Give an unqualified opinion of the financial statements

      C   Force the directors to change the treatment of the item in the accounts

      D   Persuade the directors to change the treatment of the item in the accounts   **(2 marks)**

---

10   The external auditor has a duty to report on the truth and fairness of the financial statements and to report any reservations. The auditor is normally given a number of powers by statute to enable the statutory duties to be carried out.

      List three powers that are usually granted to the auditor by statute.   **(3 marks)**

---

11   Which one of the powers listed below is unlikely to be granted to the auditor by legislation?

      A   The right access at all times to the books, records, documents and accounts of the entity

      B   The right to be notified of, attend and speak at meetings of equity holders

      C   The right to correct financial statements if the auditor believes the statements do not show a true and fair view

      D   The right to require officers of the entity to provide whatever information and explanations thought necessary for the performance of the duties of the auditor   **(2 marks)**

---

12   Which of the following is the most appropriate definition of an external audit?

      A   An external audit is an exercise carried out by auditors in order to give an opinion on whether the financial statements of a company are true and fair.

      B   An external audit is an exercise carried out by auditors in order to give assurance to shareholders on the effectiveness and efficiency of management.

      C   An external audit is performed by management to identify areas of deficiency within a company and to make recommendations to mitigate those deficiencies.

      D   The external audit is an exercise performed by auditors to provide assurance that the company will continue to operate in the future.   **(2 marks)**

---

13   The external auditors have completed the audit of GQ for the year ended 30 June 2008 and have several outstanding differences of opinion that they have been unable to resolve with the management of GQ. The senior partner of the external auditors has reviewed these outstanding differences and concluded that individually and in aggregate the differences are not material.

      Which ONE of the following audit opinions will the external auditors use for GQ's financial statements for the year ended 30 June 2008?

      A   An unqualified opinion

      B   An adverse opinion

      C   An emphasis of matter

      D   A qualified opinion   **(2 marks)**

---

14   In no more than 25 words, state the objective of an external audit.   **(2 marks)**

                                                       (Total = 29 marks)

3 Objective test questions: Ethics
40 mins

1   A professional accountant in business may be involved in a wide variety of work. Which of these functions will he **not** be carrying out?

     A   Preparing financial statements
     B   Auditing financial statements
     C   Preparing budgets and forecasts
     D   Preparing the management letter provided to the auditors   **(2 marks)**

2   A professional accountant is required under the CIMA Code to comply with five fundamental principles. These include:

     A   Integrity, Objectivity, Reliability
     B   Professional competence and due care, Confidentiality, Integrity
     C   Morality, Objectivity, Professional behaviour
     D   Efficiency, Confidentiality, Professional competence and due care   **(2 marks)**

3   A qualified accountant holds a number of shares in his employing company, and has become eligible for a profit-related bonus for the first time. What type of threat could this represent to his objectivity when preparing the company's financial statements?

     A   Self-interest
     B   Self-review
     C   Intimidation
     D   Familiarity   **(2 marks)**

4   Three of the following are recognised advantages of a principles based approach to ethical codes. Which is the exception?

     A   Encourages proactive discussion of issues
     B   Encourages consistent application of rules
     C   Suits complex situations and evolving environments
     D   Encourages professional development   **(2 marks)**

5   While out to lunch, you run into a client at the sandwich bar. In conversation, she tells you that she expects to inherit from a recently deceased uncle, and asks you how she will be affected by inheritance tax, capital gains tax and other matters – which you have not dealt with, in detail, for some years.

     Which of the following principles of the CIMA Code of Ethics is raised by this scenario?

     A   Professional competence and due care
     B   Integrity
     C   Professional behaviour
     D   Confidentiality   **(2 marks)**

6   While at a party at the weekend, you meet a client of yours who is clearly very concerned about some VAT issues. You know enough about VAT to carry out your daily work, but you are not an expert on the areas of imports and exports on which your client is asking your opinion.

     What ethical issue does this situation raise?

     A   Objectivity
     B   Professional competence and due care
     C   Professional behaviour
     D   Confidentiality   **(2 marks)**

7   The CIMA Code of Ethics for Professional Accountants sets out five principles that a professional accountant is required to comply with. Three of these principles are professional behaviour, integrity and objectivity. List the other two.   **(2 marks)**

8   Which of the following is an advantage of a principles-based ethical code?

    A   It can easily be legally enforced.

    B   It provides rules to be followed in all circumstances

    C   It encourages compliance by requiring a professional person to actively consider the issues.

    D   It can be narrowly interpreted, making it easy for the professional to see whether or not the Code has been violated.   **(2 marks)**

9   What is meant by the fundamental principle of 'professional behaviour'?

    A   Compliance with relevant laws and regulations and avoidance of any action that discredits the profession

    B   Being straightforward and honest in all professional and business relationships

    C   Not allowing professional judgement to be affected by bias, undue influence or business considerations

    D   Maintaining a high level of technical expertise through continuing professional development   **(2 marks)**

10   Which of the following is **not** a circumstance where disclosure of confidential information is permitted under the CIMA Code?

    A   Disclosure of information when authorised by the client

    B   Disclosure of information to advance the interests of a new client

    C   Disclosure of information to protect the professional interests of an accountant in a legal action

    D   Disclosure of information when required by law   **(2 marks)**

11   Which of these is **not** a source of ethical codes for accountants?

    A   IFAC

    B   CIMA

    C   APB

    D   HMRC   **(2 marks)**

Total = 22 marks

4   Section B questions: Regulation   45 mins

(a)   The International Accounting Standards Board (IASB) *Framework for the Preparation and Presentation of Financial Statements (Framework)* defines the elements of financial statements.

    Required

    Explain each of the elements, illustrating each with an example.   **(5 marks)**

    P7 5/08

(b)   The IASB's *Framework* identifies four principal qualitative characteristics of financial information.

    Required

    Identify and explain each of the four principal qualitative characteristics of financial information listed in the IASB's *Framework*.   **(5 marks)**

    P7 11/05

(c)   C is a small developing country which passed legislation to create a recognised professional accounting body two years ago. At the same time as the accounting body was created, new regulations governing financial reporting requirements of entities were passed. However, there are currently no accounting standards in C.

C's government has asked the new professional accounting body to prepare a report setting out the country's options for developing and implementing a set of high quality local accounting standards. The government request also referred to the work of the IASB and its International Financial Reporting Standards.

Required

As an advisor to the professional accounting body, outline three options open to C for the development of a set of high quality local accounting standards. Identify one advantage and one disadvantage of each option. **(5 marks)**

`P7 5/06`

(d) *The Framework for the Preparation and presentation of Financial Statements* (Framework) was first published in 1989 and was adopted by The International Accounting Standards Board (IASB)

Explain the purposes of the *Framework*. **(5 marks)**

`P7 5/07`

(e) EK publishes various types of book and occasionally produces films which it sells to major film distributors.

(i) On 31 March 20X7, EK acquired book publishing and film rights to the next book to be written by an internationally acclaimed author, for $1 million. The author has not yet started writing the book but expects to complete it in 20X9.

(ii) Between 1 June and 31 July 20X7, EK spent $500,000 exhibiting its range of products at a major international trade fair. This was the first time EK had attended this type of event. No new orders were taken as a direct result of the event, although EK directors claim to have made valuable contacts that should generate additional sales or additional funding for films in the future. No estimate can be made of additional revenue at present.

(iii) During the year, EK employed an external consultant to redesign EK's corporate logo and to create advertising material to improve EK's corporate image. The total cost of the consultancy was $800,000.

EK's directors want to treat all of the above items of expenditure as assets.

Required

Explain how EK should treat these items of expenditure in its financial statements for the year ended 31 October 20X7 with reference to the International Accounting Standard Board's (IASB) *Framework for the Preparation and Presentation of Financial Statements (Framework)* and relevant International Financial Reporting Standards. **(5 marks)**

`P7 5/08`

(Total = 25 marks)

5 Section B questions: External audit   36 mins

(a) Selected balances in HF's financial records at 30 April 20X9 were as follows:

	$000
Revenue	15,000
Profit	1,500
Property, plant and equipment – net book value	23,000
Inventory	1,500

After completing the required audit work the external auditors of HF had the following observations:

(1) Inventory with a book value of $500 is obsolete and should be written off.

(2) Development expenditure net book value of $600,000, relating to the development of a new product line, has been capitalised and amortised in previous years but the project has now been abandoned, (after 30 April X9).

(3) Decommissioning costs relating to HF's production facilities, estimated to be $5,000,000 in 17 years time is being provided for, over 20 years, at $250,000 a year.

Assume there are no other material matters outstanding.

As external auditor you have just completed a meeting with HF management. At the meeting HF management decided the following:

- Item (1) is not material, so it is not necessary to write off the obsolete inventory.
- Item (2) the development expenditure should be written off against current year profits.
- Item (3) the decommissioning cost will continue to be provided for over 20 years.

Required

(i) Explain whether or not the management's decisions taken in the meeting are correct for items (1) and (2). **(2 marks)**

(ii) Explain whether you agree with the management's treatment of the decommissioning costs in item (3) and explain the type of audit report that should be issued, giving your reasons. **(3 marks)**

(Total = 5 marks)

`P7 5/09`

(b) Explain the circumstances in which an audit report will express each of the following:

(i) A qualified opinion
(ii) A disclaimer of opinion
(iii) An adverse opinion **(5 marks)**

(c) An auditor, in carrying out his statutory duty, may sometimes find himself to be in conflict with the directors of the company. What statutory rights does he have to assist him in discharging his responsibility to the shareholders? **(5 marks)**

(d) DC is carrying out three different construction contracts. The balances and results for the year to 30 September 2006 were as follows:

Contract	1	2	3
Contract end date	30 Sept 2013	31 Dec 2010	30 Sept 2010
	$m	$m	$m
Profit/(loss) recognised for year	2	2.3	(0.6)
Expected total profit/(loss) on contract	12	5.0	(3.0)

DC's management have included $3.7m profit in the profit for the year ended 30 September 2006.

No allowance has been made in the income statement for the future loss expected to arise on contract 3, as management consider the loss should be offset against the expected profits on the other two contracts.

EA & Co are DC's external auditors. EA & Co consider that the profit in relation to long term contracts for the year ended 30 September 2006 should be $1.3m, according to IAS 11 *Construction Contracts*. Assume that EA & Co have been unable to persuade DC's management to change their treatment of the long term contract profit/loss.

Required

(i) Explain the objective of an external audit.

(ii) Identify, with reasons, the type of audit report that would be appropriate for EA & Co to use for DC's financial statements for the year ended 30 September 2006. Briefly explain what information should be included in the audit report in relation to the contracts.

Your answer should refer to appropriate International Standards on Auditing (ISA). **(5 marks)**

`P7 11/06`

(Total = 20 marks)

6   Section B questions: Ethics   27 mins

  (a)   The CIMA Code of Ethics sets out fundamental principles and a conceptual framework for applying them. How does this approach work and how does it differ from a rules-based system?   **(5 marks)**

  (b)   The CIMA Code of Ethics sets out five fundamental principles. List and briefly explain each of these principles.   **(5 marks)**

  (c)   The CIMA Code of Ethics is principles based. Describe the advantages and disadvantages of a principles-based ethical code.   **(5 marks)**

                                                 (Total = 15 marks)

Part B: Single Company Financial Accounts

Questions 7 to 33 cover Single Company Financial Accounts, the subject of Part B of the BPP Study Text for F1.

7 Objective test questions: Presentation — 43 mins

1 Which, if any, of the following statements about limited liability companies are correct, according to IAS 1 (revised)?

   1   Companies must produce their financial statements within one year after their reporting period.

   2   The accounting policies adopted by a company must be disclosed by note.

   3   The accounting records of a limited liability company must be open to inspection by a member of the company at all times.

   A   2 only
   B   2 and 3 only
   C   1 and 3 only
   D   None of the statements is correct   **(2 marks)**

2 Which of the following items can appear in a company's statement of changes in equity, according to IAS 1 (revised) *Presentation of financial statements?*

   1   Total comprehensive income for the period
   2   Dividends paid
   3   Surplus on revaluation of properties
   4   Proceeds of issuance of share capital

   A   All four items
   B   1, 2 and 3 only
   C   1, 3 and 4 only
   D   2 and 4 only   **(2 marks)**

3 Which of the following items are required by IAS 1 (revised) *Presentation of financial statements* to be disclosed in the financial statements of a limited liability company?

   1   Authorised share capital
   2   Finance costs
   3   Staff costs
   4   Depreciation

   A   1 and 4 only
   B   1 , 2 and 3 only
   C   2, 3 and 4 only
   D   All four items   **(2 marks)**

4 Which of the following constitute a change of accounting policy according to IAS 8 *Accounting policies, changes in accounting estimates and errors?*

   1   A change in the basis of valuing inventory

   2   A change in depreciation method

   3   Depreciation that was previously treated as part of cost of sales is now shown under administrative expenses

   4   Adopting an accounting policy for a new type of transaction not previously dealt with

   A   1 and 2
   B   2 and 3
   C   1 and 3
   D   2 and 4   **(2 marks)**

5   Which of the following items would qualify for treatment as a change in accounting estimate, according to IAS 8 (revised) *Accounting policies, changes in accounting estimates and errors?*

1   Provision for obsolescence of inventory
2   Correction necessitated by a material error
3   A change as a result of the adoption of a new International Accounting Standard
4   A change in the useful life of a non-current asset

A   All four items
B   2 and 3 only
C   1 and 3 only
D   1 and 4 only   **(2 marks)**

6   A change in accounting policy is accounted for by:

A   Changing the current year figures but not previous year's figures
B   Retrospective application
C   No alteration of any figures but disclosure in the notes
D   No alteration of any figures nor disclosure in the notes   **(2 marks)**

7   Which one of the following would be regarded as a change of accounting policy under IAS 8 *Accounting policies, changes in accounting estimates and errors?*

A   An entity changes its method of depreciation of machinery from straight line to reducing balance.

B   An entity has changed its method of valuing inventory from FIFO to weighted average.

C   An entity changes its method of calculating the provision for warranty claims on its products sold.

D   An entity disclosed a contingent liability for a legal claim in the previous year's accounts. In the current year, a provision has been made for the same legal claim.   **(2 marks)**

8   Shah changes the depreciation method for its motor vehicles from the straight line method to the reducing balance method. How would this be treated in the financial statements?

A   Changing the current year figures but not previous year's figures
B   Retrospective application
C   No alteration of any figures but disclosure in the notes
D   No alteration of any figures nor disclosure in the notes   **(2 marks)**

9   IAS 8 – *Accounting Policies, Changes in Accounting Estimates and Errors* specifies the definition and treatment of a number of different items. Which of the following is NOT specified by IAS 8?

A   The effect of a change in an accounting estimate
B   Prior period adjustments
C   Provisions
D   Errors   **(2 marks)**

10   IAS 1 (revised) *Presentation of financial statements* requires some items to be disclosed on the face of the financial statements and others to be disclosed in the notes.

1   Depreciation
2   Revenue
3   Closing inventory
4   Finance cost
5   Dividends

Which two of the above have to be shown on the face of the statement of comprehensive income, rather than in the notes:

A   1 and 4
B   3 and 5
C   2 and 3
D   2 and 4   **(2 marks)**

11 IAS 1 (revised) *Presentation of Financial Statements* encourages an analysis of expenses to be presented on the face of the statement of comprehensive income. The analysis of expenses must use a classification based on either the nature of expense, or its function, within the entity such as:

1   Raw materials and consumables used;
2   Distribution costs;
3   Employee benefit costs;
4   Cost of sales;
5   Depreciation and amortisation expense.

Which of the above would be disclosed on the face of the statement of comprehensive income if a manufacturing entity uses analysis based on function?

A   1, 3 and 4
B   2 and 4
C   1 and 5
D   2, 3 and 5   **(2 marks)**

12 Which one of the following would be regarded as a chance of accounting estimate according to IAS 8 *Accounting policies, changes in accounting estimates and errors*?

A   An entity started valuing inventory using the weighted average cost basis. Inventory was previously valued on the FIFO basis.
B   An entity started revaluing its properties, as allowed by IAS 16 *Property, plant and equipment*. Previously, all property, plant and equipment had been carried at cost less accumulated depreciation.
C   A material error in the inventory valuation methods caused the closing inventory at 31 March 2008 to be overstated by $900,000.
D   An entity created a provision for claims under its warranty of products sold during the year. 5% of sales revenue had previously been set as the required provision amount. After an analysis of three years sales and warranty claims the calculation of the provision amount has been changed to a more realistic 2% of sales.

(2 marks)

(Total = 24 marks)

8 Section B questions: Presentation   18 mins

(a) Suggest reasons why companies should be expected to publish accounts using standard formats saying why and to whom the specific information shown in the formats would be useful.   **(5 marks)**

(b) The following is an extract from the trial balance of CE at 31 March 20X6:

	$'000	$'000
Administration expenses	260	
Cost of sales	480	
Interest paid	190	
Interest bearing borrowings		2,200
Inventory at 31 March 20X6	220	
Property, plant and equipment at cost	1,500	
Property, plant and equipment, depreciation to 31 March 20X5		540
Distribution costs	200	
Revenue		2,000

Notes:

(i)   Included in the closing inventory at the year end was inventory at a cost of $35,000, which was sold during April 20X6 for $19,000.

(ii) Depreciation is provided for on property, plant and equipment at 20% per year using the reducing balance method. Depreciation is regarded as cost of sales.

(iii)   A member of the public was seriously injured while using one of CE's products on 4 October 20X5. Professional legal advice is that CE will probably have to pay $500,000 compensation.

Required

Prepare CE's statement of comprehensive income for the year ended 31 March 20X6 down to the line 'profit before tax'. **(5 marks)**

P7 5/06

(Total = 10 marks)

9   Objective test questions: Statements of cash flows   43 mins

1   The following is an extract from a statement of cash flows prepared by a trainee accountant.

	$'000
Cash flows from operating activities	
Profit before taxation	3,840
Adjustments for	
Depreciation	(1,060)
Loss on sale of building	210
	2,990
Increase in inventories	(490)
Decrease in trade payables	290
Net cash from operating activities	2,790

Which of the following criticisms of this extract are correct?

1   Depreciation should have been added, not deducted.
2   Loss on sale of building should have been deducted, not added.
3   Increase in inventories should have been added, not deducted.
4   Decrease in trade payables should have been deducted, not added.

A   1 and 4
B   2 and 3
C   1 and 3
D   2 and 4   **(2 marks)**

2   In the year ended 31 December 20X4 a company sold some plant which had cost $100,000 for $20,000. At the time of sale the carrying value of the plant was $18,000.

Which of the following correctly states the treatment of the transaction in the company's statement of cash flows?

	Proceeds of sale	*Profit on sale*
A	Cash inflow under financing activities	Deducted from profit in calculating cash flow from operating activities.
B	Cash inflow under investing activities	Added to profit in calculating cash flow from operating activities.
C	Cash inflow under financing activities	Added to profit in calculating cash flow from operating activities.
D	Cash inflow under investing activities	Deducted from profit in calculating cash flow from operating activities. **(2 marks)**

3   Which of the following items should not appear in a company's statement of cash flows?

1   Proposed dividends
2   Dividends received
3   Bonus issue of shares
4   Surplus on revaluation of a non-current asset
5   Proceeds of sale of an investment not connected with the company's trading activities

A	1, 2, 3 and 5
B	3 and 4 only
C	1, 3 and 4
D	2 and 5	(2 marks)

4   Which, if any, of the following statements about statements of cash flows are correct according to IAS 7 *Statement of Cash Flows*?

1   The direct and indirect methods produce different figures for operating cash flow.

2   In calculating operating cash flow using the indirect method, an increase in inventory is added to operating profit.

3   Figures shown in the statement of cash flows should include sales taxes.

4   The final figure in the statement of cash flows is the increase or decrease in cash at bank.

A	1 and 4
B	2 and 3
C	2 only
D	None of the statements is correct.	(2 marks)

5   The statement of financial position of R, a limited liability company, at 31 December 20X3 and 20X4 included these figures.

	31 December	
	20X3	*20X4*
	$m	*$m*
Property, plant and equipment: cost	40	50
Accumulated depreciation	(10)	(14)
	30	36

The statement of comprehensive income for the year ended 31 December 20X4 showed the following figures.

| Depreciation charge for year | $6m |
| Loss on sales of property, plant and equipment | $1m |

The company purchased new property, plant and equipment costing $16m during the year.

What figure should appear in the company's statement of cash flows for 20X4 for receipts from the sale of property, plant and equipment?

A	$3m
B	$5m
C	$4m
D	The figure cannot be calculated from the information provided.	(2 marks)

6   A statement of cash flows shows the increase or decrease in cash and cash equivalents in the period.

Which of the following items are included in this movement?

1   Cash at bank

2   Overdraft at bank

3   Current asset investments readily convertible into known amounts of cash and which can be sold without disrupting the company's business.

4   Equity investments.

A	All four items
B	1, 2 and 3 only
C	1 and 2 only
D	1 and 3 only	(2 marks)

7   Which of the following should appear in a statement of cash flows according to IAS 7 *Statement of Cash Flows*?

    1   Dividends paid on preference shares
    2   Interest capitalised as part of the cost of a non-current asset
    3   Cash flows resulting from share issues

    A   All three items
    B   1 and 2 only
    C   1 and 3 only
    D   2 and 3 only   **(2 marks)**

8   The IAS 7 format for a statement of cash flows using the indirect method opens with adjustments to net profit before taxation to arrive at cash flow from operating activities.

    Which of the following lists consists only of items that would be deducted in that calculation?

    A   Loss on sale of non-current assets, increase in inventories, decrease in trade payables
    B   Depreciation, increase in trade receivables, decrease in trade payables
    C   Increase in trade receivables, profit on sale of non-current assets, decrease in trade payables
    D   Profit on sale of non-current assets, increase in trade payables, decrease in trade receivables

                                                                           (2 marks)

9   A company's accounting records contain the following figures.

	$'000
Sales for year	3,600
Purchases for year	2,400
Receivables: 31 December 20X2	600
31 December 20X3	700
Payables: 31 December 20X2	300
31 December 20X3	450
Salaries and other expenses paid during 20X3, excluding interest	760

    What figure should appear in the company's statement of cash flows for 20X3 for cash generated from operations, based on these figures?

    A $490,000
    B $390,000
    C $1,250,000
    D   None of these figures   **(2 marks)**

10   At 30 September 20X5, BY had the following balances, with comparatives:

As at 30 September	20X5	20X4
	$'000	$'000
Non-current tangible assets		
Property, plant and equipment	260	180
Equity and reserves		
Property, plant and equipment revaluation surplus	30	10

The statement of comprehensive income for the year ended 30 September 20X5 included:

Gain on disposal of an item of equipment	$10,000
Depreciation charge for the year	$40,000

Notes to the accounts:

Equipment disposed of had cost $90,000. The proceeds received on disposal were $15,000.

Calculate the property, plant and equipment purchases that BY would show in its statement of cash flows for the year ended 30 September 20X5, as required by IAS 7 *Statement of Cash Flows*.   **(4 marks)**

11   At 1 October 20X4, BK had the following balance:

Accrued interest payable $12,000 credit

During the year ended 30 September 20X5, BK charged interest payable of $41,000 to its statement of comprehensive income. The closing balance on accrued interest payable account at 30 September 20X5 was $15,000 credit.

How much interest paid should BK show on its statement of cash flows for the year ended 30 September 20X5?

A $38,000
B $41,000
C $44,000
D $53,000   **(2 marks)**

P7 11/05

(Total = 24 marks)

10   Section B question: Statements of cash flows   9 mins

The following financial information relates to FC for the year ended 31 March 20X8.

FC
STATEMENT OF COMPREHENSIVE INCOME FOR THE YEAR ENDED 31 MARCH 20X8

	$'000
Revenue	445
Cost of sales	(220)
Gross profit	225
Other income	105
	330
Administrative expenses	(177)
Finance costs	(20)
Profit before tax	133
Income tax expense	(43)
Profit for the year	90

The following administrative expenses were incurred in the year.

	$'000
Wages	70
Other general expenses	15
Depreciation	92
	177

Other income:	
Rentals received	45
Gain on disposal of non-current assets	60
	105

Statement of financial position extracts at:

	31 March 20X8	31 March 20X7
	$'000	$'000
Inventories	40	25
Trade receivables	50	45
Trade payables	(30)	(20)

Required

Prepare FC's statement of cash flows for the year ended 31 March 20X8, down to the line 'Cash generated from operations', using the direct method.   **(5 marks)**

P7 5/08

11 Dickson

27 mins

Below are the statements of financial position of Dickson Co as at 31 March 20X6 and 31 March 20X5, together with the income statement for the year ended 31 March 20X6.

STATEMENT OF FINANCIAL POSITION AS AT 31 MARCH

	20X6 $'000	20X5 $'000
Non-current assets		
Property, plant and equipment	825	637
Goodwill	100	100
Development expenditure	290	160
	1,215	897
Current assets		
Inventories	360	227
Trade receivables	274	324
Investments	143	46
Cash	29	117
	806	714
Total assets	2,021	1,611
Equity		
Share capital – $1 ordinary shares	500	400
Share premium	350	100
Revaluation surplus	160	60
Retained earnings	151	152
	1,161	712
Non-current liabilities		
6% loan notes	150	100
Finance lease liabilities	100	80
Deferred tax	48	45
	298	225
Current liabilities		
Trade payables	274	352
Finance lease liabilities	17	12
Current tax	56	153
Loan note interest	5	–
Dividends	78	103
Bank overdraft	132	54
	562	674
Total equity and liabilities	2,021	1,611

INCOME STATEMENT FOR THE YEAR ENDED 31 MARCH 20X6

	$'000
Revenue	1,476
Cost of sales	(962)
Gross profit	514
Other expenses	(157)
Finance costs	(15)
Profit before tax	342
Income tax expense	(162)
Profit for the year	180

Notes:

(1) Goodwill arose on the acquisition of unincorporated businesses. During the year ended 31 March 20X6 expenditure on development projects totalled $190,000.

(2) During the year ended 31 March 20X6 items of property, plant and equipment with a carrying value of $103,000 were sold for $110,000. Depreciation charged in the year on property, plant and equipment totalled $57,000. Dickson purchased $56,000 of property, plant and equipment by means of finance leases, payments being made in arrears on the last day of each accounting period.

(3) The current asset investments are government bonds and management has decided to class them as cash equivalents.

(4) The new loan notes were issued on 1 April 20X5. Finance cost includes loan note interest and finance lease finance charges only.

(5) During the year Dickson made a 1 for 8 bonus issue capitalising its retained earnings followed by a rights issue.

(6) Dividends declared during the period totalled $131,000.

Required

Prepare a statement of cash flows for the year ended 31 March 20X6 for Dickson Co in accordance with IAS 7 *Statement of cash flows,* using the indirect method. **(15 marks)**

12 Tex (FATP Pilot paper/amended)   45 mins

The following information has been extracted from the draft financial statements of Tex, a manufacturing company.

TEX
STATEMENT OF COMPREHENSIVE INCOME FOR THE YEAR ENDED 30 SEPTEMBER 20X1

	$'000
Revenue	15,000
Cost of sales	(9,000)
Gross profit	6,000
Other operating expenses	(2,300)
	3,700
Finance cost	(124)
Profit before taxation	3,576
Income tax expense	(1,040)
Profit for the year	2,536

TEX
STATEMENT OF FINANCIAL POSITION AS AT 30 SEPTEMBER 20X1

	20X1		20X0	
	$'000	$'000	$'000	$'000
Assets				
Property, plant and equipment		18,160		14,500
Current assets				
Inventories	1,600		1,100	
Trade receivables	1,500		800	
Bank	150		1,200	
		3,250		3,100
Total assets		21,410		17,600

	20X1		20X0	
	$'000	$'000	$'000	$'000
Equity and liabilities				
Equity:				
Share capital		10,834		7,815
Retained earnings		6,536		5,000
		17,370		12,815
Non-current liabilities				
Interest-bearing borrowing	1,700		2,900	
Deferred tax	600		400	
		2,300		3,300
Current liabilities				
Trade payables	700		800	
Taxation	1,040		685	
		1,740		1,485
Total equity and liabilities		21,410		17,600

Property, plant and equipment

	Property $'000	Plant $'000	Total $'000
Cost			
30 September 20X0	8,400	10,800	19,200
Additions	2,800	5,200	8,000
Disposals	–	(2,600)	(2,600)
30 September 20X1	11,200	13,400	24,600
Depreciation			
30 September 20X0	1,300	3,400	4,700
Disposals	–	(900)	(900)
Charge for year	240	2,400	2,640
30 September 20X1	1,540	4,900	6,440
Net book value			
30 September 20X1	9,660	8,500	18,160
30 September 20X0	7,100	7,400	14,500

The plant that was disposed of during the year was sold for $730,000.

All additions to property, plant and equipment were purchased for cash.

Dividends paid during the year were $1,000,000.

Required

(a)   Prepare Tex's statement of cash flows for the year ended 30 September 20X1.   **(13 marks)**

(b)   During the year to 30 September 20X2 Tex had the following results:

TEX
STATEMENT OF COMPREHENSIVE INCOME FOR THE YEAR ENDED 30 SEPTEMBER 20X2

	$'000
Revenue	18,000
Cost of sales	(8,900)
Gross profit	9,100
Other operating expenses	(5,000)
	4,100
Finance cost	(120)
Profit before taxation	3,980
Income tax expense	(1,300)
Profit for the year	2,680

Extract from cash book for year to 30 September 20X2:

	$'000
Other operating expenses (all paid by the year end)	2,000
Loan interest paid	120
Cash received from customers	16,700
Cash paid to suppliers	8,300
Tax paid	1,040
Dividend paid	1,000

Purchases of inventories totalled $9m for the year to 30 September 20X2.

There are no additions or disposals of property, plant or equipment. Depreciation is charged to other operating expenses in the statement of comprehensive income.

There is no movement on share capital or non-current liabilities.

Required

Prepare the statement of financial position for Tex at 30 September 20X2.   **(12 marks)**

(Total = 25 marks)

13 AG (FATP 5/05/amended)   45 mins

The financial statements of AG are given below:

STATEMENT OF FINANCIAL POSITION AS AT	31 March 20X5		31 March 20X4	
	$'000	$'000	$'000	$'000
Non-current assets				
Property, plant and equipment	3,600		3,900	
Goodwill	800		900	
Development expenditure	370	4,770	400	5,200
Current assets				
Inventories	685		575	
Trade receivables	515		420	
Cash and cash equivalents	1,082	2,282	232	1,227
Total assets		7,052		6,427
Equity				
Share capital	2,600		1,900	
Share premium account	750		400	
Revaluation surplus	425		300	
Retained earnings	1,360		1,415	
Total equity		5,135		4,015
Non-current liabilities				
8% redeemable preference shares	500		–	
10% loan notes	0		1,000	
5% loan notes	500		500	
Deferred tax	250		200	
Total non-current liabilities		1,250		1,700
Current liabilities				
Trade payables	480		350	
Income tax	80		190	
Accrued expenses	107		172	
Total current liabilities		667		712
Total equity and liabilities		7,052		6,427

STATEMENT OF COMPREHENSIVE INCOME FOR THE YEAR ENDED 31 MARCH 20X5

	$'000
Revenue	7,500
Cost of sales	(4,000)
Gross profit	3,500
Distribution costs	(900)
Administrative expenses	(2,400)
Finance costs	(65)
Profit before tax	135
Income tax expense	(90)
Profit for the year	45

Additional information

(a)   On 1 April 20X4, AG issued 1,400,000 $0.50 ordinary shares at a premium of 50%.

(b)   On 1 May 20X4, AG purchased and cancelled all its 10% loan notes at par.

(c)   On 1 October 20X4, AG issued 500,000 $1.00 8% preference shares at par. The preference shares are redeemable at par in 20X9.

(c)   Non-current tangible assets include properties which were revalued upwards by $125,000 during the year.

(d)   Non-current tangible assets disposed of in the year had a net book value of $75,000; cash received on disposal was $98,000. Any gain or loss on disposal has been included under cost of sales.

(e)   Cost of sales includes $80,000 for development expenditure amortised during the year.

(f)   Administrative expenses includes $100,000 for goodwill written-off during the year.

(g)   Depreciation charged for the year was $720,000.

(h)   The accrued expenses balance includes interest payable on the loan notes of $87,000 at 31 March 20X4 and $12,000 at 31 March 20X5. Dividends on the redeemable 8% preference shares were paid on 31 March 20X5.

(i)   The income tax expense for the year to 31 March 20X5 is made up as follows:

	$'000
Corporate income tax	40
Deferred tax	50
	90

(j)   Dividends paid on ordinary shares during the year were $100,000.

Required

Prepare a statement of cash flows, using the indirect method, for AG for the year ended 31 March 20X5, in accordance with IAS 7 *Statement of cash flows*.   **(25 marks)**

14 CJ (FATP 5/06/amended)   45 mins

The financial statements of CJ for the year to 31 March 20X6 were as follows:

STATEMENTS OF FINANCIAL POSITION AS AT	31 March 20X6		31 March 20X5	
	$'000	$'000	$'000	$'000
Assets				
Non-current assets				
Property	19,160		18,000	
Plant and equipment	8,500		10,000	
Available for sale investments	2,100		2,100	
		29,760		30,100
Current assets				
Inventory	2,714		2,500	
Trade receivables	2,106		1,800	
Cash at bank	11,753		0	
Cash in hand	409		320	
		16,982		4,620
Total assets		46,742		34,720
Equity and liabilities				
Equity				
Ordinary shares $0.50 each	12,000		7,000	
Share premium	10,000		5,000	
Revaluation surplus	4,200		2,700	
Retained earnings	2,809		1,510	
		29,009		16,210
Non-current liabilities				
Interest bearing borrowings	13,000		13,000	
Provision for deferred tax	999	13,999	800	13,800
Current liabilities				
Bank overdraft	0		1,200	
Trade and other payables	1,820		1,700	
Corporate income tax payable	1,914		1,810	
		3,734		4,710
Total equity and liabilities		46,742		34,720

STATEMENT OF COMPREHENSIVE INCOME FOR THE YEAR TO 31 MARCH 20X6

	$'000
Revenue	31,000
Cost of sales	(19,000)
Gross profit	12,000
Administrative expenses	(3,900)
Distribution costs	(2,600)
	5,500
Finance cost	(1,302)
Profit before tax	4,198
Income tax expense	(2,099)
Profit for the year	2,099
Other comprehensive income:	
Gain on property revaluation	1,500
Total comprehensive income for the year	3,599

Additional information

(a)   On 1 April 20X5, CJ issued 10,000,000 $0.50 ordinary shares at a premium of 100%.

(b)   Properties were revalued by $1,500,000 during the year.

(c)   Plant disposed of in the year had a net book value of $95,000; cash received on disposal was $118,000.

(d)   Depreciation charged for the year was properties $2,070,000 and plant and equipment $1,985,000.

(e)   The trade and other payables balance includes interest payable of $650,000 at 31 March 20X5 and $350,000 at 31 March 20X6.

(f)   Dividends paid during the year, $800,000 comprised last year's final dividend plus the current year's interim dividend.

Dividends payable are not accrued.

(g)   Income tax expense comprises:

	$
Corporate income tax	1,900,000
Deferred tax	199,000
	2,099,000

Required

(a)   Prepare CJ's statement of cash flows for the year ended 31 March 20X6, in accordance with IAS 7 *Statement of cash flows*.   **(15 marks)**

(b)   CJ commenced a long-term contract in early 20X6. The details are as follows:

	$'000
Total contract price	5,000
Costs to date	700
Expected further costs to complete	2,500
Progress billings	500
Percentage completed	20%

CJ did not include any of these amounts in its financial statements. No payment has yet been received and it has not yet made any payments to its suppliers or subcontractors.

Required

Redraft CJ's statement of financial position at 31 March 20X6 to include the results of the long-term contract. Ignore any tax implications. (This does not affect your answer to (a).)   **(10 marks)**

(Total = 25 marks)

15   DN (FATP 11/06/amended)   45 mins

DN's draft financial statements for the year ended 31 October 20X6 are as follows:

DN
STATEMENT OF COMPREHENSIVE INCOME FOR THE YEAR TO 31 OCTOBER 20X6

	$'000	$'000
Revenue		2,600
Cost of sales		
Parts and sub-assemblies	(500)	
Labour	(400)	
Overheads	(400)	
		(1,300)
Gross profit		1,300
Administrative expenses	(300)	
Distribution costs	(100)	
		(400)
Profit from operations		900
Finance cost		(110)
Profit before tax		790
Income tax expense		(140)
Profit for the year		650
Other comprehensive income		
Gain on revaluation of property		300
Total comprehensive income for the year		950

DN
STATEMENT OF FINANCIAL POSITION AS AT

	31 October 20X6		31 October 20X5	
	$'000	$'000	$'000	$'000
Assets				
Non-current assets				
Property, plant and equipment		4,942		4,205
Current assets				
Inventories	190		140	
Trade receivables	340		230	
Cash and cash equivalents	2,318		45	
		2,848		415
Total assets		7,790		4,620
Equity and liabilities				
Equity				
Equity shares of $0.50 each	1,300		1,000	
Share premium	300		0	
Revaluation surplus	400		0	
Retained earnings	2,060		1,410	
Total equity		4,060		2,410
Non-current liabilities				
Bank loans		3,500		2,000
		7,560		4,410
Current liabilities		230		210
Total equity and liabilities		7,790		4,620

Additional information

(a) Property, plant and equipment comprises:

	20X6	20X5
	$'000	$'000
Property	3,100	2,800
Plant and equipment	1,842	1,405

(b) Plant and equipment sold during the year for $15,000 had a carrying amount of $10,000. The profit on disposal of $5,000 has been included in overheads.

(c) Properties were revalued on 31 October 20X6.

(d) DN made an equity share issue on 31 October 20X6.

(e) DN's funding includes two bank loans:

- $1,500,000 6% loan commenced 30 June 20X6, due for repayment 29 June 20X9
- $2,000,000 7% loan repaid early on 1 July 20X6

(f) Tax paid for the year was $120,000.

(g) Current liabilities:

	20X6	20X5
	$'000	$'000
Trade payables	105	85
Interest payable	55	75
Tax payable	70	50
Total current liabilities	230	210

(h) No dividends were declared or paid during the year.

(i) Overheads include the annual depreciation charge of $100,000 for property and $230,000 for plant and equipment.

Required

(a) Prepare DN's statement of cash flows for the year ended 31 October 20X6, using the indirect method, in accordance with IAS 7 *Statement of cash flows*. **(15 marks)**

(b) Over the next twelve months DN expects to make sales of $3,300,000, which will require purchases of $1,700,000. Inventory levels will remain constant.

It expects to collect $3,100,000 from customers and pay $1,600,000 to suppliers. Interest costs will be the same as 20X6 and the tax charge is estimated at $60,000. DN will clear both tax and interest payable by the year end.

No purchases or disposals of non-current assets are planned. Depreciation will be $330,000 and DN intends to hold other expenses to $500,000, which will be paid in cash.

Required

Draft DN's projected statement of financial position at 31 October 20X7.   **(10 marks)**

(Total = 25 marks)

16 HZ (FATP 5/09/amended)   45 mins

The accountant of HZ started preparing the financial statements for the year ended 31 March 20X9, but was suddenly taken ill. The **draft** financial statements for HZ for the year ended 31 March 20X9 are given below:

HZ STATEMENTS OF FINANCIAL POSITION AT	31 MARCH 20X9		31 MARCH 20X8	
	$000	$000	$000	$000
Assets				
Non-current assets				
Property, plant and equipment	5,854		6,250	
Goodwill	217		350	
Other intangible assets	28	6,099	170	6,770
Current assets				
Inventories	890		750	
Trade receivables	1,074		545	
Cash and cash equivalents	717		300	
		2,681		1,595
Total assets		8,780		8,365
Equity and liabilities				
Equity share capital	2,873		2,470	
Share premium account	732		530	
Revaluation surplus	562		400	
Retained earnings	1,661		1,840	
Total equity		5,828		5,240
Non-current liabilities				
Preference shares	942		–	
10% loan notes	–		1,250	
5% loan notes	700		700	
Deferred tax	312		250	
Total non-current liabilities		1,954		2,200
Current liabilities				
Trade payables	744		565	
Income tax	117		247	
Provision	120		–	
Accrued interest on loan notes	17		113	
Total current liabilities		998		925
Total equity and liabilities		8,780		8,365

STATEMENT OF COMPREHENSIVE INCOME FOR THE YEAR ENDED 31 MARCH 20X9

	$000
Revenue	9,900
Cost of sales	(5,200)
Gross profit	4,700
Distribution costs	(1,195)
Administrative expenses	(2,990)
Profit from operations	415
Finance costs	(122)
Profit before tax	293
Income tax expense	(182)
Profit for the year	111

Additional information:

(i)   Non-current tangible assets include properties which were revalued upwards during the year.

(ii)   Non-current tangible assets disposed of in the year had a net book value of $98,000; cash received on their disposal was $128,000. Any gain or loss on disposal has been included under cost of sales.

(iii) During the year goodwill became impaired. The impairment was charged to cost of sales.

(iv)   Depreciation charged for the year was $940,000, included in cost of sales.

(v)   On 1 April 20X8, HZ issued 806,000 $0.50 equity shares at a premium of 50%.

(vi)   On 1 April 20X8, HZ issued 1,000,000 5% cumulative $1 preferred shares at par, redeemable at 10% premium on 1 April 20Y8. Issue costs of $70,000 have been paid and correctly deducted from the non-current liability balance. The constant annual rate of interest is 6.72%.

(vii) The other intangible assets relate to research and development expenditure.

       Development expenditure of $170,000 no longer met the IAS 38 criteria as at 31 March 20X9 and was written off.

(viii) On 1 May 20X8, HZ purchased and cancelled all its 10% loan notes at par plus accrued interest (included in finance costs).

(ix)   Ordinary dividends paid during the year were $290,000 and preferred share dividends paid were $50,000.

(x)   HZ has been advised that it is probably going to lose a court case and has provided $120,000 for the estimated cost of this case. This is included in administrative expenses.

Required

Prepare a statement of cash flows, using the indirect method, for HZ for the year ended 31 March 20X9, in accordance with IAS 7 *Statement of cash flows*.   **(25 marks)**

17 Objective test questions: Non-current assets, inventories and construction contracts I   49 mins

1   The components of the cost of a major item of equipment are given below.

	$
Purchase price	780,000
Import duties	117,000
Sales tax (refundable)	78,000
Site preparation	30,000
Installation	28,000
Initial operating losses before the asset reaches planned performance	50,000
Estimated cost of dismantling and removal of the asset, recognised as a provision under IAS 37 *Provisions, contingent liabilities and contingent assets*	100,000
	1,183,000

What amount may be recognised as the cost of the asset, according to IAS 16 *Property, plant and equipment?*

- A $956,000
- B $1,105,000
- C $1,055,000
- D $1,183,000   **(2 marks)**

---

2   Which of the following statements about IAS 36 *Impairment of assets* are correct?

1   Non-current assets must be checked annually for evidence of impairment.

2   An impairment loss must be recognised immediately in the income statement, except that all or part of a loss on a revalued asset should be charged against any related revaluation surplus.

3   If individual assets cannot be tested for impairment, it may be necessary to test a group of assets as a unit.

- A   1 and 2 only
- B   1 and 3 only
- C   2 and 3 only
- D   1, 2 and 3   **(2 marks)**

---

3   Which of the following statements is correct?

1   Negative goodwill should be shown in the statement of financial position as a deduction from positive goodwill.

2   IAS 38 allows goodwill to be written off immediately against reserves as an alternative to capitalisation.

3   As a business grows, internally generated goodwill may be revalued upwards to reflect that growth.

4   Internally developed brands must not be capitalised.

- A   1 and 4
- B   2 and 3
- C   3 only
- D   4 only   **(2 marks)**

---

4   Which of the following accounting policies would contravene International Accounting Standards if adopted by a company?

1   Goodwill on acquisitions is written off immediately against reserves.

2   Land on which the company's buildings stand is not depreciated.

3   Internally generated brands are capitalised at fair value as advised by independent consultants.

4   In calculating depreciation, the estimated useful life of an asset is taken as half the actual estimated useful life as a measure of prudence.

- A   1, 3 and 4
- B   2 and 4 only
- C   1 and 3 only
- D   All four are unacceptable   **(2 marks)**

---

5   Which of the following items should be included in arriving at the cost of the inventory of finished goods held by a manufacturing company, according to IAS 2 *Inventories?*

1   Carriage inwards on raw materials delivered to factory
2   Carriage outwards on goods delivered to customers
3   Factory supervisors' salaries
4   Factory heating and lighting
5   Cost of abnormally high idle time in the factory
6   Import duties on raw materials

A   1, 3, 4 and 6
B   1, 2, 4 ,5 and 6
C   3, 4 and 6
D   2, 3 and 5   (2 marks)

6   Which of the following statements about IAS 2 *Inventories* are correct?

1   Production overheads should be included in cost on the basis of a company's actual level of activity in the period.

2   In arriving at the net realisable value of inventories, trade discounts and settlement discounts must be deducted.

3   In arriving at the cost of inventories, FIFO, LIFO and weighted average cost formulas are acceptable.

4   It is permitted to value finished goods inventories at materials plus labour cost only, without adding production overheads.

A   1 only
B   2 only
C   3 only
D   None of them   (2 marks)

7   The position of a construction contract at 30 June 20X6 is as follows.

	$
Contract price	900,000
At 30 June 20X6	
Costs to date	720,000
Estimated costs to completion	480,000
Progress payments invoiced and received	400,000
Percentage complete	60%

What figures should appear for this contract in the accounts at 30 June 20X6, according to IAS 11 *Construction contracts*?

	Statement of comprehensive income		Statement of financial position	
A	Sales revenue	$540,000	Receivables	$140,000
	Costs	$840,000		
B	Sales revenue	$540,000		
	Costs	$720,000		
C	Sales revenue	$540,000	Amount due from customer	$20,000
	Costs	$840,000		
D	Sales revenue	$540,000	Receivables	$140,000
	Costs	$720,000		

(2 marks)

8   The following measures relate to a non-current asset:

(i)   Net book value $20,000
(ii)   Net realisable value $18,000
(iii)   Value in use $22,000
(iv)   Replacement cost $50,000

The recoverable amount of the asset is

A $18,000
B $20,000
C $22,000
D $50,000   (2 marks)

9 BL started a contract on 1 November 20X4. The contract was scheduled to run for two years and has a sales value of $40 million.

At 31 October 20X5, the following details were obtained from BL's records:

	$m
Costs incurred to date	16
Estimated costs to completion	18
Percentage complete at 31 October 20X5	45%

Applying IAS 11 *Construction contracts*, how much revenue and profit should BL recognise in its statement of comprehensive income for the year ended 31 October 20X5? **(2 marks)**

10 CI purchased equipment on 1 April 20X2 for $100,000. The equipment was depreciated using the reducing balance method at 25% per year. CI's year end is 31 March.

Depreciation was charged up to and including 31 March 20X6. At that date, the recoverable amount was $28,000.

Calculate the impairment loss on the equipment according to IAS 36 Impairment of Assets. **(3 marks)**

The following data are given for sub-questions 11 and 12 below

CN started a three year contract to build a new university campus on 1 April 20X5. The contract had a fixed price of $90 million.

CN incurred costs to 31 March 20X6 of $77 million and estimated that a further $33 million would need to be spent to complete the contract.

CN uses the percentage of cost incurred to date to total cost method to calculate stage of completion of the contract.

11 Calculate revenue earned on the contract to 31 March 20X6, according to IAS 11 Construction Contracts. **(2 marks)**

12 State how much gross profit/loss CN should recognise in its statement of comprehensive income for the year ended 31 March 20X6, according to IAS 11 Construction Contracts. **(2 marks)**

13 IAS 16 *Property, Plant and Equipment* requires an asset to be measured at cost on its original recognition in the financial statements.

EW used its own staff, assisted by contractors when required, to construct a new warehouse for its own use.

Which ONE of the following costs would NOT be included in attributable costs of the non-current asset?

A Clearance of the site prior to work commencing.

B Professional surveyors' fees for managing the construction work.

C EW's own staff wages for time spent working on the construction.

D An allocation of EW's administration costs, based on EW staff time spent on the construction as a percentage of the total staff time. **(2 marks)**

(Total = 27 marks)

18 Objective test questions: Non-current assets, inventories and construction contracts II 63 mins

1 A company purchased a machine for $50,000 on 1 January 20X1. It was judged to have a 5-year life with a residual value of $5,000. On 31 December 20X2 $15,000 was spent on an upgrade to the machine. This extended its remaining useful life to 5 years, with the same residual value. During 20X3, the market for the product declined and the machine was sold on 1 January 20X4 for $7,000.

What was the loss on disposal?

A $31,000
B $35,000
C $31,600
D $35,600 (2 marks)

2 A cash generating unit comprises the following:

	$m
Building	20
Plant and equipment	10
Goodwill	5
Current assets	10
	45

Following a downturn in the market, an impairment review has been undertaken and the recoverable amount of the cash generating unit is estimated to be $25m.

What is the carrying value of the building after adjusting for the impairment loss?

A $11m
B $10m
C $12.5m
D $20m (2 marks)

3 In less than 30 words, define 'impairment'. (2 marks)

4 Which of the following is *not* true regarding IAS 2 *Inventories*?

A Fixed production overheads must be allocated to items of inventory on the basis of the normal level of production.

B Plant lying idle will lead to a higher fixed overhead allocation to each unit.

C An abnormally high level of production will lead to a lower allocation of fixed production overhead to each unit

D Unallocated overheads must be recognised as an expense in the period in which they are incurred.

(2 marks)

5 In less than 20 words define *fair value*. (2 marks)

The following data is to be used to answer sub-questions 6 and 7 below

X acquired the business and assets from the owners of an unincorporated business: the purchase price was satisfied by the issue of 10,000 equity shares with a nominal market value of $10 each and $20,000 cash. The market value of X shares at the date of acquisition was $20 each.

The assets acquired were:

• Net tangible non-current assets with a book value of $20,000 and current value of $25,000.
• Patents for a specialised process valued by a specialist valuer at $15,000.
• Brand name, valued by a specialist brand valuer on the basis of a multiple of earnings at $50,000.

- Publishing rights of the first text from an author that the management of X expects to become a best seller. The publishing rights were a gift from the author to the previous owners at no cost. The management of X has estimated the future value of the potential best seller at $100,000. However, there is no reliable evidence available to support the estimate of the management.

6   In no more than **30 words**, explain the accounting treatment to be used for the publishing rights of the first text.   **(2 marks)**

7   Calculate the value of goodwill to be included in the accounts of X for this purchase.   **(4 marks)**

8   An item of plant and equipment was purchased on 1 April 20X1 and for $100,000. At the date of acquisition its expected useful life was 10 years. Depreciation was provided on a straight line basis, with no residual value.

On April 1 20X3, the asset was revalued to $95,000. On 1 April 20X4, the useful life of the asset was reviewed and the remaining useful life was reduced to 5 years, a total useful life of 8 years.

Calculate the amounts that would be included in the statement of financial position for the asset cost/valuation and provision for accumulated depreciation at 31 March 20X5.   **(4 marks)**

9   IAS 16 *Property, Plant and Equipment* provides definitions of terms relevant to non-current assets. Complete the following sentence, **in no more than 10 words**.

'Depreciable amount is ...'   **(2 marks)**

10   Which ONE of the following items would CM recognise as subsequent expenditure on a non-current asset and capitalise it as required by IAS 16 *Property, Plant and Equipment*?

A   CM purchased a furnace five years ago, when the furnace lining was separately identified in the accounting records. The furnace now requires relining at a cost of $200,000. When the furnace is relined it will be able to be used in CM's business for a further five years.

B   CM's office building has been badly damaged by a fire. CM intends to restore the building to its original condition at a cost of $250,000.

C   CM's delivery vehicle broke down. When it was inspected by the repairers it was discovered that it needed a new engine. The engine and associated labour costs are estimated to be $5,000.

D   CM closes its factory for two weeks every year. During this time, all plant and equipment has its routine annual maintenance check and any necessary repairs are carried out. The cost of the current year's maintenance check and repairs was $75,000.   **(2 marks)**

11   DS purchased a machine on 1 October 20X2 at a cost of $21,000 with an expected useful economic life of six years, with no expected residual value. DS depreciates its machines using the straight line basis.

The machine has been used and depreciated for three years to 30 September 20X5. New technology was invented in December 20X5, which enabled a cheaper, more efficient machine to be produced; this technology makes DS's type of machine obsolete. The obsolete machine will generate no further economic benefit or have any residual value once the new machines become available. However, because of production delays, the new machines will not be available on the market until 1 October 20X7.

Calculate how much depreciation DS should charge to profit or loss for the year ended 30 September 20X6, as required by IAS 16 *Property, Plant and Equipment*.   **(3 marks)**

12   IAS 38 *Intangible Assets* sets out six criteria that must be met before an internally generated intangible asset can be recognised.

List FOUR of IAS 38's criteria for recognition.   **(4 marks)**

13   Details from DV's long-term contract, which commenced on 1 May 20X6, at 30 April 20X7:

	$'000
Invoiced to client for work done	2,000
Costs incurred to date:	
Attributable to work completed	1,500
Inventory purchased, but not yet used	250
Progress payment received from client	900
Expected further costs to complete project	400
Total contract value	3,000

DV uses the percentage of costs incurred to total costs to calculate attributable profit.

Calculate the amount that DV should recognise in its statement of comprehensive income for the year ended 30 April 20X7 for revenue, cost of sales and attributable profits on this contract according to IAS 11 *Construction Contracts*.

(4 marks)

(Total = 35 marks)

19   Section B questions: Non-current assets, inventories and construction contracts   54 mins

(a)   (i)   Discuss the criteria which IAS 38 *Intangible assets* states should be used when considering whether research and development expenditure should be written off in an accounting period or carried forward.

(ii)   Discuss to what extent these criteria are consistent with the fundamental accounting assumptions within IAS 1.   (5 marks)

(b)   'The cost of inventories should comprise all costs of purchase, costs of conversion and other costs incurred in bringing the inventories to their present location and condition' (IAS 2).

This statement results in problems of a practical nature in arriving at the amount at which inventories and short term work in progress are stated in the accounts.

Required

Comment on the above statement identifying and discussing both the accounting policy and the problems 'of a practical nature' that may arise when computing the amount at which inventories and short term work in progress are stated in financial accounts.   (5 marks)

(c)   A new type of delivery vehicle, when purchased on 1 April 20X0 for $20,000, was expected to have a useful life of four years. It now appears that the original estimate of the useful life was too short, and the vehicle is now expected to have a useful life of six years, from the date of purchase. All delivery vehicles are depreciated using the straight-line method and are assumed to have zero residual value.

Required

As the trainee management accountant, draft a memo to the transport manager explaining whether it is possible to change the useful life of the new delivery vehicle. Using appropriate International Accounting Standards, explain how the accounting transactions relating to the delivery vehicle should be recorded in the statement of comprehensive income for the year ended 31 March 20X3 and the statement of financial position at that date   (5 marks)

P7 Pilot paper

(d)   BI owns a building which it uses as its offices, warehouse and garage. The land is carried as a separate non-current tangible asset in the statement of financial position.

BI has a policy of regularly revaluing its non-current tangible assets. The original cost of the building in October 20X2 was $1,000,000; it was assumed to have a remaining useful life of 20 years at that date, with no residual value. The building was revalued on 30 September 20X4 by a professional valuer at $1,800,000.

BI also owns a brand name which it acquired 1 October 20X0 for $500,000. The brand name is being amortised over 10 years.

The economic climate had deteriorated during 20X5, causing BI to carry out an impairment review of its assets at 30 September 20X5. BI's building was valued at a market value of $1,500,000 on 30 September 20X5 by an independent valuer. A brand specialist valued BI's brand name at market value of $200,000 on the same date.

BI's management accountant calculated that the brand name's value in use at 30 September 20X5 was $150,000.

Required

Explain how BI should report the events described above and quantify any amounts required to be included in its financial statements for the year ended 30 September 20X5. **(5 marks)**

P7 11/05

(e) DV purchased two buildings on 1 September 1996. Building A cost $200,000 and had a useful economic life of 20 years. Building B cost $120,000 and had a useful life of 15 years. DV's accounting policies are to revalue buildings every five years and depreciate them over their useful economic lives on the straight line basis. DV does not make an annual transfer from revaluation surplus to retained profits for excess depreciation.

DV received the following valuations from its professionally qualified external valuer:

31 August 2001	Building A	$180,000
	Building B	$75,000
31 August 2006	Building A	$100,000
	Building B	$30,000

Required

Calculate the gains or impairments arising on the revaluation of Buildings A and B at 31 August 2006 and identify where they should be recognised in the financial statements of DV. **(5 marks)**

P7 11/06

(f) HS, a contractor, signed a two year fixed price contract on 31 March 20X8 for $300,000 to build a bridge. Total costs were originally estimated at $240,000.

At 31 March 20X9, HS extracted the following figures from its financial records:

	$000
Contract value	300
Costs incurred to date	170
Estimated costs to complete	100
Progress payments received	130
Value of work completed	165

HS calculates the stage of completion of contracts using the value of work completed as a proportion of total contract value.

Required

Calculate the following amounts for the contract that should be shown in HS's financial statements:

Statement of comprehensive income:

- Revenue recognised for the year ended 31 March 20X9;
- Profit recognised for the year ended 31 March 20X9.

Statement of financial position:

- Gross amount due to/from the customer at 31 March 20X9, stating whether it is an asset or liability.

(5 marks)

P7 5/09

(Total = 30 marks)

20 Geneva   27 mins

Geneva Co is a company involved in the building industry and often has a number of major construction contracts which fall into two or more accounting periods.

During the year ended 31 December 20X8, Geneva Co enters into three construction contracts as follows:

	Contract		
	Lausanne	Bern	Zurich
	$'000	$'000	$'000
Fixed contract price	2,000	2,000	2,000
Payments on account	1,080	950	800
Costs incurred to date	1,000	1,100	640
Estimated costs to complete the contract	600	1,100	1,160
Estimate percentage of work completed	60%	50%	35%

Required

Show how each contract would be reflected in the statement of financial position and statement of comprehensive income of Geneva Co for the year ended 31 December 20X8. **(5 marks each)**

(Total = 15 marks)

21 Objective test questions: Capital transactions and financial instruments   47 mins

1   A company made an issue of 100,000 ordinary shares of 50c at $1.10 each. The cash received was correctly recorded in the cash book but the whole amount was entered into ordinary share capital account.

Which of the following journal entries will correct the error made in recording the issue?

		Debit	Credit
		$	$
A	Share capital account	10,000	
	Share premium account		10,000
B	Cash	60,000	
	Share premium account		60,000
C	Share capital account	60,000	
	Share premium account		60,000
D	Share premium account	60,000	
	Share capital account		60,000

(2 marks)

2   A company issued 1,000,000 $1 shares at $1.50 each payable as follows.

On application (including premium)	70c
On allotment	30c
First and final call	50c

All monies were received except for the call due from a holder of 10,000 shares. These shares were subsequently forfeited and reissued at $1.60 per share.

What *total* will be credited to share premium account as a result of this issue?

A $501,000
B $506,000
C $511,000
D   None of the above   **(2 marks)**

3   At 1 January 20X4, a company's share capital consisted of 1,000,000 ordinary shares of 50c each, and there was a balance of $800,000 on its share premium account.

During 20X4, the following events took place.

1 March   The company made a bonus issue of 1 share for every 2 held, using the share premium account.

1 July   The company issued 600,000 shares at $2 per share.

1 October   The company made a rights issue of 1 share for every 3 held at $1.80 per share.

What are the balances on the company's share capital and share premium accounts at 31 December 20X4?

	Share capital $	Share premium $
A	1,400,000	2,860,000
B	2,800,000	1,460,000
C	1,800,000	2,320,000
D	1,400,000	2,360,000

(2 marks)

---

4   A company has forfeited shares for non-payment of calls, but has not yet reissued them.

How, if at all, will the forfeited shares be shown in the company's statement of financial position?

A   As a deduction from called up share capital
B   As an asset under investments
C   As a current asset under receivables
D   No item appears in the statement of financial position for the shares   **(2 marks)**

---

5   Which of the following are normally permitted uses for a company's share premium account?

1   Issuing fully paid bonus shares
2   Being repaid to members as part of an authorised reduction of share capital
3   Writing off preliminary expenses of company formation
4   Writing off subsequent share issue expenses

A   1, 2 and 4 only
B   1, 3 and 4 only
C   2, 3 and 4 only
D   All four are permitted   **(2 marks)**

---

6   Which of the following statements regarding share issues is incorrect?

A   **Application** is where potential shareholders apply for shares in the company and send cash to cover their application

B   **Allotment** is when the company allocates shares to the successful applicants and returns cash to unsuccessful applicants

C   A **call** is where the purchase value is payable in instalments. The company will 'call' for instalments.

D   If a shareholder fails to pay a call his allotment is cancelled and his money returned to him. His shares may then be reissued.   **(2 marks)**

---

7   IAS 32 *Financial Instruments – Disclosure and Presentation* classifies issues shares as either equity instruments or financial liabilities. An entity has the following categories of funding in its statement of financial position:

1   A preference share that is redeemable for cash at a 10% premium on 30 May 2015.
2   An ordinary share which is not redeemable and has no restrictions on receiving dividends.
3   A loan note that is redeemable at par in 2020.
4   A cumulative preference share that is entitled to receive a dividend of 7% a year.

Applying IAS 32, how would **each** of the above be categorised on the statement of financial position?

	As an equity instrument	As a financial liability
A	1 and 2	3 and 4
B	2 and 3	1 and 4
C	2	1, 3 and 4
D	1, 2 and 3	4

(2 marks)

8   BN is a listed entity and has the following balances included in its opening statement of financial position:

	$000
Equity	
Equity shares, $1 shares, fully paid	750
Share premium	250
Retained earnings	500
	1,500

BN reacquired 100,000 of its shares and classified them as 'treasury shares'. BN still held the treasury shares at the year end.

How should BN classify the treasury shares on its closing statement of financial position in accordance with IAS 32 *Financial instruments – presentation?*

A   As a non-current asset investment.
B   As a deduction from equity.
C   As a current asset investment.
D   As a non-current liability.

(2 marks)

9   R issued 500,000 new $1 equity shares on 1 April 20X2. The issue price of the share was $1.50 per share. Applicants paid $0.20 per share with their applications and a further $0.80 per share on allotment. All money was received on time.

A final call of $0.50 per share was made on 31 January 20X3. One holder of 5,000 shares failed to pay the call by the due date and the shares were forfeited. The forfeited shares were reissued for $1 per share on 31 March 20X3.

Which of the following is the correct set of accounting entries to record the reissue of the forfeited shares?

	Investment in own shares account	Bank account	Investment in own shares account	Share premium account	
A	$5,000 credit	$5,000 debit	$2,500 debit	$2,500 credit	
B	$5,000 credit	$5,000 debit	0	0	
C	$5,000 credit	$5,000 debit	$2,500 credit	$2,500 debit	
D	$5,000 debit	$5,000 credit	$2,500 credit	$2,500 debit	**(2 marks)**

The following data applies to questions 10 and 11.

On 1 January 20X8 PX issued 10m 7% $1 preference shares, redeemable after 4 years at a 5% premium. Issue charges amount to $500,000 and the effective interest rate is 10%.

10   What is the total finance charge on the issue?   **(3 marks)**

11   At what amount will the preference shares be shown in the statement of financial position at 31 December 20X9?   **(3 marks)**

12   Which ONE of the following gives the true meaning of "treasury shares"?

A   Shares owned by a country's Treasury
B   An entity's own shares purchased by the entity and still held at the period end
C   An entity's own shares purchased by the entity and resold before the period end at a gain
D   An entity's own shares purchased by the entity and cancelled

(2 marks)

(Total = 26 marks)

22 Objective test questions: Accounting standards I 65 mins

1   A company leases some plant on 1 January 20X4. The cash price of the plant is $9,000, and the company leases it for four years, paying four annual instalments of $3,000 beginning on 31 December 20X4.

The company uses the sum of the digits method to allocate interest.

What is the interest charge for the year ended 31 December 20X5?

   A $900
   B $600
   C $1,000
   D $750   **(2 marks)**

2   A company leases some plant on 1 January 20X4. The cash price is $9,000, and the company is to pay four annual instalments of $3,000, beginning on 1 January 20X4.

The company uses the sum of the digits method to allocate interest.

What is the interest charge for the year ended 31 December 20X5?

   A $750
   B $500
   C $900
   D $1,000   **(2 marks)**

3   Which of the following statements about IAS 10 *Events after the reporting period* are correct?

   1   Notes to the financial statements must give details of all material adjusting events reflected in those financial statements.

   2   Notes to the financial statements must give details of non-adjusting events affecting users' ability to understand the company's financial position.

   3   Financial statements should not be prepared on a going concern basis if after the end of the reporting period the directors have decided to liquidate the company.

   A   All three statements are correct.
   B   1 and 2 only
   C   1 and 3 only
   D   2 and 3 only   **(2 marks)**

4   A company's statement of comprehensive income showed a profit before tax of $1,800,000

After the year end and before the financial statements were authorised for issue, the following events took place.

   1   The value of an investment held at the year end fell by $85,000.

   2   A customer who owed $116,000 at the year end went bankrupt owing a total of $138,000.

   3   Inventory valued at cost $161,000 in the statement of financial position was sold for $141,000.

   4   Assets with a carrying value at the year end of $240,000 were unexpectedly expropriated by government.

What is the company's profit after making the necessary adjustments for these events?

   A $1,399,000
   B $1,579,000
   C $1,664,000
   D   None of these figures   **(2 marks)**

5 Which of the following events after the reporting period would normally be classified as *adjusting*, according to IAS 10 *Events after the reporting period*?

    1   Destruction of a major non-current asset
    2   Issue of shares and loan notes
    3   Discovery of error or fraud
    4   Evidence of impairment in value of a property as at the year end
    5   Purchases and sales of non-current assets

    A   1, 2 and 5 only
    B   3 and 4 only
    C   3, 4 and 5 only
    D   1, 3 and 4 only   **(2 marks)**

6 Which of the following events after the reporting period would normally be classified as *non-adjusting*, according to IAS 10 *Events after the reporting period*?

    1   Opening new trading operations
    2   Sale of goods held at the year end for less than cost
    3   A customer is discovered to be insolvent
    4   Announcement of plan to discontinue an operation
    5   Expropriation of major assets by government

    A   2 and 3 only
    B   1, 2 and 3 only
    C   2, 3, 4 and 5 only
    D   1, 4 and 5 only   **(2 marks)**

7 In compiling its financial statements, the directors of a company have to decide on the correct treatment of the following items.

    1   An employee has commenced an action against the company for wrongful dismissal. The company's solicitors estimate that the ex-employee has a 40 per cent chance of success in the action.

    2   The company has guaranteed the overdraft of another company, not at present in any financial difficulties. The possibility of a liability arising is thought to be remote.

    3   Shortly after the year end, a major installation owned by the company was destroyed in a flood. The company's going concern status is not affected.

What are the correct treatments for these items, assuming all are of material amount?
    A   All three should be disclosed by note.
    B   A provision should be made for item 1 and items 2 and 3 disclosed by note.
    C   Items 1 and 3 should be disclosed by note, with no disclosure for item 2.
    D   Item 1 should be disclosed by note. No disclosure is required for items 2 and 3.   **(2 marks)**

8 Which of the following statements about IAS 37 *Provisions, contingents liabilities and contingent assets* are correct?

    1   Provisions should be made for constructive obligations (those arising from a company's pattern of past practice) as well as for obligations enforceable by law.

    2   Discounting may be used when estimating the amount of a provision if the effect is material.

    3   A restructuring provision must include the estimated costs of retraining or relocating continuing staff.

    4   A restructuring provision may only be made when a company has a detailed plan for the reconstruction and a firm intention to carry it out.

    A   All four statements are correct
    B   1, 2 and 4 only
    C   1, 3 and 4 only
    D   2, 3 and 4 only   **(2 marks)**

9   Which of the following criteria must be present in order for a company to recognise a provision?

    1   There is a present obligation as a result of past events.
    2   It is probable that a transfer of economic benefits will be required to settle the obligation.
    3   A reliable estimate of the obligation can be made.

    A   All three criteria must be present.
    B   1 and 2 only
    C   1 and 3 only
    D   2 and 3 only   **(2 marks)**

---

10   Which **one** of the following would be treated as a non-adjusting event after the reporting period, as required by IAS 10 *Events after the Reporting Period*, in the financial statements of AN for the period ended 31 January 20X5? The financial statements were approved for publication on 15 May 20X5.

    A   Notice was received on 31 March 20X5 that a major customer of AN had ceased trading and was unlikely to make any further payments.

    B   Inventory items at 31 January 20X5, original cost $30,000, were sold in April 20X5 for $20,000.

    C   During 2004, a customer commenced legal action against AN. At 31 January 20X5, legal advisers were of the opinion that AN would lose the case, so AN created a provision of $200,000 for the damages claimed by the customer. On 27 April 20X5, the court awarded damages of $250,000 to the customer.

    D   There was a fire on 2 May 20X5 in AN's main warehouse which destroyed 50% of AN's total inventory.   **(2 marks)**

---

11   DT's final dividend for the year ended 31 October 20X5 of $150,000 was declared on 1 February 20X6 and paid in cash on 1 April 20X6. The financial statements were approved on 31 March 20X6.

    The following statements refer to the treatment of the dividend in the accounts of DT:

    1   The payment clears an accrued liability set up as at 31 October 20X5.

    2   The dividend is shown as a deduction in the statement of comprehensive income for the year ended 31 October 20X6.

    3   The dividend is shown as an accrued liability as at 31 October 20X6.

    4   The $150,000 dividend was shown in the notes to the financial statements at 31 October 20X5.

    5   The dividend is shown as a deduction in the statement of changes in equity for the year ended 31 October 20X6.

    Which of the above statements reflect the correct treatment of the dividend?

    A   1 and 2
    B   1 and 4
    C   3 and 5
    D   4 and 5   **(2 marks)**

---

12   List the THREE criteria specified in IAS 37 *Provisions, Contingent Liabilities and Contingent Assets* that must be satisfied before a provision is recognised in the financial statements.   **(3 marks)**

---

13 DH has the following two legal claims outstanding:

- A legal action against DH claiming compensation of $700,000, filed in February 20X7. DH has been advised that it is probable that the liability will materialise.

- A legal action taken by DH against another entity, claiming damages of $300,000, started in March 20X4. DH has been advised that it is probable that it will win the case.

How should DH report these legal actions in its financial statements for the year ended 30 April 20X7?

	Legal action against DH	Legal action taken by DH
A	Disclose by a note to the accounts	No disclosure
B	Make a provision	No disclosure
C	Make a provision	Disclose as a note
D	Make a provision	Accrue the income

(2 marks)

14 Define an operating segment as per IFRS 8 *Operating segments*. (3 marks)

15 Which ONE of the following is a criteria for determining a reportable segment under IFRS 8 *Operating segments*?

A   Its revenue is 15% or more of the total revenue of all segments
B   Its revenue is 10% or more of the total revenue of all operating segments
C   Its assets are 10% or more of the combined assets of all operating segments
D   Its assets are 15% or more of the combined assets of all operating segments (2 marks)

16 Which ONE of the following material items would be classified as a non-adjusting event in HL's financial statements for the year ended 31 December 20X8 according to IAS 10 *Events after the reporting period*?

HL's financial statements were approved for publication on 8 April 20X9.

A   On 1 March 20X9, HL's auditors discovered that, due to an error during the count, the closing inventory had been undervalued by $250,000.

B   Lightning struck one of HL's production facilities on 31 January 20X9 and caused a serious fire. The fire destroyed half of the factory and its machinery. Output was severely reduced for six months.

C   One of HL's customers commenced court action against HL on 1 December 20X8. At 31 December 20X8, HL did not know whether the case would go against it or not. On 1 March 20X9, the court found against HL and awarded damages of $150,000 to the customer.

D   On 15 March 20X9, HL was advised by the liquidator of one of its customers that it was very unlikely to receive any payments for the balance of $300,000 that was outstanding at 31 December 20X8. (2 marks)

17 Which of the following are required by IFRS 8 *Operating segments* to be disclosed in an entity's financial statements, if they are included in the measure of segment profit or loss to be reported to the chief operating decision maker?

(i)   Revenues from transactions with other operating segments within the entity
(ii)   Cost of sales
(iii) Amortisation
(iv)   Income tax expense
(v)   Administrative expenses and distribution costs

A   (i), (ii) and (v)
B   (ii), (iii) and (iv)
C   (ii), (iii) and (v)
D   (i), (iii) and (iv)

(2 marks)

(Total = 36 marks)

23 Objective test questions: Accounting standards II   86 mins

1   IAS 37 *Provisions, contingent liabilities and contingent assets* governs the recognition of contingent items. Which of the following statements about contingencies, if any, are correct according to IAS 37?

   1   A contingent liability should be disclosed by note if it is probable that an obligation will arise and its amount can be estimated reliably.

   2   A contingent asset should be disclosed by note if it is probable that it will arise.

   3   An entity should not recognise a contingent asset.

   A   None of the statements is correct.
   B   1 and 2
   C   2 and 3
   D   All of the statements are correct.   (2 marks)

2   IAS 24 *Related party disclosures* governs disclosures required for transactions between a company and parties deemed to be related to it.

   Which of the following parties will normally be held to be related parties of a company?

   1   Its subsidiary companies
   2   Its directors
   3   Close family of the company's directors
   4   Providers of finance to the company
   5   A customer or supplier with whom the company has a significant volume of business

   A   All of the parties listed
   B   1, 2, 3 and 4 only
   C   1, 2 and 3 only
   D   3, 4 and 5 only   (2 marks)

3   Which of the following statements defines a finance lease?

   A   A short term hire agreement
   B   A long term hire agreement where the legal title in the asset passes on the final payment
   C   A long term hire agreement where substantially all the risks and rewards of ownership are transferred
   D   A long term hire agreement where the hirer is responsible for maintenance of the asset   (2 marks)

4   An asset is hired under a finance lease with a deposit of $30,000 on 1 January 20X1 plus 8 six monthly payments in arrears of $20,000 each. The fair value of the asset is $154,000. The finance charge is to be allocated using the sum of the digits method.

   What is the finance charge for the year ending 31 December 20X3?

   A $7,000
   B $8,000
   C $10,000
   D $11,000   (2 marks)

5   The directors of Robin (year end 31 December 20X6) were informed on 27 February 20X7 that a serious fire at one of the company's factories had stopped production there for at least six months to come. On 3 March 20X7 the directors of Robin were informed that a major customer had gone into liquidation owing a substantial amount to Robin as at the year end. The liquidator was pessimistic about the prospect of recovering anything for unsecured creditors. The financial statements for the year ended 31 December 20X6 were approved on 20 March 20X7.

   In accordance with IAS 10 *Events after the reporting period*, how should the two events be treated in the financial statements?

	Fire	Liquidation
A	Accrued in accounts	Disclosed in notes
B	Disclosed in notes	Disclosed in notes
C	Accrued in accounts	Accrued in accounts
D	Disclosed in notes	Accrued in accounts (2 marks)

6   In which of the following circumstances would a provision be recognised under IAS 37 *Provisions, contingent liabilities and contingent assets* in the financial statements for the year ending 31 March 20X6?

     1   A board decision was made on 15 March to close down a division with potential costs of $100,000. At 31 March the decision had not been communicated to managers, employees or customers.

     2   There are anticipated costs from returns of a defective product in the next few months of $60,000. In the past all returns of defective products have always been refunded to customers.

     3   It is anticipated that a major refurbishment of the company Head Office will take place from June onwards costing $85,000.

     A   1 and 2 only
     B   2 and 3 only
     C   2 only
     D   3 only   **(2 marks)**

7   According to IAS 24 *Related party disclosures*, which of the following would be presumed to be a related party of Fredo unless it can be demonstrated otherwise?

     A   The bank which has given a loan to Fredo
     B   The husband of the managing director of Fredo
     C   Fredo's major supplier
     D   The assistant accountant of Fredo   **(2 marks)**

8   List the three criteria set out in IAS 37 *Provisions, Contingent Liabilities and Contingent Assets* for the recognition of a provision.   **(3 marks)**

9   AP has the following two legal claims outstanding:

     •   A legal action claiming compensation of $500,000 filed against AP in March 20X4.

     •   A legal action taken by AP against a third party, claiming damages of $200,000 was started in January 20X3 and is nearing completion.

     In both cases, it is more likely than not that the amount claimed will have to be paid.

     How should AP report these legal actions in its financial statements for the year ended 31 March 20X5?

	Legal action against AP	*Legal action by AP*
A	Disclose by a note	No disclosure
B	Make a provision	No disclosure
C	Make a provision	Disclose as a note
D	Make a provision	Accrue the income

     (2 marks)

10   Which one of the following would be regarded as a related party of BS?

     A   BX, a customer of BS.

     B   The president of the BS Board, who is also the chief executive officer of another entity, BU, that supplies goods to BS.

     C   BQ, a supplier of BS.

     D   BY, BS's main banker.   **(2 marks)**

11   An item of machinery leased under a five year finance lease on 1 October 20X3 had a fair value of $51,900 at date of purchase.

     The lease payments were $12,000 per year, payable in arrears.

     If the sum of digits method is used to apportion interest to accounting periods, calculate the finance cost for the year ended 30 September 20X5.   **(3 marks)**

12   Which one of the following would require a provision to be created by BW at its year end of 31 October 20X5?

    A   The government introduced new laws on data protection which come into force on 1 January 20X6. BW's directors have agreed that this will require a large number of staff to be retrained. At 31 October 20X5, the directors were waiting on a report they had commissioned that would identify the actual training requirements.

    B   At the year end, BW is negotiating with its insurance provider about the amount of an insurance claim that it had filed. On 20 November 20X5, the insurance provider agreed to pay $200,000.

    C   BW makes refunds to customers for any goods returned within 30 days of sale, and has done so for many years.

    D   A customer is suing BW for damages alleged to have been caused by BW's product. BW is contesting the claim and, at 31 October 20X5, the directors have been advised by BW's legal advisers it is very unlikely to lose the case.   **(2 marks)**

13   IAS 18 *Revenue recognition* defines when revenue may be recognised on the sale of goods.

    List four of the five conditions that IAS 18 requires to be met for income to be recognised.   **(4 marks)**

The following data are given for sub-questions 14 and 15 below

CS acquired a machine, using a finance lease, on 1 January 20X4. The machine had an expected useful life of 12,000 operating hours, after which it would have no residual value.

The finance lease was for a five-year term with rentals of $20,000 per year payable in arrears. The cost price of the machine was $80,000 and the implied interest rate is 7.93% per year. CS used the machine for 2,600 hours in 20X4 and 2,350 hours in 20X5.

14   Using the actuarial method, calculate the non-current liability and current liability figures required by IAS 17 *Leases* to be shown in CS's statement of financial position at 31 December 20X5.   **(3 marks)**

15   Calculate the non-current asset – property, plant and equipment net book value that would be shown in CS's balance sheet at 31 December 20X5. Calculate the depreciation charge using the machine hours method.   **(2 marks)**

16   On 31 March 20X7, DT received an order from a new customer, XX, for products with a sales value of $900,000. XX enclosed a deposit with the order of $90,000.

    On 31 March 20X7, DT had not completed credit referencing of XX and had not despatched any goods. DT is considering the following possible entries for this transaction in its financial statements for the year ended 31 March 20X7.

    1   Include $900,000 in income statement revenue for the year
    2   Include $90,000 in income statement revenue for the year
    3   Do not include anything in income statement revenue for the year
    4   Create a trade receivable for $810,000
    5   Create a trade payable for $90,000

    According to IAS 18 *Revenue Recognition*, how should DT record this transaction in its financial statements for the year ended 31 March 20X7?

    A   1 and 4
    B   2 and 5
    C   3 and 4
    D   3 and 5   **(2 marks)**

The following data are given for sub questions 17 and 18 below

Company X closed one of its divisions 12 months ago. It has yet to dispose of one remaining machine. The carrying value of the machine at the date when business ceased was $750,000. It was being depreciated at 25% on a reducing balance basis. Company X has been advised that the fair value of the machine is $740,000 and expects to incur costs of $10,000 in making the sale. It has located a probable buyer but the sale will not be completed before the year end.

17   At what amount should the machine be shown in the year end financial statements of Company X?

    A $750,000
    B $562,500
    C $740,000
    D $730,000   **(2 marks)**

18   Where should the carrying value of the machine be shown in Company X's statement of financial position?

    A   Under non-current assets
    B   Under current assets
    C   Included within inventory
    D   Included within receivables   **(2 marks)**

19   GD's financial reporting period is 1 September 2007 to 31 August 2008.

Which ONE of the following would be classified as a non-adjusting event according to IAS 10 *Events after the reporting period*?

Assume all amounts are material and that GD's financial statements have not yet been approved for publication.

    A   On 30 October 2008, GD received a communication stating that one of its customers had ceased trading and gone into liquidation. The balance outstanding at 31 August 2008 was unlikely to be paid.

    B   At 31 August 2008, GD had not provided for an outstanding legal action against the local government administration for losses suffered as a result of incorrect enforcement of local business regulations. On 5 November 2008, the court awarded GD $50,000 damages.

    C   On 1 October 2008, GD made a rights issue of 1 new share for every 3 shares held at a price of $175. The market price on that date was $200.

    D   At 31 August 2008, GD had an outstanding insurance claim of $150,000. On 10 October 2008, the insurance company informed GD that it would pay $140,000 as settlement.   **(2 marks)**

20   Which ONE of the following would **NOT** normally be treated as a related party of HJ in accordance with IAS 24 *Related party disclosures*?

    A   XX, HJ's largest customer, accounts for 75% of HJ's turnover
    B   HJ2, a subsidiary of HJ, that does not trade with HJ
    C   HJA, an associate of HJ
    D   A shareholder of HJ, holding 25% of HJ's equity shares

                                                                 (2 marks)

21   HP entered into an operating lease for a machine on 1 May 20X7 with the following terms:

    •   Five years non-cancellable lease
    •   12 months rent free period from commencement
    •   Rent of $12,000 per annum payable at $1,000 a month from month 13 onwards
    •   Machine useful life 15 years

Calculate the amount that should be charged to profit or loss in HP's financial statements in respect of the lease, for each of the years ended 30 April 20X8 and 30 April 20X9.

                                                                       (3 marks)

                                                                (Total = 48 marks)

24 Section B questions: Accounting standards I   72 mins

(a)   The following definitions have been taken from the International Accounting Standards Committee's *Framework for the Preparation and Presentation of Financial Statements.*

*   'An asset is a resource controlled by the entity as a result of past events and from which future economic benefits are expected to flow to the entity.'

*   'A liability is a present obligation of the entity arising from past events, the settlement of which is expected to result in an outflow from the entity of resources embodying economic benefits.'

IAS 17 *Leases* requires lessees to capitalise finance leases in their financial statements.

Required

Explain how IAS 17's treatment of finance leases applies the definitions of assets and liabilities.

(5 marks)

(b)   NDL drilled a new oil well, which started production on 1 March 20X3. The licence granting permission to drill the new oil well included a clause that requires NDL to 'return the land to the state it was in before drilling commenced'.

NDL estimates that the oil well will have a 20-year production life. At the end of that time, the oil well will be de-commissioned and work carried out to reinstate the land. The cost of this de-commissioning work is estimated to be $20 million.

Required

As the trainee management accountant, draft a memo to the production manager explaining how NDL must treat the de-commissioning costs in its financial statements for the year to 31 March 20X3. Your memo should refer to appropriate International Accounting Standards.   **(5 marks)**

P7 Pilot paper

(c)   BJ is an entity that provides a range of facilities for holidaymakers and travellers.

At 1 October 20X4 these included:

*   a short haul airline operating within Europe; and
*   a travel agency specialising in arranging holidays to more exotic destinations, such as Hawaii and Fiji.

BJ's airline operation has made significant losses for the last two years. On 31 January 20X5, the directors of BJ decided that, due to a significant increase in competition on short haul flights within Europe, BJ would close all of its airline operations and dispose of its fleet of aircraft. All flights for holiday makers and travellers who had already booked seats would be provided by third party airlines. All operations ceased on 31 May 20X5.

On 31 July 20X5, BJ sold its fleet of aircraft and associated non-current assets for $500 million, the carrying value at that date was $750 million.

At the balance sheet date, BJ were still in negotiation with some employees regarding severance payments. BJ has estimated that in the financial period October 20X5 to September 20X6, they will agree a settlement of $20 million compensation.

The closure of the airline operation caused BJ to carry out a major restructuring of the entire entity. The restructuring has been agreed by the directors and active steps have been taken to implement it. The cost of restructuring to be incurred in year 20X5/20X6 is estimated at $10 million.

Required

Explain how BJ should report the events described above and quantify any amounts required to be included in its financial statements for the year ended 30 September 20X5. (Detailed disclosure notes are not required.)   **(5 marks)**

P7 11/05

(d)   CB is an entity specialising in importing a wide range of non-food items and selling them to retailers. George is CB's president and founder and owns 40% of CB's equity shares:

- CB's largest customer, XC, accounts for 35% of CB's revenue. XC has just completed negotiations with CB for a special 5% discount on all sales.

- During the accounting period, George purchased a property from CB for $500,000. CB had previously declared the property surplus to its requirements and had valued it at $750,000.

- George's son, Arnold, is a director in a financial institution, FC. During the accounting period, FC advanced $2 million to CB as an unsecured loan at a favourable rate of interest.

Required

Explain, with reasons, the extent to which each of the above transactions should be classified and disclosed in accordance with IAS 24 *Related Party Disclosures* in CB's financial statements for the period. **(5 marks)**

`P7 5/06`

(e)   CR issued 200,000 $10 redeemable 5% preference shares at par on 1 April 20X5. The shares were redeemable on 31 March 20Y0 at a premium of 15%. Issue costs amounted to $192,800.

Required

(a)   Calculate the total finance cost over the life of the preference shares. **(2 marks)**

(b)   Calculate the annual charge to the income statement for finance expense, as required by IAS 39 Financial Instruments: Recognition and Measurement, for each of the five years 20X6 to 20Y0. Assume the constant annual rate of interest as 10%. **(3 marks)**

(Total = 5 marks)

`P7 5/06`

(f)   You are in charge of the preparation of the financial statements for DF. You are nearing completion of the preparation of the accounts for the year ended 30 September 20X6 and two items have come to your attention.

(i)   Shortly after a senior employee left in April 20X6, a number of accounting discrepancies were discovered. With further investigation, it became clear that fraudulent activity had been going on. DF has calculated that, because of the fraud, the profit for the year ended 30 September 20X5 had been overstated by $45,000.

(ii)   On 1 September 20X6, DF received an order from a new customer enclosing full payment for the goods ordered; the order value was $90,000. DF scheduled the manufacture of the goods to commence on 28 November 20X6. The cost of manufacture was expected to be $70,000. DF's management want to recognise the $20,000 profit in the statement of comprehensive income for the year ended 30 September 20X6. It has been suggested that the $90,000 should be recognised as revenue and a provision of $70,000 created for the cost of manufacture.

DF's statement of comprehensive income for the year ended 30 September 20X5 showed a profit of $600,000. The draft statement of comprehensive income for the year ended 30 September 20X6 showed a profit of $700,000. The 30 September 20X5 accounts were approved by the directors on 1 March 20X6.

Required

Explain how the events described above should be reported in the financial statements of DF for the years ended 30 September 20X5 and 20X6. **(5 marks)**

`P7 11/06`

(g)   On 1 June 20X6 the directors of DP commissioned a report to determine possible actions they could take to reduce DP's losses. The report, which was presented to the directors on 1 December 20X6, proposed that DP cease all of its manufacturing activities and concentrate on its retail activities. The directors formally approved the plan to close DP's factory. The factory was gradually shut down, commencing on 5 December 20X6, with production finally ceasing on 15 March 20X7. All employees had ceased working or had been transferred to other facilities in the company, by 29 March 20X7. The plant and equipment was removed and sold for $25,000 (net book value $95,000) on 30 March 20X7.

The factory and building are being advertised for sale but had not been sold by 31 March 20X7. The carrying value of the land and building at 31 March 20X7, based on original cost, was $750,000. The estimated net realisable value of the land and building at 31 March 20X7 was $1,125,000.

Closure costs incurred (and paid) up to 31 March 20X7 were $620,000.

The cash flows, revenues and expenses relating to the factory were clearly distinguishable from DP's other operations. The output of the factory was sold directly to third parties and to DP's retail outlets. The manufacturing facility was shown as a separate segment in DP's segmental information.

Required

With reference to relevant International Accounting Standards, explain how DP should treat the factory closure in its financial statements for the year ended 31 March 20X7. **(5 marks)**

(h) On 1 September 20X7, the Directors of EK decided to sell EK's retailing division and concentrate activities entirely on its manufacturing division.

The retailing division was available for immediate sale, but EK had not succeeded in disposing of the operation by 31 October 20X7. EK identified a potential buyer for the retailing division, but negotiations were at an early stage. The Directors of EK are certain that the sale will be completed by 31 August 20X8.

The retailing division's carrying value at 31 August 20X7 was:

	$'000
Non-current tangible assets – property, plant and equipment	300
Non-current tangible assets – goodwill	100
Net current assets	43
Total carrying value	443

The retailing division has been valued at $423,000, comprising:

	$'000
Non-current tangible assets – property, plant and equipment	320
Non-current tangible assets – goodwill	60
Net current assets	43
Total carrying value	423

EK's directors have estimated that EK will incur consultancy and legal fees for the disposal of $25,000.

Required

(i) Explain whether EK can treat the sale of its retailing division as a 'discontinued operation', as defined by IFRS 5 *Non-current Assets held for Sale and Discontinued Operations*, in its financial statements for the year ended 31 October 20X7. **(3 marks)**

(ii) Explain how EK should treat the retailing division in its financial statements for the year ended 31 October 20X7, assuming the sale of its retailing division meets the classification requirements for a disposal group (IFRS 5). **(2 marks)**

(Total = 5 marks)

P7 11/07

(Total = 40 marks)

25 Section B questions: Accounting standards II · 72 mins

(a) IAS 37 defines the meaning of a provision and sets out when a provision should be recognised.

Required

Using the IAS 37 definition of a provision, explain how a provision meets the International Accounting Standards Board's *Framework for the Preparation and Presentation of Financial Statements'* definition of a liability. **(5 marks)**

P7 Pilot paper

(b) A lessee leases a non-current asset on a non-cancellable lease contract of five years, the details of which are:

- The asset has a useful life of five years.
- The rental is $21,000 per annum payable at the end of each year.
- The lessee also has to pay all insurance and maintenance costs.
- The fair value of the asset was $88,300.

The lessee uses the sum of digits method to calculate finance charges on the lease.

Required

Prepare statement of comprehensive income and statement of financial position extracts for years one and two of the lease. **(5 marks)**

P7 Pilot paper

(c) AE has a three year contract which commenced on 1 April 20X4. At 31 March 20X5, AE had the following balances in its ledger relating to the contract:

	$'000	$'000
Total contract value		60,000
Cost incurred up to 31 March 20X5:		
Attributable to work completed	21,000	
Inventory purchased for use in 20X5/6	3,000	24,000
Progress payments received		25,000
Other information:		
Expected further costs to completion		19,000

At 31 March 20X5, the contract was certified as 50% complete.

Required

Prepare the statement of comprehensive income and statement of financial position extracts showing the balances relating to this contract, as required by IAS 11 *Construction contracts*. **(5 marks)**

P7 5/05

(d) A five year finance lease commenced on 1 April 20X3. The annual payments are $30,000 in arrears. The fair value of the asset at 1 April 20X3 was $116,000. Use the sum of digits method for interest allocations and assume that the asset has no residual value at the end of the lease term.

Required

In accordance with IAS 17 *Leases*:

(i) Calculate the amount of finance cost that would be charged to the statement of comprehensive income for the year ended 31 March 20X5

(ii) Prepare statement of financial position extracts for the lease at 31 March 20X5. **(5 marks)**

P7 5/05

(e) CD is a manufacturing entity that runs a number of operations including a bottling plant that bottles carbonated soft drinks. CD has been developing a new bottling process that will allow the bottles to be filled and sealed more efficiently.

The new process took a year to develop. At the start of development, CD estimated that the new process would increase output by 15% with no additional cost (other than the extra bottles and their contents).

Development work commenced on 1 May 20X5 and was completed on 20 April 20X6. Testing at the end of the development confirmed CD's original estimates.

CD incurred expenditure of $180,000 on the above development in 20X5/X6.

CD plans to install the new process in its bottling plant and start operating the new process from 1 May 20X6.

CD's year end is 30 April.

Required

(i)   Explain the requirements of IAS 38 *Intangible Assets* for the treatment of development costs.

(3 marks)

(ii)   Explain how CD should treat its development costs in its financial statements for the year ended 30 April 20X6.   **(2 marks)**

(Total = 5 marks)

`P7 5/06`

(f)   On 1 April 20X5, DX acquired plant and machinery with a fair value of $900,000 on a finance lease. The lease is for five years with the annual lease payments of $228,000 being paid in advance on 1 April each year. The interest rate implicit in the lease is 13.44%. The first payment was made on 1 April 20X5.

Required

(i)   Calculate the finance charge in respect of the lease that will be shown in DX's income statement for the year ended 31 March 20X7.

(ii)   Calculate the amount to be shown as a current liability and a non-current liability in DX's balance sheet at 31 March 20X7.

(All workings should be to the nearest $'000.)   **(5 marks)**

`P7 5/07`

(g)   The objective of IAS 24 *Related Party Disclosures* is to ensure that financial statements disclose the effect of the existence of related parties.

Required

With reference to IAS 24, explain the meaning of the terms 'related party' and 'related party transaction'.

(5 marks)

`P7 11/07`

(h)   EJ publishes trade magazines and sells them to retailers. EJ has just concluded negotiations with a large supermarket chain for the supply of a large quantity of several of its trade magazines on a regular basis.

EJ has agreed a substantial discount on the following terms:

- The same quantity of each trade magazine will be supplied each month;
- Quantities can only be changed at the end of each six month period;
- Payment must be made six monthly in advance.

The supermarket paid $150,000 on 1 September 20X7 for six months supply of trade magazines to 29 February 20X8. At 31 October 20X7, EJ had supplied two months of trade magazines.

EJ estimates that the cost of supplying the supermarket each month is $20,000.

Required

(i)   State the criteria in IAS 18 *Revenue* for income recognition.   **(2 marks)**

(ii)   Explain, with reasons, how EJ should treat the above in its financial statements for the year ended 31 October 20X7.   **(3 marks)**

`P7 11/07`

(Total = 5 marks)

(Total = 40 marks)

26 AZ (FATP Pilot paper/amended)   45 mins

AZ is a quoted manufacturing entity. Its finished products are stored in a nearby warehouse until ordered by customers. AZ has been re-organising the business to improve performance.

The trial balance for AZ at 31 March 20X3 was as follows:

	$'000	$'000
7% Loan Notes (redeemable 20X7)		18,250
Retained earnings at 31 March 20X2		14,677
Administrative expenses	16,020	
Bank and Cash	25,820	
Cost of goods manufactured in the year to 31 March 20X3 (excluding depreciation)	94,000	
Distribution costs	9,060	
Dividends received		1,200
Equity shares $1 each, fully paid		19,000
Interest paid	639	
Inventory at 31 March 20X2	4,852	
Plant and Equipment	30,315	
Allowance for depreciation at 31 March 20X2:		
Plant and Equipment		6,060
Vehicles		1,670
Allowance for doubtful trade receivables		600
Restructuring costs	121	
Sales revenue		124,900
Trade payables		8,120
Trade receivables	9,930	
Vehicles	3,720	
	194,477	194,477

Additional information provided

(a) Non-current assets are being depreciated as follows:

Plant & Equipment   20% per annum straight line
Vehicles   25% per annum reducing balance

Depreciation of plant and equipment is considered to be part of cost of sales, while depreciation of vehicles should be included under distribution costs.

(b) Tax due for the year to 31 March 20X3 is estimated at $15,000.

(c) The closing inventory at 31 March 20X3 was $5,180,000.

(d) The 7% loan notes are 10-year loans due for repayment by 31 March 20X7. AZ incurred no other interest charges in the year to 31 March 20X3.

(e) The restructuring costs in the trial balance represent the cost of the final phase of a major fundamental restructuring of the entity to improve competitiveness and future profitability.

(f) The auditors have drawn attention to the following issues not reflected in the trial balance:

(i) Inventory brought forward at the beginning of the year had been understated by $500,000.

(ii) Items included in closing inventory at cost of $1.2m were damaged in transit. They will require remedial work costing $250,000 and can then be sold for $1.35m.

(iii) Administrative expenses include $600,000 paid on leasing a machine from 1 April 20X2. This should not have been treated as an operating lease. It is actually a finance lease. The original cost of the machine was $2m and the agreement provides for four annual payments in arrears of $600,000. The interest rate implicit in the lease is 7.7%.

Required

Prepare AZ's statement of comprehensive income for the year to 31 March 20X3, a statement of financial position at that date, and a statement of changes in equity for the year. These should be in a form suitable for presentation to the shareholders, in accordance with the requirements of International Accounting Standards.

Notes to the financial statements are NOT required, but all workings must be clearly shown. DO NOT prepare a statement of accounting policies. **(25 marks)**

27 AF (FATP 5/05/amended)   45 mins

AF is a furniture manufacturing entity. The trial balance for AF at 31 March 20X5 was as follows:

	$'000	$'000
6% loan notes (redeemable 20Y0)		1,500
Retained earnings at 31 March 20X4		388
Administrative expenses	1,540	
Available for sale investments at market value 31 March 20X4	1,640	
Bank and cash	822	
Cost of sales	3,463	
Distribution costs	1,590	
Dividend paid 1 December 20X4	275	
Interest paid on loan notes – half year to 30 September 20X4	45	
Inventory at 31 March 20X5	1,320	
Investment income received		68
Land and buildings at cost	5,190	
Ordinary shares of $1 each, fully paid		4,500
Plant and equipment at cost	3,400	
Provision for deferred tax		710
Accumulated depreciation at 31 March 20X4: Buildings		1,500
Accumulated depreciation at 31 March 20X4: Plant and equipment		1,659
Revaluation surplus		330
Sales revenue		8,210
Share premium		1,380
Trade payables		520
Trade receivables	1,480	
	20,765	20,765

Additional information provided

(a)   Available for sale investments are carried in the financial statements at market value. The market value of the available for sale investments at 31 March 20X5 was $1,750,000.

(b)   There were no sales or purchases of non-current assets or available for sale investments during the year ended 31 March 20X5.

(c)   Income tax due for the year ended 31 March 20X5 is estimated at $250,000. The tax rate is 30%. There is no balance outstanding in relation to previous years' corporate income tax. At 31 March 20X5 capital allowances exceed depreciation by $2,700,000.

(d)   Depreciation is charged on buildings using the straight-line basis at 3% each year. The cost of land included in land and buildings is $2,000,000. Plant and equipment is depreciated using the reducing balance method at 20%. Depreciation is regarded as a cost of sales.

(e)   AF entered into a non-cancellable five year operating lease on 1 April 20X4 to acquire machinery to manufacture a new range of kitchen units. Under the terms of the lease, AF will receive the first year rent free, then $62,500 is payable for four years commencing in year two of the lease. The machine is estimated to have a useful economic life of 20 years.

(f)   The 6% loan notes are 10 year loans due for repayment in March 20Y0. AF incurred no other finance costs in the year to 31 March 20X5.

Required

Prepare the statement of comprehensive income of AF for the year to 31 March 20X5, a statement of changes in equity and a statement of financial position at that date, in a form suitable for presentation to the shareholders and in accordance with the requirements of International Financial Reporting Standards.

Notes to the financial statements are **not** required, but all workings must be clearly shown.   **(25 marks)**

28 BG (FATP 11/05/amended)   45 mins

BG provides office cleaning services to a range of organisations in its local area. BG operates through a small network of depots that are rented spaces situated in out-of-town industrial developments. BG has a policy to lease all vehicles on operating leases.

The trial balance for BG at 30 September 20X5 was as follows:

	$'000	$'000
10% bonds (redeemable 20Y0)		150
Administrative expenses	239	
Bank and cash	147	
Bond interest paid – half year to 31 March 20X5	8	
Cost of cleaning materials consumed	101	
Direct operating expenses (including cleaning staff)	548	
Dividend paid	60	
Equipment and fixtures, cost at 30 September 20X5	752	
Equity shares $1 each, fully paid		200
Income tax	9	
Inventory of cleaning materials at 30 September 20X5	37	
Investment income received		11
Provision for deferred tax		50
Accumulated depreciation at 30 September 20X4:		
Equipment and fixtures		370
Provision for legal claim balance at 30 September 20X4		190
Retained earnings at 30 September 20X4		256
Revenue		1,017
Share premium		40
Trade payables		24
Trade receivables	346	
Vehicle operating lease rentals paid	61	
	2,308	2,308

Additional information

(a)   The income tax balance in the trial balance is a result of the underprovision of tax for the year ended 30 September 20X4.

(b)   The taxation due for the year ended 30 September 20X5 is estimated at $64,000 and the deferred tax provision needs to be increased by $15,000.

(c)   Equipment and fixtures are depreciated at 20% per annum straight line. Depreciation of equipment and fixtures is considered to be part of direct cost of sales. BG's policy is to charge a full year's depreciation in the year of acquisition and no depreciation in the year of disposal.

(d)   The 10% bonds were issued in 20X0.

(e)   BG paid an interim dividend during the year, but does not propose to pay a final dividend as profit for the year is well below expectations.

(f)   At 30 September 20X4, BG had an outstanding legal claim from a customer alleging that BG had caused a major fire in the customer's premises. BG was advised that it would very probably lose the case, so a provision of $190,000 was set up at 30 September 20X4. During 20X5, new evidence was discovered and the case against BG was dropped. As there is no further liability, the directors have decided that the provision is no longer required.

Required

(a) Prepare the statement of comprehensive for BG for the year to 30 September 20X5 and a statement of financial position at that date, in a form suitable for presentation to the shareholders and in accordance with the requirements of International Financial Reporting Standards. Do NOT prepare a statement of changes in equity.

(15 marks)

BG currently has 9 vans leased on operating leases. All of the leases were taken out on 1 October 20X3 when the vans were new and priced at $20,000 each. At that time BG could have acquired them under finance leases, paying 3 annual instalments of $8,000 for each van on 1 October 20X3, 20X4 and 20X5. The directors are wondering whether this would have been a better option.

Required

(b) Redraft the retained earnings balance at 30 September 20X5 of BG as it would be if the vans had been acquired as above under finance leases and depreciated at 20% per annum. Assume an interest rate of 21.53% pa.

(10 marks)

(Total = 25 marks)

29 DZ (FATP 5/07/amended)   45 mins

DZ is a manufacturing entity and produces one group of products, known as product Y.

DZ's trial balance at 31 March 20X7 is shown below.

	$'000	$'000
Administration expenses	891	
Bank and cash	208	
Cash received on disposal of land		1,500
Cash received on disposal of plant		5
Cost of raw materials purchased in year	2,020	
Direct production labour costs	912	
Distribution costs	462	
Equity shares $1 each, fully paid		1,000
Inventory of finished goods at 31 March 20X6	240	
Inventory of raw materials at 31 March 20X6	132	
Land at valuation at 31 March 20X6	1,250	
Plant and equipment at cost at 31 March 20X6	4,180	
Production overheads (excluding depreciation)	633	
Property at cost at 31 March 20X6	11,200	
Provision for depreciation at 31 March 20X6 (see notes (d) and (e))		
Property		1,900
Plant and equipment		2,840
Research and development (see note (f))	500	
Retained earnings at 31 March 20X6		4,797
Revaluation surplus at 31 March 20X6		2,100
Revenue		8,772
Trade payables		748
Trade receivables	1,059	
Accruals		25
	23,687	23,687

Further information

(a) The property cost of $11,200,000 consisted of land $3,500,000 and buildings $7,700,000.

(b) During the year, DZ disposed of non-current assets as follows.

- A piece of surplus land was sold on 1 March 20X7 for $1,500,000
- Obsolete plant was sold for $5,000 scrap value on the same date
- All the cash received is included in the trial balance

Details of the assets sold were:

Asset type	Cost	Revalued amount	Accumulated dep'n
Land	$500,000	$1,250,000	$0
Plant and equipment	$620,000		$600,000

(c) On 31 March 20X7, DZ revalued its properties to $9,800,000 (land $4,100,000 and buildings $5,700,000).

(d) Buildings are depreciated at 5% per annum on the straight line basis. Buildings depreciation is treated as 80% production overhead and 20% administration.

(e) Plant and equipment is depreciated at 25% per annum using the reducing balance method, the depreciation being treated as a production overhead

(f) Product Y was developed in-house. Research and development is carried out on a continuous basis to ensure that the product range continues to meet customer demands. The research and development figure in the trial balance is made up as follows.

	$'000
Development costs capitalised in previous years	867
Less amortisation to 31 March 20X6	534
	333
Research costs incurred in the year to 31 March 20X7	119
Development costs (all meet IAS 38 *Intangible Assets* criteria) incurred in the year to 31 March 20X7	48
Total	500

(g) Development costs are amortised on a straight line basis at 20% per annum.

(h) Research and development costs are treated as cost of sales when charged to the income statement.

(i) DZ charges a full year's amortisation and depreciation in the year of acquisition and none in the year of disposal.

(j) Inventory of raw materials at 31 March 20X7 was $165,000. Inventory of finished goods at 31 March 20X7 was $270,000.

(k) The directors estimate the income tax charge on the year's profits at $811,000. ✓

(l) No interim dividend was paid during the year.

Required

(a) Prepare DZ's property, plant and equipment note to the accounts for the year ended 31 March 20X7.

(6 marks)

(b) Prepare the statement of comprehensive income and a statement of changes in equity for the year to 31 March 20X7 and a statement of financial position at that date, in a form suitable for presentation to the shareholders and in accordance with the requirements of International Financial Reporting Standards.

(All workings should be to the nearest $'000). **(19 marks)**

Notes to the financial statements are NOT required (except as specified in part (a) of the question) but ALL workings must be clearly shown. Do NOT prepare a statement of accounting policies.

(Total = 25 marks)

30 FZ (FATP 5/08 amended)   45 mins

FZ is an entity which owns a number of factories that specialise in packaging and selling fresh dairy products in bulk to wholesale entities and large supermarkets. FZ also own a chain of small newsagents' shops.

At its meeting on 1 January 20X8, the Board of FZ decided that, to maximise its strategic opportunities, it would sell the newsagents' shops and concentrate on its dairy product business.

FZ's trial balance at 31 March 20X8 is shown below.

	Notes	$'000	$'000
5% Loan notes (redeemable 20Z0)			1,000
Administrative expenses		440	
Cash and cash equivalents		853	
Cash received on disposal of vehicles			15
Cost of goods sold		4,120	
Distribution costs		432	
Equity dividend paid		500	
Factory buildings at valuation		12,000	
Goodwill		300	
Inventory at 31 March 20X8		900	
Newsagents shops at cost		6,200	
Ordinary shares $1 each, fully paid at 31 March 20X8			5,000
Plant and equipment		2,313	
Provision for deferred tax at 31 March 20X7			197
Provision for property, plant and equipment depreciation at 31 March 20X7	(c)		3,337
Retained earnings at 31 March 20X7			5,808
Revaluation surplus			190
Sales revenue			10,170
Share premium at 31 March 20X8			3,000
Trade payables			417
Trade receivables		929	
Vehicles at cost		147	
		29,134	29,134

Additional information

(a) The newsagents' shops were valued at $5,000,000 by an external valuer on 1 January 20X8. On the same date, a prospective buyer expressed an interest at that price. At 31 March 20X8, detailed negotiations were continuing, with the sale expected to be concluded by 31 July 20X8, for the full valuation of $5,000,000.

The net book values (all included in the relevant figures in the trial balance) of the assets relating to the newsagents' shops at 1 January 20X8, before revaluation, were:

	$'000
Goodwill	300
Newsagents' shops	4,960
	5,260

The newsagents' shops are regarded as a cash generating unit. The cost of selling the shops is estimated at $200,000.

The revenue and expenses of the newsagents' shops for the year ended 31 March 20X8, all included in the trial balance figures, were as follows.

	$'000
Revenue	772
Cost of sales	580
Administrative expenses	96
Distribution costs	57

The sales agreement provides for all employee contracts to be transferred to the new owners of the shops.

Loan note interest does not relate to newsagents shops.

(b)   At their meeting on 1 February 20X8, the directors of FZ agreed a $2,000,000 reorganisation package for all of FZ, excluding the newsagents' shops. The restructuring was announced to the staff on 16 February 20X8. it was scheduled to begin implementation on 1 July 20X8 and to be completed by 31 December 20X8. The reorganisation package covered staff retraining, staff relocation and development of new computer systems.

(c)   Property, plant and equipment depreciation at 31 March 20X7 comprised:

	$'000
Factory buildings	720
Plant and equipment	1,310
Vehicles	67
Newsagents' shops	1,240

(d)   On 1 May 20X8, FZ was informed that one of its customers, X, had ceased trading. The liquidators advised FZ that it was very unlikely to receive payment of any of the $62,000 due from X at 31 March 20X8.

(e)   The taxation due for the year ended 31 March 20X8 is estimated at $920,000 (net of tax credit for newsagents' shops of $120,000) and the deferred tax provision needs to be increased to $237,000 (all relating to continuing activities).

(f)   Depreciation is to be charged on non-current assets as follows.

- Factory buildings, straight line basis at 3%
- Plant and equipment, straight line basis at 20%
- Newsagents' shops, straight line basis at 10%

These items of depreciation are regarded as a cost of sales.

- Vehicles, reducing balance at 25%

This depreciation is regarded as a distribution cost.

FZ provides a full year's depreciation in the year of purchase and no depreciation in the year of sale.

(g)   During the year, FZ disposed of old vehicles for $15,000. The original cost of these vehicles was $57,000 and accumulated depreciation at 31 March 20X7 was $52,000.

(h)   The revaluation surplus arose when the factory buildings were revalued in 20X5.

(i)   During the year, FZ raised new capital by making a rights issue of 1,000,000 $1 equity shares at $1.50 each. All rights were taken up and all amounts are included in the trial balance.

(j)   The 5% loan notes were issued in 20X0.

(k)   FZ want to disclose the minimum information allowed by IFRS in its primary financial statements.

Required

(a)   Explain, with reasons, how items (a) and (b) above should be treated in FZ's financial statements for the year ended 31 March 20X8.   **(5 marks)**

(b)   Prepare FZ's statement of comprehensive income for the year to 31 March 20X8 and a statement of financial position at that date, in a form suitable for presentation to the shareholders and in accordance with the requirements of International Financial Reporting Standards.   **(20 marks)**

Notes to the financial statements are not required, but all workings must be clearly shown. Do not prepare a statement of accounting policies.   **(Total = 25 marks)**

31 GZ (FATP 11/08 amended)   45 mins

GZ is a small mining entity which operated a single gold mine for many years. The gold mine ceased operations on 31 October 20X7 and was closed on 1 January 20X8.

On 1 November 20X7, GZ commenced operating a new silver mine.

The trial balance for GZ at 31 October 20X8 was as follows:

	$'000	$'000
Administrative expenses	1,131	
Bank & cash	1,240	
Decommissioning and landscaping expenses of gold mine (see note (c))	1,008	
Direct operating expenses (excluding depreciation)	5,245	
Distribution costs	719	
Dividend paid 1 March 20X8	550	
Equity shares $1 each, fully paid		5,000
Finance lease payable at 1 November 20X7 (see note (g))		900
Government operating license, silver mine at cost (see note (b))	100	
Income tax	13	
Inventory at 31 October 20X8	2,410	
Investment income received		218
Mine properties at cost (see note (d))	6,719	
Plant (finance lease) at 1 November 20X7 (see note (g))	900	
Plant and equipment at 31 October 20X7 (excluding finance lease)	3,025	
Plant lease rentals paid in year	160	
Provision for decommissioning gold mine at 31 October 20X7		950
Provision for deferred tax at 31 October 20X7		731
Provision for depreciation at 31 October 20X7:		
Mine properties (see note (d))		2,123
Plant and equipment		370
Receipt from sale of plant (see note (c))		2
Retained earnings at 31 October 20X7		1,790
Revenue		9,600
Suspense account (see note (g))		1,820
Trade payables		2,431
Trade receivables	2,715	
	25,935	25,935

Additional information provided:

(a)   Each mine requires a government operating licence for 20 years and is expected to be productive for that time. After 20 years, the mine will be closed and decommissioned.

(b)   On 1 November 20X7, GZ received a government operating licence to operate the new silver mine. The licence cost $100,000 and is for 20 years. Included in the licence is a condition that, on closure of the mine, all above-ground structures must be removed and the ground landscaped. GZ has estimated this cost and discounted it to a present value of $3,230,000 at 31 October 20X8. The trial balance excludes this decommissioning provision.

(c)   On 1 January 20X8, GZ closed its gold mine. The $950,000 shown in the trial balance provision as "provision for decommissioning gold mine" has been charged against profits in the previous year. The removal of buildings and other above ground structures, landscaping and other decommissioning costs was complete at 31 October 20X8; the actual cost incurred was $1,008,000. GZ sold old plant and equipment from the gold mine for $2,000 (original cost $200,000, net book value $5,000). The gold mine property is now surplus to GZ's requirements. At 31 October 20X8, the gold mine property had a market value of $520,000 with estimated selling and legal costs of $27,000.

(d)   The mine property balances in the trial balance comprised:

Mine property	Gold mine	Silver mine	Total
	$'000	$'000	$'000
Cost	2,623	4,096	6,719
Provision for depreciation	2,123	0	2,123
	500	4,096	4,596

(e) Income tax due for the year ended 31 October 20X8 is estimated at $375,000. The deferred tax provision needs to be reduced by $60,000.

(f) Depreciation is charged on mining property using the straight-line basis at 5% per annum. Plant and equipment is depreciated using the reducing balance method at 25%. The depreciation policy is to charge a full year's depreciation in the year of acquisition and no depreciation in the year of disposal. Depreciation is regarded as a cost of production.

(g) GZ entered into a non-cancellable seven-year finance lease on 1 November 20X7 to acquire mining machinery. Under the terms of the lease, GZ will make annual payments of $160,000 in arrears, the first payment being made on 31 October 2008. The machinery is estimated to have a useful economic life of seven years. The fair value of the machinery at 1 November 20X7 was $900,000. GZ allocates finance charges using the sum of digits method.

(h) The final dividend for the year to 31 October 20X7 was paid on 1 March 20X8.

(i) GZ made a new issue of 1,400 equity shares on 31 October 20X8 at a premium of 30%. The cash received was debited to the bank account and credited to the suspense account.

Required

(a) Prepare GZ's Property, Plant and Equipment note to the financial statements for the year to 31 October 20X8. **(6 marks)**

(b) Prepare GZ's statement of comprehensive income and a statement of changes in equity for the year to 31 October 20X8 and a statement of financial position at that date, in a form suitable for presentation to the shareholders and in accordance with the requirements of International Financial Reporting Standards. (All workings should be to the nearest $'000).

Notes to the financial statements, except as indicated in part (a) above, are NOT required, but all workings must be clearly shown. Do NOT prepare a statement of accounting policies. **(19 marks)**

(Total = 25 marks)

32 XY (Specimen Paper) 45 mins

XY's trial balance at 31 March 20X9 is shown below:

	Notes	$000	$000
Administrative expenses		303	
Available for sale investments	(ii)	564	
Cash and cash equivalents		21	
Cash received on disposal of land			48
Cost of goods sold		908	
Distribution costs		176	
Equity dividend paid	(ix)	50	
Income tax	(iii)	12	
Inventory at 31 March 20X9		76	
Land at cost – 31 March 20X8	(v)	782	
Long term borrowings	(viii)		280
Ordinary Shares $1 each, fully paid at 31 March 20X9	(vii)		500
Property, plant and equipment – at cost 31 March 20X8	(vi)	630	
Provision for deferred tax at 31 March 20X8	(iv)		19
Property, plant and equipment depreciation at 31 March 20X8	(vi)		378
Retained earnings at 31 March 20X8			321
Revaluation surplus at 31 March 20X8			160
Revenue			1,770
Share premium at 31 March 20X9			200
Trade payables			56
Trade receivables		210	
		3,732	3,732

Additional information provided:

(i)   XY trades in Country X. In Country X, the corporate tax on profits is at a rate of 25%. Tax depreciation is deductible as follows: 50% of additions to property, plant and equipment in the accounting period in which they are recorded; 25% per year of the written-down value in subsequent accounting periods except that in which the asset is disposed of. No tax depreciation is allowed on land.

(ii)   Available for sale investments are carried in the financial statements at market value. The market value of the available for sale investments at 31 March 20X9 was $608,000. There were no purchases or sales of available for sale investments during the year.

(iii)   The income tax balance in the trial balance is a result of the underprovision of tax for the year ended 31 March 20X8.

(iv)   The taxation due for the year ended 31 March 20X9 is estimated at $96,000. The tax depreciation cumulative allowances at 31 March 20X8 for property, plant and equipment were $453,000.

(v)   Land sold during the year had a book value of $39,000. The fair value of the remaining land at 31 March 20X9 was $729,000.

(vi)   Property, plant and equipment is depreciated at 20% per annum straight line. Depreciation of property, plant and equipment is considered to be part of cost of sales. XY's policy is to charge a full year's depreciation in the year of acquisition and no depreciation in the year of disposal.

(vii)   XY issued 100,000 equity shares on 31 October 20X8 at a premium of 50%. The cash received was correctly entered into the financial records and is included in the trial balance.

(viii) Long term borrowings consist of a loan taken out on 1 April 20X8 at 5% interest per year. No loan interest has been paid at 31 March 20X9.

(ix)   XY paid a final dividend of $50,000 for the year ended 31 March 20X8.

Required

(a)   Calculate the deferred tax amounts relating to property, plant and equipment, that are required to be included in XY's statement of comprehensive income for the year ended 31 March 20X9 and its statement of financial position at that date. Ignore all other deferred tax implications.   **(5 marks)**

(b)   Prepare XY's statement of comprehensive income and statement of changes in equity for the year to 31 March 20X9 and a statement of financial position at that date, in a form suitable for presentation to the shareholders and in accordance with the requirements of International Financial Reporting Standards.
(20 marks)

Notes to the financial statements are NOT required, but all workings must be clearly shown. Do NOT prepare a statement of accounting policies.   **(Total = 25 marks)**

33 EZ (5/10)   45 mins

EZ's trial balance at 31 March 20X9 is shown below:

	Notes	$'000	$'000
Administrative expenses		86	
Cash and cash equivalents		22	
Cost of goods sold		418	
Distribution costs		69	
Equity dividend paid	(v)	92	
Inventory at 31 March 20X9		112	
Land market value – 31 March 20X8	(i)	700	
Lease	(ix)	15	
Long term borrowings	(vii)		250
Equity Shares $1 each, fully paid at 31 March 20X9	(vi)		600
Property, plant and equipment – at cost 31 March 20X8	(iii)	480	
Provision for deferred tax at 31 March 20X8	(ii)		30
Provision for property, plant and equipment dep'n at 31 March 20X8	(iv)		144
Retained earnings at 31 March 20X8			181
Revaluation reserve at 31 March 20X8			10
Revenue			720
Share premium at 31 March 20X9	(vi)		300
Suspense	(iii)		2
Trade payables			32
Trade receivables	(viii)	275	
		2,269	2,269

Additional information provided:

(i)   Land is carried in the financial statements at market value. The market value of the land at 31 March 20X9 was $675,000. There were no purchases or sales of land during the year.

(ii)   The tax due for the year ended 31 March 20X9 is estimated at $18,000. Deferred tax is estimated to decrease by $10,000.

(iii)   During the year EZ disposed of old equipment for $2,000. No entry has been made in the accounts for this transaction except to record the cash received in the cash book and in the suspense account. The original cost of the equipment sold was $37,000 and its book value at 31 March 20X8 was $7,000.

(iv)   Property, plant and equipment is depreciated at 10% per year straight line. Depreciation of property, plant and equipment is considered to be part of cost of sales. EZ's policy is to charge a full year's depreciation in the year of acquisition and no depreciation in the year of disposal.

(v)   During the year EZ paid a final dividend of $92,000 for the year ended 31 March 20X8.

(vi)   EZ issued 200,000 equity shares on 30 September 20X8 at a premium of 50%.

(vii)   Long term borrowings consist of a loan taken out on 1 April 20X8 at 4% interest per year. No loan interest has been paid at 31 March 20X9.

(viii) On 22 April 20X9 EZ discovered that ZZZ, its largest customer, had gone into liquidation. EZ has been informed that it is very unlikely to receive any of the $125,000 balance outstanding at 31 March 20X9.

(ix)   On 1 April 20X8 EZ acquired additional vehicles on a 2½ year (30 months) operating lease. The lease included an initial 6 months rent-free period as an incentive to sign the lease. The lease payments were $2,500 per month commencing on 1 October 20X8.

Required

Prepare EZ's statement of comprehensive income and statement of changes in equity for the year to 31 March 20X9 and a statement of financial position at that date, in a form suitable for presentation to the shareholders and in accordance with the requirements of International Financial Reporting Standards.

Notes to the financial statements are NOT required, but all workings must be clearly shown. Do NOT prepare a statement of accounting policies.   **(25 marks)**

Part C: Group Financial Statements

Questions 34 to 40 cover Group Financial Statements, the subject of Part C of the BPP Study Text for F1.

34   Objective test questions: Consolidated financial statements

38 mins

1   Fanta acquired 100% of the ordinary share capital of Tizer on 1 October 20X7.

On 31 December 20X7 the share capital and retained earnings of Tizer were as follows:

	$'000
Ordinary shares of $1 each	400
Retained earnings at 1 January 20X7	100
Retained profit for the year ended 31 December 20X7	80
	580

The profits of Tizer have accrued evenly throughout 20X1. Goodwill arising on the acquisition of Tizer was $30,000.

What was the cost of the investment in Tizer?

A $400,000
B $580,000
C $610,000
D $590,000

(2 marks)

2   Mercedes has owned 100% of Benz for many years. At 31 March 20X9 the retained earnings of Mercedes were $450,000 and the consolidated retained earnings of the group were $560,000. Mercedes has no other subsidiaries.

During the year ended 31 March 20X9, Benz had sold goods to Mercedes for $50,000. Mercedes still had these goods in inventory at the year end. Benz uses a 25% mark up on all goods.

What were the retained earnings of Benz at 31 March 20X9?

A $110,000
B $60,000
C $170,000
D $120,000

(2 marks)

3   Oldsmobile, a company with subsidiaries, purchased 35% of the ordinary share capital of Chevrolet for $50,000 on 1 April 20X8.

Chevrolet's statement of financial position at 31 March 20X9 was as follows:

	$'000
Net assets	55

	$'000
Ordinary share capital ($1 shares)	15
Retained earnings at 1 April 20X8	20
Net profit for the year ended 31 March 20X9	20
	55

During the year to 31 March 20X9 Chevrolet paid out a total dividend to its shareholders of $10,000. Oldsmobile considers that its investment in Chevrolet has been impaired by $6,000.

At what amount should Oldsmobile's investment in Chevrolet be shown in its consolidated statement of financial position as at 31 March 20X9?

A $57,000
B $50,500
C $47,500
D $44,000

(2 marks)

4   Ruby owns 30% of Emerald. During the year to 31 December 20X8 Emerald sold goods to Ruby for
      $160,000. Emerald applies a one-third mark up on cost. Ruby still had 25% of these goods in inventory
      at the year end.

      What amount should be deducted from consolidated retained earnings in respect of this transaction?

      A $40,000
      B $3,000
      C $10,000
      D $4,000   (2 marks)

5   Colossal acquired 100% of the $100,000 ordinary share capital of Enormous for $300,000 on 1 January
      20X9 when the retained earnings of Enormous were $156,000. At the date of acquisition the fair value
      of plant held by Enormous was $20,000 higher than its carrying value. This plant had a remaining life of
      4 years at the acquisition date.

      At 31 December 20X9 retained earnings are as follows:

                                                                                                  $
      Colossal   275,000
      Enormous   177,000

      Colossal considers that goodwill on acquisition is impaired by 50%.

      What are group retained earnings at 31 December 20X9?

      A $279,000
      B $284,000
      C $296,000
      D $291,000   (3 marks)

6   On 1 April 20X7 Rhino acquired 40% of the share capital of Hippo for $120,000, when the retained
      earnings of Hippo were $80,000. During the year Rhino sold goods to Hippo for $30,000, including a
      profit margin of 25%. These goods were still in inventory at the year end.

      At 31 March 20X8 the retained earnings of Hippo were $140,000.

      At what amount should Rhino's interest in Hippo be shown in the consolidated statement of financial
      position at 31 March 20X8?

      A $173,000
      B $144,000
      C $141,000
      D $105,000   (2 marks)

The following information is relevant for questions 7 and 8

On 1 January 20X6 A purchased 100,000 ordinary shares in B for $210,000. At that date B's retained
earnings amounted to $90,000 and the fair value of its assets was equal to their book values.

Four years later, on 31 December 20X9, the statements of financial position of the two companies were:

	A	B
	$	$
Sundry net assets	200,000	260,000
Shares in B	210,000	-
	410,000	260,000
Ordinary shares of $1	200,000	100,000
Retained earnings	210,000	160,000
	410,000	260,000

The share capital of B has remained unchanged since 1 January 20X6. Goodwill is impaired by 50%.

7   What amount should appear in the group consolidated statement of financial position at 31 December
        20X9 for goodwill?

        A $25,000
        B $20,000
        C $10,000
        D $14,000   (2 marks)

8   What amount should appear in the consolidated statement of financial position at 31 December 20X9 for
        group retained earnings?

        A $270,000
        B $338,000
        C $370,000
        D $280,000   (2 marks)

The following information is relevant for questions 9 and 10

H acquired 100% of the share capital of S on 1 January 20X9 for $350,000.

The statements of financial position of the two companies at 31 December 20X9 were as follows:

	H	S
	$	$
Sundry assets	590,000	290,000
Investment in S	350,000	-
	940,000	290,000
Issued share capital - $1 shares	400,000	140,000
Share premium account	320,000	50,000
Retained earnings at 1 January 20X9	140,000	60,000
Profit for year to 31 December 20X9	80,000	40,000
	940,000	290,000

There have been no changes in the share capital or share premium account of either company since 1
January 20X9. There was no impairment of goodwill.

9   What figure for goodwill should appear in the consolidated statement of financial position of the H group
        at 31 December 20X9?

        A $60,000
        B $100,000
        C $150,000
        D $160,000   (2 marks)

10   What figure for group retained earnings should appear in the consolidated statement of financial position
        of the H group at 31 December 20X9?

        A $260,000
        B $220,000
        C $320,000
        D $200,000   (2 marks)

                                                                                        (Total = 21 marks)

35 Goose and Gander   45 mins

You are provided with the draft accounts of Goose and Gander at 31 December 20X8.

STATEMENTS OF COMPREHENSIVE INCOME FOR THE YEAR ENDED 31 DECEMBER 20X8

	Goose $'000	Gander $'000
Revenue	5,000	1,000
Cost of sales	2,900	600
Gross profit	2,100	400
Other expenses	1,700	320
Net profit	400	80
Tax	130	25
Profit for the year	270	55

STATEMENTS OF FINANCIAL POSITION AT 31 DECEMBER 20X8

	$'000	$'000
Non-current assets		
Property, plant and equipment	2,000	200
Current assets		
Inventory	500	120
Trade receivables	650	40
Bank and cash	390	35
	1,540	195
	3,540	395
Equity and liabilities		
Equity		
Share capital	500	100
Share premium	1500	–
Revaluation surplus	50	–
Retained earnings	350	200
	2,400	300
Current liabilities		
Trade payables	1,010	70
Tax	130	25
	1,140	95
	3,540	395

The following information is also available:

(a)   Goose acquired 100% of the issued share capital of Gander (100,000 $1 shares) on 1 January 20X8 by issuing 4 new $1 shares in Goose in exchange for every 5 shares in Gander. The fair value of Goose's shares on the date of exchange was $5.50. The retained earnings of Gander were $185,000 on the date of acquisition. The acquisition of Gander has not been reflected in the draft accounts of Goose at 31 December 20X8.

(b)   On 31 December 20X8 Goose despatched goods which cost $80,000 to Gander, at an invoiced cost of $100,000. Gander received the goods on 2 January 20X9 and recorded the transaction then.

(c)   Included in the draft accounts of Goose at 31 December 20X8 is a property with a carrying value of $100,000. Due to recent urban development, the fair value of the property increased to $200,000 at 31 December 20X8. Goose has a policy of revaluing properties, but has yet to reflect this increase in its draft accounts.

Required

(a)   Prepare a draft consolidated statement of comprehensive income and a draft consolidated statement of financial position for the Goose Group at 31 December 20X8.   **(20 marks)**

(b)   Explain why consolidated financial statements are useful to the users of financial statements (as opposed to just the parent company's separate (entity) financial statements). **(5 marks)**

(Total = 25 marks)

36 Molecule | 45 mins

Molecule is the parent company of Atom and owns 30% of Electron. The following are the statements of financial position for all three companies as at 31 October 20X7.

	Molecule $'000	Atom $'000	Electron $'000
Assets			
Non-current assets			
Property, plant and equipment	3,000	3,300	2,000
Investments: shares in Atom at cost	4,545	–	–
shares in Electron at cost	800	–	–
Current assets			
Inventory	1,500	800	400
Receivables	1,800	750	300
Bank	600	350	150
	3,900	1,900	850
Total assets	12,245	5,200	2,850
Equity and liabilities			
Equity			
$1 ordinary shares	9,000	4,000	2,000
Retained earnings	1,325	200	600
	10,325	4,200	2,600
Current liabilities			
Payables	1,220	200	150
Tax	700	800	100
Total equity and liabilities	12,245	5,200	2,800

The following information is also available.

(a)   Molecule purchased all of the shares in Atom some years ago when Atom had retained earnings of $60,000. All goodwill on acquisition has been fully written off as impaired in prior years. Molecule purchased its shares in Electron on 1 November 20X6 when Electron had retained earnings of $300,000.

(b)   During the year Molecule sold goods with an invoice value of $240,000 to Atom. These goods were invoiced at cost plus 20%. Half of the goods are still in Atom's inventory at the year end.

(c)   Atom owes Molecule $30,000 at 31 October 20X7 for goods it purchased during the year.

(d)   Molecule wants to recognise an impairment of $100,000 in respect of its investment in Electron.

(e)   Molecule has identified that a receivable of $450,000 from a customer who went bankrupt in August 20X5 was included in its accounts at 31 October 20X6. This balance was known to be irrecoverable at the previous year end, but no adjustments were made. Molecule wishes to correct this error, but has not yet made any adjustments to the 31 October 20X7 accounts.

Required

(a)   Calculate the goodwill on acquisition of Atom.   **(2 marks)**

(b)   Prepare the consolidated statement of financial position for the Molecule group as at 31 October 20X7.

        Note. A working should be included for group retained earnings. Disclosure notes are not required.

        (20 marks)

(c)   A company that owns less than 50% of the shares of another company will regard it as an 'associate' if it is able to exert 'significant influence'. Identify three circumstances that might demonstrate 'significant influence'.   **(3 marks)**

(Total = 25 marks)

37 Parsley   45 mins

You are provided with the following financial statements for Parsley, a limited liability company, and its subsidiary Sage

STATEMENT OF COMPREHENSIVE INCOME FOR THE YEAR ENDED 31 DECEMBER 20X9

		Parsley $'000	Sage $'000
Sales revenue		135,000	74,000
Cost of sales		(70,000)	(30,000)
Gross profit		65,000	44,000
Distribution costs		(7,500)	(6,200)
Administrative expenses		(19,000)	(7,784)
Income from Sage:	loan note interest	4	–
	dividends	8,000	–
Interest payable		–	(16)
Profit before tax		46,504	30,000
Income tax expense		(10,000)	(9,000)
Profit for the year		36,504	21,000

STATEMENTS OF FINANCIAL POSITION AS AT 31 DECEMBER 20X9

	Parsley		Sage	
Assets	$'000	$'000	$'000	$'000
Non-current assets				
Property, plant and equipment		74,000		39,050
Investments:				
$1 ordinary shares in Sage at cost		30,000		–
Sage loan notes		50		–
		104,050		39,050
Current assets				
Inventory	10,630		4,498	
Receivables	18,460		12,230	
Bank	13,400		1,344	
		42,490		18,072
Total assets		146,540		57,122
Equity and liabilities				
Equity				
$1 ordinary shares		80,000		25,000
Retained earnings		37,540		15,000
		117,540		40,000
Non-current liabilities				
8% Loan note		–		200
Current liabilities				
Payables	6,000		1,922	
Tax	11,000		7,000	
Dividends payable	12,000		8,000	
		29,000		16,922
Total equity and liabilities		136,540		57,122

The following information is also available:

(a)   Parsley purchased 100% of the $1 ordinary shares in Sage on 1 January 20X8. At that date Sage's retained earnings were $2,000,000.

(b)   Parsley's annual impairment review of goodwill on acquisition of Sage valued it at $2,250,000 at 31 December 20X9.

(c)   During the year ended 31 December 20X9 Parsley sold goods which originally cost $8,000,000 to Sage for $12,000,000. Sage still had 25% of these goods in inventory at 31 December 20X9.

(d)   Sage owed Parsley $1,800,000 at 31 December 20X9 for some of the goods Parsley supplied during the year.

(e)   Parsley owns $50,000 of Sage's loan notes. The interest is paid annually in arrears at 31 December. Interest for the year ended 31 December 20X9 is included in Sage's payables. Parsley has also included the interest in its receivables.

(f)   All dividends were declared but not paid prior to the year end.

Required

(a)   Calculate the goodwill arising on the acquisition of Sage.   **(2 marks)**

(b)   Prepare the following financial statements for Parsley:

    (i)   The consolidated statement of comprehensive income for the year ended 31 December 20X9.

    (6 marks)

    (ii)   The consolidated statement of financial position as at 31 December 20X9.

    Note. A working should be included for the retained earnings. Disclosure notes are not required.

    (14 marks)

(c)   Explain the accounting treatment of intra-group trading in consolidated accounts.   **(3 marks)**

    (Total = 25 marks)

38 Tom, Dick and Harry   45 mins

The following statements of financial position have been prepared as at 31 October 20X9.

	Tom		Dick		Harry	
	$'000	$'000	$'000	$'000	$'000	$'000
Non-current assets						
Property, plant and equipment		205		120		220
Investments						
100,000 shares in Dick Ltd at cost		200		–		–
60,000 shares in Harry Ltd at cost		115		–		–
Current assets						
Inventory	100		70		90	
Receivables	170		40		70	
Bank	190		30		50	
		460		140		210
		980		260		430
Equity and liabilities						
$1 ordinary shares	500		100		200	
Retained earnings	370		130		150	
		870		230		350
Current liabilities						
Trade payables		110		30		80
		980		260		430

Additional information

(a)   Tom purchased all the share capital of Dick on 1 November 20X8 for $200,000. The previous owners of Dick needed to sell quickly as they were in financial difficulty. The book value of Dick's net assets on the date of acquisition was $190,000. A valuation exercise performed by a reputable firm showed that the fair value of Dick's property, plant and equipment at that date was $50,000 greater than book value. The increase in fair value was not accounted for in the books of Dick. If Dick had re-valued its non-current assets at 31 October 20X8, an addition of $2,000 would have been made to the depreciation charged for 20X8/20X9.

(b)   Tom sold goods for $25,000 to Dick during the year. The price included a 25% mark up. 40% of them are still held in inventory by Dick.

(c)   Tom's investment in Harry was acquired on 31 October 20X5 when the retained earnings of Harry were $130,000. The fair value of Harry's assets were the same as their net book value at the date of acquisition. At 31 October 20X9, the investment in Harry is impaired by $4,000.

Required

(a)   (i)   Calculate the goodwill on acquisition of Dick.

        (ii)   Explain the treatment required by IFRS 3 for a bargain purchase that creates negative goodwill.

        (6 marks)

(b)   Prepare the consolidated statement of financial position for the Tom Group as at 31 October 20X9.

        (19 marks)

        (Total = 25 marks)

39 PSA (Specimen Paper)   45 mins

The draft summarised statements of financial position at 31 March 20X9 for three entities, P, S and A are given below.

	P		S		A	
	$000	$000	$000	$000	$000	$000
Non-current Assets						
Property, plant and equipment		40,000		48,000		34,940
Investments:						
40,000 Ordinary shares in S at cost		60,000				
Loan to S		10,000				
8,000 Ordinary shares in A at cost		13,000				
		123,000		48,000		34,940
Current Assets						
Inventory	8,000		12,000		8,693	
Current a/c with S	8,000		–		–	
Trade receivables	17,000		11,000		10,106	
Cash and cash equivalents	1,000		3,000		3,033	
		34,000		26,000		21,832
Total Assets		157,000		74,000		56,772
Equity and Liabilities						
Equity shares of $1 each		100,000		40,000		20,000
Retained earnings		21,000		13,000		7,800
		121,000		53,000		27,800
Non-current liabilities						
Borrowings		26,000		10,000		10,000
Current liabilities						
Trade payables	10,000		5,000		18,972	
Current a/c with P	–		6,000		–	
		10,000		11,000		18,972
Total Equity and Liabilities		157,000		74,000		56,772

Additional information:

(i)   P's acquired all of S's equity shares on 1 April 20X8 for $60,000,000 when S's retained earnings were $6,400,000. P also advanced S a ten year loan of $10,000,000 on 1 April 20X8.

(ii)   The fair value of S's property, plant and equipment on 1 April 20X8 exceeded its book value by $1,000,000. The excess of fair value over book value was attributed to buildings owned by S. At the date of acquisition these buildings had a remaining useful life of 20 years. P's accounting policy is to depreciate buildings using the straight line basis.

(iii)   At 31 March 20X9 $250,000 loan interest was due and had not been paid. Both P and S had accrued this amount at the year end.

(iv) P purchased 8,000,000 of A's equity shares on 1 April 20X8 for $13,000,000 when A's retained earnings were $21,000,000. P exercises significant influence over all aspects of A's strategic and operational decisions.

(v) S posted a cheque to P for $2,000,000 on 30 March 20X9 which did not arrive until 7 April 20X9.

(vi) No dividends are proposed by any of the entities.

(vii) P occasionally trades with S. In March 20X9 P sold S goods for $4,000,000. P uses a mark up of one third on cost. On 31 March 20X9 all the goods were included in S's closing inventory and the invoice for the goods was still outstanding.

(viii) P's directors do not want to consolidate A. They argue that they do not control A, therefore it does not need to be consolidated. They insist that A should appear in the consolidated statement of financial position at cost of $13,000,000.

Required

(a) Draft a response that explains to P's directors the correct treatment of A in the consolidated financial statements. Include comments on any ethical issues involved. **(5 marks)**

(b) Prepare a Consolidated Statement of Financial Position for the P Group of entities as at 31 March 20X9, in accordance with the requirements of International Financial Reporting Standards. **(20 marks)**

Notes to the financial statements are not required but all workings must be shown. **(Total = 25 marks)**

40 AX (5/10)   45 mins

AX holds shares in two other entities, AS and AA.

AX purchased 100% of AS shares on 1 April 20X8 for $740,000, when the fair value was $75,000 more than book value. The excess of fair value over book value was attributed to land held by AS.

At 1 April 20X8 the retained earnings of AS showed a debit balance of $72,000.

AX purchased 120,000 ordinary shares in AA on 1 April 20X8 for $145,000 when AA's retained earnings were $49,000. AX is able to exercise significant influence over all aspects of AA's strategic and operational decisions. At 1 April 20X8 the fair values of AA's assets were the same as their net book value.

The draft summarised financial statements for the three entities as at 31 March 20X9 are given below.

DRAFT SUMMARISED STATEMENT OF FINANCIAL POSITION AS AT 31 MARCH 20X9

	AX		AS		AA	
	$'000	$'000	$'000	$'000	$'000	$'000
Non-current Assets						
Property, plant and equipment	1,120		700		740	
Investments:						
600,000 Ordinary shares in AS at cost	740		–		–	
120,000 Ordinary shares in AA at cost	145		–		–	
		2,005		700		740
Current Assets						
Inventory	205		30		14	
Trade receivables	350		46		30	
Cash and cash equivalents	30		–		11	
		585		76		55
Total Assets		2,590		776		795

	AX		AS		AA	
	$'000	$'000	$'000	$'000	$'000	$'000
Equity and Liabilities						
Equity shares of $1 each		1,500		600		550
Retained earnings		518		15		100
		2,018		615		650
Non-current liabilities						
Borrowings	360		80		109	
Deferred tax	120		16		10	
		480		96		119
Current liabilities						
Trade payables	92		29		15	
Tax (see additional information (i))	–		16		11	
Bank overdraft	–		20		–	
		92		65		26
Total Equity and Liabilities		2,590		776		795

SUMMARISED STATEMENT OF COMPREHENSIVE INCOME FOR THE YEAR ENDED 31 MARCH 20X9

	AX	AS	AA
	$'000	$'000	$'000
Revenue	820	285	147
Cost of sales	(406)	(119)	(52)
	414	166	95
Administrative expenses	(84)	(36)	(14)
Distribution costs	(48)	(22)	(11)
	(282)	(108)	(70)
Finance cost	(18)	(5)	(8)
	264	103	62
Income Tax (see additional information (i))		(16)	(11)
Profit for the year		87	51

Additional information:

(i) AX is deemed resident in Country X for tax purposes. In Country X, the corporate tax on profits is at a rate of 25%. All expenses other than depreciation, amortisation, entertaining, taxes paid to other public bodies and donations to political parties are tax deductible.

(ii) AX has not yet calculated its tax charge for the year to 31 March 20X9. AX's cost of sales includes a depreciation charge of $31,000 for property, plant and equipment. Included in administrative expenses are entertaining expenses of $4,000. AX's property, plant and equipment qualified for tax depreciation allowances of $49,000 for the year ended 31 March 20X9.

(iii) In the year since acquisition AS sold goods for $55,000 to AX of which $25,000 remained in AX's closing inventory at 31 March 20X9. AS uses a mark up of 25% on cost. All invoices from AS for the goods had been paid by the year end.

(iv) No dividends are proposed by any of the entities.

Required

(a) Calculate the estimated amount of corporate income tax that AX will be due to pay for the year ended 31 March 20X9 and any required adjustment to the provision for deferred tax at that date. **(5 marks)**

(b) Prepare a consolidated statement of comprehensive income for the AX Group of entities for the year ended 31 March 20X9 and a consolidated statement of financial position as at that date.

Notes to the financial statements are not required but all workings must be shown. **(20 marks)**

(Total = 25 marks)

Part D: Principles of business taxation

Questions 41 to 47 cover Principles of business taxation, the subject of Part D of the BPP Study Text for F1.

41   Objective test questions: General principles of taxation   65 mins

1   Which of the following powers is *not* available to tax authorities.

    A   Power to review and query filed returns
    B   Power to detain company officials
    C   Power to request special returns
    D   Power to enter and search premises   **(2 marks)**

2   Complete the blanks:

    Direct taxation is charged directly on the .... or .... that is intended to pay the tax.   **(2 marks)**

3   In 1776, Adam Smith proposed that an acceptable tax should meet four characteristics. Three of these characteristics were certainty, convenience and efficiency.

    Identify the FOURTH characteristic.

    A   Neutrality
    B   Transparency
    C   Equity
    D   Simplicity   **(2 marks)**

4   Define tax evasion.   **(2 marks)**

5   List (using no more than five words per item) the four main sources of tax rules in a country.   **(4 marks)**

6   The effective incidence of a tax is on

    A   the date the tax is actually paid.
    B   the person or entity that finally bears the cost of the tax.
    C   the date the tax assessment is issued.
    D   the person or entity receiving the tax assessment.   **(2 marks)**

7   In no more than 15 words, define the meaning of 'competent jurisdiction'.   **(2 marks)**

8   Which **one** of the following powers is a tax authority least likely to have granted to them?

    A   Power of arrest.
    B   Power to examine records.
    C   Power of entry and search.
    D   Power to give information to other country's tax authorities.   **(2 marks)**

9   An entity sells furniture and adds a sales tax to the selling price of all products sold. A customer purchasing furniture from the entity has to pay the cost of the furniture plus the sales tax. The customer therefore bears the cost of the sales tax.

    This is referred to as

    A   Formal incidence
    B   Indirect incidence
    C   Effective incidence
    D   Direct incidence   **(2 marks)**

10   List three possible reasons why governments set deadlines for filing returns and/or paying taxes.   **(3 marks)**

11 What is 'hypothecation'?

    A   Process of earmarking tax revenues for specific types of expenditure
    B   Estimation of tax revenue made by the tax authorities for budget purposes
    C   Refund made by tax authorities for tax paid in other countries
    D   Payment of taxes due to tax authorities, net of tax refunds due from tax authorities   **(2 marks)**

12 Explain briefly THREE major principles of modern taxation.   **(3 marks)**

13 Which ONE of the following is NOT an advantage for the tax authority of deduction of tax at source?

    A   The total amount of tax due for the period is easier to calculate
    B   Tax is collected earlier
    C   Administration costs are borne by the entity deducting tax
    D   Tax is deducted before income is paid to the taxpayer   **(2 marks)**

14 HD sells office stationery and adds a sales tax to the selling price of all products sold. A customer purchasing goods from HD has to pay the cost of the goods plus the sales tax.

HD pays the sales tax collected to the tax authorities.

From the perspective of HD the sales tax would be said to have

    A   formal incidence
    B   effective incidence
    C   informal incidence
    D   ineffective incidence   **(2 marks)**

15 The 'tax gap' is the difference between:

    A   When a tax payment is due and the date it is actually paid

    B   The tax due calculated by the entity and the tax demanded by the tax authority

    C   The amount of tax due to be paid and the amount actually collected

    D   The date when the entity was notified by the tax authority of the tax due and the date the tax should be paid   **(2 marks)**

16 Which of the following is a source of tax rules?

    A   International accounting standards
    B   Local company legislation
    C   International tax treaties
    D   Domestic accounting practice   **(2 marks)**

(Total = 36 marks)

42 Objective test questions: Types of taxation I   79 mins

1 Country X uses a Pay-As-You-Earn (PAYE) system for collecting taxes from employees. Each employer is provided with information about each employee's tax position and tables showing the amount of tax to deduct each period. Employers are required to deduct tax from employees and pay it to the revenue authorities on a monthly basis

From the perspective of the government, list THREE advantages of the PAYE system.   **(3 marks)**

2 Where is employee tax recorded in a set of financial accounts?

    A   Charged to employee costs in the income statement
    B   Charged to cost of sales in the income statement
    C   Included as a payable in the balance sheet
    D   Included as a receivable in the balance sheet   **(2 marks)**

3 Complete the following equation.

Accounting profit + ? – non-taxable income – tax allowable expenditure = ? **(2 marks)**

4 A withholding tax is

A tax withheld from payment to the tax authorities.
B tax paid less an amount withheld from payment.
C tax deducted at source before payment of interest or dividends.
D tax paid on increases in value of investment holdings. **(2 marks)**

5 BM has a taxable profit of $30,000 and receives a tax assessment of $3,000.

BV has a taxable profit of $60,000 and receives a tax assessment of $7,500.

BM and BV are resident in the same tax jurisdiction.

This tax could be said to be

A A progressive tax
B A regressive tax
C A direct tax
D A proportional tax **(2 marks)**

6 State two reasons why a group of entities might want to claim group loss relief rather than use the loss in the entity to which it relates. (Group loss relief is where, for tax purposes the loss for the year of one entity in the group is offset against the profit of the year of one or more other entities in the group.) **(2 marks)**

7 DR makes a taxable profit of $400,000 and pays an equity dividend of $250,000. Income tax on DR's profit is at a rate of 25%.

Equity shareholders pay tax on their dividend income at a rate of 30%.

If DR and its equity shareholders pay a total of $175,000 tax between them, what method of corporate income tax is being used in that country?

A The classical system
B The imputation system
C The partial imputation system
D The split rate system **(2 marks)**

8 A full imputation system of corporate income tax is one where an entity is taxable on

A all of its income and gains whether they are distributed or not. The shareholder is liable for taxation on all dividends received.

B all of its income and gains whether they are distributed or not, but all the underlying corporation tax on the distribution is passed to the shareholder as a tax credit.

C all of its income and gains whether they are distributed or not, but only part of the underlying corporation tax is passed to the shareholder as a tax credit.

D its retained profits at one rate and on its distributed profits at another (usually lower) rate of tax. **(2 marks)**

9 Company Z has a factory in Malaysia with retail outlets in Hong Kong. The company's registered office is in London but the head office is located in the Cayman Islands. All board meetings take place in the Cayman Islands. Where is Company Z's country of residence?

A Malaysia
B Hong Kong
C England
D Cayman Islands **(2 marks)**

10 The European Union (EU) is an example of a supranational body. In not more than 20 words, describe the effect the EU has on its member states' tax rules. **(2 marks)**

11   Name four payments that are usually affected by withholding tax.   **(2 marks)**

12   Name three methods of giving double taxation relief.   **(2 marks)**

13   Double tax relief is used to:

A   Ensure that you do not pay tax twice on any of your income.
B   Mitigate taxing overseas income twice.
C   Avoid taxing dividends received from subsidiaries in the same country twice.
D   Provide relief where a company pays tax at double the normal rate.   **(2 marks)**

14   Corporate residence for tax purposes can be determined in a number of ways, depending on the country concerned.

Which ONE of the following is NOT normally used to determine corporate residence for tax purposes?

A   The country from which control of the entity is exercised.
B   The country of incorporation of the entity.
C   The country where management of the entity hold their meetings.
D   The country where most of the entity's products are sold.   **(2 marks)**

15   An entity, DP, in Country A receives a dividend from an entity in Country B. The gross dividend of $50,000 is subject to a withholding tax of $5,000 and $45,000 is paid to DP.

Country A levies a tax of 12% on overseas dividends.

Country A and Country B have both signed a double taxation treaty based on the OECD model convention and both apply the credit method when relieving double taxation.

How much tax would DP be expected to pay in Country A on the dividend received from the entity in Country B?

A $400
B $1,000
C $5,400
D $6,000   **(2 marks)**

16   Where a resident entity runs an overseas operation as a branch of the entity, certain tax implications arise.

Which one of the following does not usually apply in relation to an overseas branch?

A   Assets can be transferred to the branch without triggering a capital gain
B   Corporate income tax is paid on profits remitted by the branch
C   Tax depreciation can be claimed on any qualifying assets used in the trade of the branch
D   Losses sustained by the branch are immediately deductible against the resident entity's income.
                                                                                                          (2 marks)

17   The following details relate to EA:

•   Incorporated in Country A.
•   Carries out its main business activities in Country B.
•   Its senior management operate from Country C and effective control is exercised from Country C.

Assume countries A, B and C have all signed double tax treaties with each other, based on the OECD model tax convention.

Which country will EA be deemed to be resident in for tax purposes?

A   Country A
B   Country B
C   Country C
D   Both Countries B and C   **(2 marks)**

18   The OECD Model tax convention defines a permanent establishment.

Which ONE of the following is not specifically listed as a "permanent establishment" by the OECD Model tax convention?

A   An office.
B   A factory.
C   An oil well.
D   A site of an 11 month construction project.   **(2 marks)**

19   Developed countries generally use three tax bases. One tax base widely used is income.

List the other TWO widely used bases.   **(2 marks)**

20   The following details are relevant:

- HC carries out its main business activities in Country A;

- HC is incorporated in Country B;

- HC's senior management exercise control from Country C, but there are no sales or purchases made in Country C;

- HC raises its finance and is quoted on the stock exchange in Country D.

Assume Countries A, B, C and D have all signed double taxation treaties with each other, based on the OECD model tax convention.

Which country will HC be deemed to be resident in for tax purposes?

A   Country A
B   Country B
C   Country C
D   Country D   **(2 marks)**

21   EB has an investment of 25% of the equity shares in XY, an entity resident in a foreign country.

EB receives a dividend of $90,000 from XY, the amount being after the deduction of withholding tax of 10%.

XY had profits before tax for the year of $1,200,000 and paid corporate income tax of $200,000.

How much underlying tax can EB claim for double taxation relief?   **(3 marks)**

(Total = 44 marks)

43   Objective test questions: Types of taxation II   113 mins

1   Excise duties are deemed to be most suitable for commodities that have certain specific characteristics.

List THREE characteristics of a commodity that, from a revenue authority's point of view, would make that commodity suitable for an excise duty to be imposed.   **(3 marks)**

2   Which of the following is an indirect tax?

A   Withholding tax
B   Employee tax
C   Sales tax
D   Company income tax   **(2 marks)**

3   The cost of a sales tax is borne by which person?

    A   The supplier of raw materials
    B   The end consumer
    C   The retailer
    D   The wholesaler   **(2 marks)**

The following data are given for sub-questions 4 and 5 below

Country D uses a value added tax (VAT) system whereby VAT is charged on all goods and services at a rate of 15%. Registered VAT entities are allowed to recover input VAT paid on their purchases.

Country E uses a multi-stage sales tax system, where a cumulative tax is levied every time a sale is made. The tax rate is 7% and tax paid on purchases is not recoverable.

DA is a manufacturer and sells products to DB, a retailer, for $500 excluding tax. DB sells the products to customers for a total of $1,000 excluding tax.

DA paid $200 plus VAT/sales tax for the manufacturing cost of its products.

4   Assume DA operates in Country D and sells products to DB in the same country.

    Calculate the net VAT due to be paid by DA and DB for the products.   **(2 marks)**

5   Assume DA operates in Country E and sells products to DB in the same country.

    Calculate the total sales tax due to be paid on all of the sales of the products.   **(2 marks)**

6   Which of the following types of taxes is regarded as an indirect tax?

    A   Taxes on income.
    B   Taxes on capital gains.
    C   Taxes on inherited wealth.
    D   Sales tax (Value added tax).   **(2 marks)**

7   AE purchases products from a foreign entity and imports them into a country A. On import, the products are subject to an excise duty of $5 per item and Value Added Tax (VAT) of 15% on cost plus excise duty.

    AE purchased 200 items for $30 each and after importing them sold all of the items for $50 each plus VAT at 15%.

    How much is due to be paid to the tax authorities for these transactions?

    A $450
    B $1,450
    C $2,050
    D $2,500   **(3 marks)**

8   Country OS has a value added tax (VAT) system where VAT is charged on all goods and services. Registered VAT entities are allowed to recover input VAT paid on their purchases.

    VAT operates at different levels in OS:

    •   Standard rate   10%
    •   Luxury rate   20%
    •   Zero rate   0%

    During the last VAT period, an entity, BZ, purchased materials and services costing $100,000, excluding VAT. All materials and services were at standard rate VAT.

    BZ converted the materials into two products Z and L; product Z is zero rated and product L is luxury rated for VAT purposes.

    During the VAT period, BZ made the following sales, excluding VAT:

            $
    Z   60,000
    L   120,000

    At the end of the period, BZ paid the net VAT due to the tax authorities.

    Assuming BZ had no other VAT-related transactions, how much VAT did BZ pay?   **(2 marks)**

9   CU manufactures clothing and operates in a country that has a Value Added Tax system (VAT). The VAT system allows entities to reclaim input tax that they have paid on taxable supplies. VAT is at 15% of the selling price at all stages of the manufacturing and distribution chain.

CU manufactures a batch of clothing and pays expenses (taxable inputs) of $100 plus VAT. CU sells the batch of clothing to a retailer CZ for $250 plus VAT. CZ unpacks the clothing and sells the items separately to various customers for a total of $600 plus VAT.

How much VAT do CU and CZ each have to pay in respect of this one batch of clothing?   **(2 marks)**

---

10   Country Z has a VAT system where VAT is charged on all goods and services. Registered VAT entities are allowed to recover input VAT paid on their purchases.

VAT operates at three different levels in Z:

-      Standard rate   15%
-      Luxury rate   22%
-      Zero rate   0%

During the last VAT period, an entity, GW, purchased materials and services costing $138,000, including VAT. All materials and services were at standard rate VAT.

GW converted the materials into two products A and B; product A is zero-rated and product B is luxury-rated for VAT purposes.

During the VAT period, GW made the following sales, including VAT:

	$
A	70,000
B	183,000

At the end of the period, GW paid the net VAT due to the tax authorities.

Assume no opening or closing inventory balances.

Assuming GW had no other VAT-related transactions, calculate GW's profit and the amount of VAT that GW paid?   **(4 marks)**

---

11   HN purchases products from a foreign country. The products cost $14 each and are subject to excise duty of $3 per item and VAT at 15%.

If HN imports 1,000 items, how much does it pay to the tax authorities for this transaction?

A $2,100
B $5,100
C $5,550
D $19,550   **(2 marks)**

---

12   Country Z has a VAT system which allows entities to reclaim input tax paid.

In Country Z, the VAT rates are:

Zero rated   0%
Standard rated   15%

FE owns and runs a small retail store. The store's sales include items that are zero rated, standard rated and exempt. FE's electronic cash register provides an analysis of sales. The figures for the three months to 30 April 20X8 were:

	Sales value, including VAT where appropriate
	$
Zero rated	13,000
Standard rated	18,400
Exempt	11,000
Total	42,400

FE's analysis of expenditure for the same period provided the following:

	Expenditure, excluding VAT $
Zero rated purchases	6,000
Standard rated purchases relating to standard rate outputs	10,000
Standard rated purchases relating to zero rate outputs	4,000
Standard rated purchases relating to exempt outputs	5,000
	25,000

Calculate the VAT due to/from FE for the three months ended 30 April 20X8. **(3 marks)**

---

13 Company G makes an accounting profit of $350,000 during the year. This includes non-taxable income of $25,000 and depreciation of $30,000. In addition, $15,000 of the expenses are disallowable for tax purposes. If the tax allowable depreciation totals $32,000, what is the taxable profit?

    A $323,000
    B $338,000
    C $352,000
    D $362,000   **(2 marks)**

---

14 Company G makes a taxable profit of $350,000 during the year. This includes adjustments for non-taxable income of $25,000, depreciation of $30,000 and $15,000 disallowed expenses. If the tax allowable depreciation totals $32,000, what is the accounting profit?

    A $323,000
    B $338,000
    C $352,000
    D $362,000   **(2 marks)**

---

15 Company G makes an accounting loss of $350,000 during the year. This includes non-taxable income of $25,000 and depreciation of $30,000. In addition, $400,000 of the expenses are disallowable for tax purposes. If the tax allowable depreciation totals $32,000, what is the taxable amount?

    A $23,000 profit
    B $23,000 loss
    C $123,000 profit
    D $123,000 profit   **(2 marks)**

---

16 Company W makes a taxable profit of $50m during the year. This is after adjustments for non-taxable income of $3m, depreciation of $15m and $1m disallowed expenses. If the tax allowable depreciation totals $4m, what is the accounting profit?

    A $38m
    B $41m
    C $58m
    D $59m   **(2 marks)**

---

17 Company M makes an accounting profit of $250,000 during the year. This includes depreciation of $45,000 and disallowable expenses of $20,000. If the tax allowable depreciation totals $30,000 and the tax rate is 30%, what is the tax payable?

    A $64,500
    B $75,000
    C $79,500
    D $85,500   **(2 marks)**

---

18 Company B makes an accounting profit of $360,000 during the year. This includes non-taxable income of $35,000 and depreciation of $40,000. In addition, $10,000 of the expenses are disallowable for tax purposes. If the tax allowable depreciation totals $30,000 and the tax rate is 20%, what is the tax payable?

    A $60,000
    B $65,000
    C $69,000
    D $72,000   **(2 marks)**

19 Company X makes an accounting profit of $500,000 during the year. This includes non-taxable income of $25,000 and depreciation of $50,000.

The finance director finds that $5,000 of the expenses are disallowable for tax purposes. If the tax allowable depreciation totals $60,000 and the tax rate is 25%, what is the tax payable?

    A $116,250
    B $117,500
    C $123,750
    D $132,500   **(2 marks)**

20 Company G makes an accounting profit of $250,000 during the year. This is after charging depreciation of $40,000 and tax disallowable expenses of $2,000. If the tax allowable depreciation totals $30,000 and the tax rate is 30%, what is the tax payable?

    A $71,400
    B $72,000
    C $77,400
    D $78,600   **(2 marks)**

21 Tax on an entity's trading profits could be referred to as:

    1   Income tax
    2   Profits tax
    3   Indirect tax
    4   Direct tax
    5   Earnings tax

Which TWO of the above would most accurately describe tax on an entity's trading profits:

    A   1 and 3
    B   1 and 4
    C   2 and 3
    D   4 and 5   **(2 marks)**

22 E has an accounting profit before tax of $95,000. The tax rate on trading profits applicable to E for the year is 25%. The accounting profit included non-taxable income from government grants of $15,000 and non-tax allowable expenditure of $10,000 on entertaining expenses.

How much tax is E due to pay for the year?   **(2 marks)**

23 AC made the following payment during the year ended 30 April 20X5:

	$'000
Operating costs (excluding depreciation)	23
Finance costs	4
Capital repayment of loans	10
Payments for the purchase of new computer equipment for use in AC's business	20

AC's revenue for the period was $45,000 and the corporate income tax rate applicable to AC's profits was 25%. The computer equipment qualifies for tax allowances of 10% per year on a straight line basis.

Calculate AC's tax payable for the year ended 30 April 20X5.   **(3 marks)**

24 Country B has a corporate income tax system that treats capital gains/losses separately from trading profits/losses. Capital gains/losses cannot be offset against trading profits/losses. All losses can be carried forward indefinitely, but cannot be carried back to previous years. Trading profits and capital gains are both taxed at 20%.

BD had no brought forward losses on 1 October 20X2. BD's results for 20X3 to 20X5 were as follows:

	Trading profit/(loss) $'000	Capital gains/(loss) $'000
Year to September 20X3	200	(100)
Year to September 20X4	(120)	0
Year to September 20X5	150	130

Calculate BD's corporate income tax due for each of the years ended 30 September 20X3 to 20X5.

(3 marks)

25 DZ recognised a tax liability of $290,000 in its financial statements for the year ended 30 September 20X5. This was subsequently agreed with and paid to the tax authorities as $280,000 on 1 March 20X6. The directors of DZ estimate that the tax due on the profits for the year to 30 September 20X6 will be $320,000. DZ has no deferred tax liability.

What is DZ's tax charge in its statement of comprehensive income for the year ended 30 September 20X6?

A $310,000
B $320,000
C $330,000
D $600,000 (2 marks)

26 DD purchased an item of plant and machinery costing $500,000 on 1 April 20X4, which qualified for 50% capital allowances in the first year, and 20% each year thereafter on the reducing balance basis.

DD's policy in respect of plant and machinery is to charge depreciation on a straight line basis over five years, with no residual value. On 1 April 20X6, DD decides to revalue the item of plant and machinery upwards, from its net book value, by $120,000.

Assuming there are no other capital transactions in the three year period and a tax rate of 30% throughout, calculate the amount of deferred tax to be shown in DD's statement of comprehensive income for the year ended 31 March 20X7, and the deferred tax provision to be included in its statement of financial position at 31 March 20X7. (4 marks)

(Total = 61 marks)

44 Objective test questions: Deferred tax   74 mins

1 A company had a credit balance brought forward on current tax of $20,000. During the year it paid tax of $18,000 and it has a provision for the current year of $50,000. It has increased the deferred tax provision by $5,000. What is the total charge to tax for the year in the statement of comprehensive income?

A $53,000
B $55,000
C $57,000
D $68,000 (2 marks)

2   A company had a debit balance brought forward on current tax of $2,000. During the year it has paid no tax and received a tax refund of $1,800. It has a provision for the current year of $30,000. It has decreased the deferred tax provision by $5,000. What is the total charge to tax for the year in the statement of comprehensive income?

    A $23,200
    B $24,800
    C $25,200
    D $35,200   **(2 marks)**

3   In accounting for deferred tax, which of the following items can give rise to temporary differences?

    1   Differences between accounting depreciation and tax allowances for capital expenditure
    2   Expenses charged in the income statement but disallowed for tax
    3   Revaluation of a non-current asset
    4   Unrelieved tax losses

    A   1, 3 and 4 only
    B   1 and 2 only
    C   3 and 4 only
    D   All four items   **(2 marks)**

4   Which of the following are examples of assets or liabilities whose carrying amount is always equal to their tax base?

    1   Accrued expenses that will never be deductible for tax purposes

    2   Accrued expenses that have already been deducted in determining the current tax liability for current or earlier periods

    3   Accrued income that will never be taxable

    4   A loan payable in the statement of financial position at the amount originally received, which is also the amount eventually repayable

    A   1 and 3 only
    B   1 and 2 only
    C   2 and 4 only
    D   All four items   **(2 marks)**

5   Which of the following statements about IAS 12 *Income taxes* are correct?

    1   Companies may discount deferred tax assets and liabilities if the effect would be material.

    2   The financial statements must disclose an explanation of the relationship between tax expense and accounting profit.

    3   Deferred tax may not be recognised in respect of goodwill unless any impairment of that goodwill is deductible for tax purposes.

    4   The tax base of an asset or liability is the amount attributed to that asset or liability for tax purposes.

    A   All the statements are correct
    B   2, 3 and 4 only are correct
    C   1 and 4 only are correct
    D   None of the statements is correct.   **(2 marks)**

6   The following information relates to an entity.

    •   At 1 January 20X8, the net book value of non-current assets exceeded their tax written down value by $850,000.

    •   For the year ended 31 December 20X8, the entity claimed depreciation for tax purposes of $500,000 and charged depreciation of $450,000 in the financial statements.

- During the year ended 31 December 20X8, the entity revalued a freehold property. The revaluation surplus was $250,000. The entity has no plans to sell the property and realise the gain in the foreseeable future.

- The tax rate was 30% throughout the year.

What is the provision for deferred tax required by IAS 12 *Income taxes* at 31 December 20X8?

A $240,000
B $270,000
C $315,000
D $345,000   (2 marks)

---

7   A company had a credit balance brought forward on current tax of $25,000. During the year it has paid no tax and received a tax refund of $2,500. It has a provision for the current year of $30,000. It has decreased the deferred tax provision by $10,000. What is the total charge to tax for the year in the statement of comprehensive income?

A $5,000 debit
B $5,000 credit
C $7,500 debit
D $7,500 credit   (2 marks)

---

8   A country had a current tax regime whereby relief is given for tax paid on dividends. What system of tax is this?   (2 marks)

---

9   A company had a credit balance brought forward on current tax of $25,000. During the year it paid tax of $27,800. It has a provision for the current year of $28,000. It has increased the deferred tax provision by $5,000. What is the total charge to tax for the year in the statement of comprehensive income?

A $31,200
B $33,000
C $33,800
D $35,800   (2 marks)

---

10   BC, a small entity, purchased its only non-current tangible asset on 1 October 20X3. The asset cost $900,000, all of which qualified for tax depreciation.

BC's asset qualified for an accelerated first year tax allowance of 50%. The second and subsequent years qualified for tax depreciation at 25% per year on the reducing balance method.

BC's accounting depreciation policy is to depreciate the asset over its useful economic life of five years, assuming a residual value of $50,000.

Assume that BC pays tax on its income at the rate of 30%.

Calculate BC's deferred tax balance required in the statement of financial position as at 30 September 20X5 according to IAS 12 *Income taxes*.   (4 marks)

---

11   On 31 March 20X6, CH had a credit balance brought forward on its deferred tax account of $642,000. There was also a credit balance on its corporate income tax account of $31,000, representing an over-estimate of the tax charge for the year ended 31 March 20X5.

CH's taxable profit for the year ended 31 March 20X6 was $946,000. CH's directors estimated the deferred tax provision required at 31 March 20X6 to be $759,000 and the applicable income tax rate for the year to 31 March 20X6 as 22%.

Calculate the income tax expense that CH will charge in its statement of comprehensive income for the year ended 31 March 20X6, as required by IAS 12 *Income taxes*.   (3 marks)

---

12   FD purchased an item of plant and machinery costing $600,000 on 1 April 20X5, which qualified for 50% capital allowances in the first year and 25% per year thereafter, on the reducing balance basis.

FD's policy in respect of plant and machinery is to charge depreciation on a straight line basis over five years, with no residual value.

On 1 April 20X7, FD carried out an impairment review of all its non-current assets. This item of plant and machinery was found to have a value in use of $240,000. FD adjusted its financial records and wrote the plant and machinery down to its value in use on 1 April 20X7.

Assuming there are no other temporary differences in the period and a tax rate of 25% per annum over the five years, calculate the amount of any deferred tax balances outstanding at 31 March 20X7 and 31 March 20X8. (Work to the nearest $1,000.) **(4 marks)**

13   EE reported accounting profits of $822,000 for the period ended 30 November 20X7. This was after deducting entertaining expenses of $32,000 and a donation to a political party of $50,000, both of which are disallowable for tax purposes.

EE's reported profit also included $103,000 government grant income that was exempt from taxation. EE paid dividends of $240,000 in the period.

Assume EE had no temporary differences between accounting profits and taxable profits.

Assume that a classical tax system applies to EE's profits and that the tax rate is 25%.

What would EE's tax payable be on its profits for the year to 30 November 20X7? **(2 marks)**

14   A government wanted to encourage investment in new non-current assets by entities and decided to change tax allowances for non-current assets to give a 100% first year allowance on all new non-current assets purchased after 1 January 20X5.

ED purchased new machinery for $400,000 on 1 October 20X5 and claimed the 100% first year allowance. For accounting purposes ED depreciated the machinery on the reducing balance basis at 25% per year. The rate of corporate income tax to be applied to ED's taxable profits was 22%.

Assume ED had no other temporary differences.

Calculate the amount of deferred tax that ED would show in its statement of financial position at 30 September 20X7.

(3 marks)

15   HF purchased an asset on 1 April 20X7 for $220,000. HF claimed a first year tax allowance of 30% and then an annual 20% writing down allowance, using the reducing balance method. HF depreciates the asset over eight years using straight line depreciation, assuming no residual value. On 1 April 20X8, HF revalued the asset and increased the net book value by $50,000. The asset's useful life was not affected. Assume there are no other temporary differences in the period and a tax rate of 25% per annum.

Calculate the amount of deferred tax movement in the year ended 31 March 20X9 and the deferred tax balance at 31 March 20X9, in accordance with IAS 12 *Income taxes*.

(4 marks)

16   CY had the following amounts for 20X3 to 20X5:

Year ended 31 December:	20X3	20X4	20X5
	$	$	$
Accounting depreciation for the year	1,630	1,590	1,530
Tax depreciation allowance for the year	2,120	1,860	1,320

At 31 December 20X2, CY had the following balances brought forward:

	$
Cost of property, plant and equipment qualifying for tax depreciation	20,000
Accounting depreciation	5,000
Tax depreciation	12,500

CY had no non-current asset acquisitions or disposals during the period 20X3 to 20X5.
Assume the corporate income tax rate is 25% for all years.
Calculate the deferred tax provision required by IAS 12 *Income taxes* at 31 December 20X5. **(3 marks)**

(Total = 41 marks)

45 Section B questions: Taxation I   45 mins

(a) Briefly explain the following taxation terminology:

    (i)   competent jurisdiction
    (ii)   hypothecation
    (iii)   taxable person
    (iv)   regressive tax structure
    (v)   tax gap.   **(5 marks)**

(b)   (i)   Give a definition of an indirect tax and explain how it works.   **(3 marks)**
    (ii)   There are two types of indirect taxes. State what these are and give two examples of each.
                                         (2 marks)

(Total = 5 marks)

(c) On 1 January 20X3, SPJ had an opening credit balance of $5,000 on its tax account, which represented the balance on the account after settling its tax liability for the previous year. SPJ had a credit balance on its deferred tax account of $1·6 million at the same date.

SPJ has been advised that it should expect to pay $1 million tax on its trading profits for the year ended 31 December 20X3 and increase its deferred tax account balance by $150,000.

Required

Prepare extracts from the statement of comprehensive income for the year ended 31 December 20X3, statement of financial position at that date and notes to the accounts showing the tax entries required.

(5 marks)

P7 Pilot paper

(d) CW owns 40% of the equity shares in Z, an entity resident in a foreign country. CW receives a dividend of $45,000 from Z; the amount received is after deduction of withholding tax of 10%. Z had before tax profits for the year of $500,000 and paid corporate income tax of $100,000.

Required

    (i)   Explain the meaning of 'withholding tax' and 'underlying tax.'   **(2 marks)**
    (ii)   Calculate the amount of withholding tax paid by CW.   **(1 mark)**
    (iii)   Calculate the amount of underlying tax that relates to CW's dividend.   **(2 marks)**

(Total = 5 marks)

P7 5/06

(e) EF is an importer and imports perfumes and similar products in bulk. EF repackages the products and sells them to retailers. EF is registered for Value Added Tax (VAT).

EF imports a consignment of perfume priced at $10,000 (excluding excise duty and VAT) and pays excise duty of 20% and VAT on the total (including duty) at 15%.

EF pays $6,900 repackaging costs, including VAT at 15% and then sells all the perfume for $40,250 including VAT at 15%.

EF has not paid or received any VAT payments to/from the VAT authorities for this consignment.

Required

    (i)   Calculate EF's net profit on the perfume consignment.
    (ii)   Calculate the net VAT due to be paid by EF on the perfume consignment.   **(Total = 5 marks)**

P7 11/07

(Total = 25 marks)

46 Section B questions: Taxation II   45 mins

(a)   Governments use a range of specific excise duties as well as general sales taxes on goods.

Required

(i)   Explain the reasons why a government might apply a specific excise duty to a category of goods.

(3 marks)

(ii)   Explain the difference between a single stage and a multi-stage sales tax.   **(2 marks)**

(Total = 5 marks)

P7 5/09

(b)   Tax authorities have various powers to enforce compliance with the tax rules.

State what these powers are and give examples of each.   **(5 marks)**

(c)   What is withholding tax and why do tax authorities use it? Give two examples of payments affected by withholding tax.   **(5 marks)**

(d)   Why do countries need to enter into double taxation agreements? What are the three main methods of giving double taxation relief?   **(5 marks)**

(e)   (i)   Explain the difference between tax avoidance and tax evasion.   **(2 marks)**

(ii)   Briefly explain the methods that governments can use to reduce tax avoidance and tax evasion.

(3 marks)

(Total = 5 marks)

(Total = 25 marks)

47 Section B questions: Taxation III   45 mins

(a)   H is a major manufacturing entity. According to the entity's records, temporary differences of $2.00 million had arisen at 30 April 20X4 because of differences between the carrying amount of non-current assets and their tax base, due to H claiming accelerated tax relief in the earlier years of the asset lives.

At 30 April 20X3, the temporary differences attributable to non-current assets were $2.30 million.

H's tax rate has been 30% in the past. On 30 April 20X4, the directors of H were advised that the rate of taxation would decrease to 28% by the time that the temporary differences on the non-current assets reversed.

Required

Prepare the note in respect of deferred tax as it would appear in the financial statements of H for the year ended 30 April 20X4. (Your answer should be expressed in $ million and you should work to two decimal places.)   **(5 marks)**

(b)   B is a retail entity. Its tax rate is 30%. It has a current tax payable brought forward from the year ended 30 April 20X3 of $750,000 and a deferred tax payable of $250,000.

On 30 April 20X4, the estimated tax charge for the year ended 30 April 20X4 was $1,400,000. The actual tax charge for the year ended 30 April 20X3 was agreed with the tax authority and settled with a payment of $720,000. The deferred tax payable needs to be increased to $300,000 as at 30 April 20X4.

Required

Prepare the notes in respect of current and deferred tax as they would appear in the financial statements of B for the year ended 30 April 20X4. (Your answer should be expressed in $ million and you should work to two decimal places.)   **(5 marks)**

(c)   DG purchased its only non-current tangible asset on 1 October 20X2. The asset cost $200,000, all of which qualified for tax depreciation. DG's accounting depreciation policy is to depreciate the asset over its useful economic life of five years, assuming no residual value, charging a full year's depreciation in the year of acquisition and no depreciation in the year of disposal.

The asset qualified for tax depreciation at a rate of 30% per year on the reducing balance method. DG sold the asset on 30 September 20X6 for $60,000.

The rate of income tax to apply to DG's profit is 20%. DG's accounting period is 1 October to 30 September.

Required

(i) Calculate DG's deferred tax balance at 30 September 20X5.

(ii) Calculate DG's accounting profit/loss that will be recognised in its statement of comprehensive income on the disposal of the asset, in accordance with IAS 16 *Property, Plant and Equipment.*

(iii) Calculate DG's tax balancing allowance/charge arising on the disposal of the asset.   **(5 marks)**

P7 11/06

(d) AB acquired non-current assets on 1 April 20X3 costing $250,000. The assets qualified for accelerated first year tax allowance at the rate of 50% for the first year. The second and subsequent years were at a tax depreciation rate of 25% per year on the reducing balance method.

AB depreciates all non-current assets at 20% a year on the straight line basis.

The rate of corporate tax applying to AB for 20X3/X4 and 20X4/X5 was 30%. Assume AB has no other qualifying non-current assets.

Required

Apply IAS 12 *Income taxes* and calculate:

(i) the deferred tax balance required at 31 March 20X4

(ii) the deferred tax balance required at 31 March 20X5

(iii) the charge to the income statement for the year ended 31 March 20X5   **(5 marks)**

P7 5/05

(e) Country X has the following tax regulations in force.

- The tax year is 1 May to 30 April

- All corporate profits are taxed at 20%

- When calculating corporate taxable income, depreciation of non-current assets cannot be charged against taxable income.

- Tax depreciation is allowed at the following rates.

  - Buildings at 5% per annum on a straight line basis
  - All other non-current tangible assets are allowed tax depreciation at 25% per annum on a reducing balance basis

- No tax allowances are allowed on land or furniture and fittings.

FB commenced trading on 1 May 20X5 when it purchased all its non-current assets.

FB's non-current asset balances were:

	Cost 1 May 20X5 $	Net book value 1 May 20X7 $	Tax written down value 1 May 20X7 $
Land	20,000	20,000	–
Buildings	80,000	73,600	72,000
Plant and equipment	21,000	1,000	11,812
Furniture and fittings	15,000	5,000	–

FB did not purchase any non-current assets between 1 May 20X5 and 30 April 20X7. On 2 May 20X7, FB disposed of all its plant and equipment for $5,000 and purchased new plant and equipment for $30,000. The new plant and equipment qualified for a first year tax allowance of 50%.

FB STATEMENT OF COMPREHENSIVE INCOME FOR THE YEAR ENDED 30 APRIL 20X8

	$
Gross profit	210,000
Administrative expenses	(114,000)
Gain on disposal of plant and equipment	4,000
Depreciation – furniture and fittings	(5,000)
Depreciation – buildings	(3,200)
Depreciation – plant and equipment	(6,000)
Distribution costs	(49,000)
	36,800
Finance cost	(7,000)
Profit before tax	29,800

Required

Calculate FB's corporate income tax due for the year ended 30 April 20X8. **(5 marks)**

(Total = 25 marks)

Mixed question banks

The following tax regime data is applicable to the mixed question banks.

Country X – Tax regime

Relevant tax rules

Corporate Profits

Unless otherwise specified, only the following rules for taxation of corporate profits will be relevant, other taxes can be ignored:

(a)   Accounting rules on recognition and measurement are followed for tax purposes.

(b)   All expenses other than depreciation, amortisation, entertaining, taxes paid to other public bodies and donations to political parties are tax deductible.

(c)   Tax depreciation is deductible as follows:

  •   50% of additions to property, plant and equipment in the accounting period in which they are recorded

  •   25% per year of the written-down value (ie cost minus previous allowances) in subsequent accounting periods except that in which the asset is disposed of

  •   No tax depreciation is allowed on land

(d)   The corporate tax on profits is at a rate of 25%.

Value Added Tax

Country X has a VAT system which allows entities to reclaim input tax paid. In country X the VAT rates are:

Zero rated   0%
Standard rated   15%

---

48   Mixed objective test questions bank 1 (Specimen Paper)   36 mins

1   Which of the following statements is correct?

   A   Tax evasion is legally arranging affairs so as to minimise the tax liability. Tax avoidance is the illegal manipulation of the tax system to avoid paying taxes due.

   B   Tax evasion is legally arranging affairs so as to evade paying tax. Tax avoidance is tax planning, legally arranging affairs so as to minimise the tax liability.

   C   Tax evasion is using loop holes in legislation to evade paying tax. Tax avoidance is the illegal manipulation of the tax system to avoid paying taxes due.

   D   Tax evasion is the illegal manipulation of the tax system to avoid paying taxes due. Tax avoidance is tax planning, legally arranging affairs so as to minimise the tax liability.   **(2 marks)**

---

2   A has been trading for a number of years and is resident for tax purposes in Country X. The tax written down value of A's property, plant and equipment was $40,000 at 31 March 20X8. A did not purchase any property, plant and equipment between 1 April 20X8 and 31 March 20X9.

A's income statement for the year ended 31 March 20X9 is as follows:

	$
Gross profit	270,000
Administrative expenses	(120,000)
Depreciation - property, plant and equipment	(12,000)
Distribution costs	(55,000)
	83,000
Finance cost	(11,000)
Profit before tax	72,000

Administration expenses include entertaining of $15,000.

What is A's income tax due for the year ended 31 March 20X9?

A   8,750
B   13,750
C   15,500
D   22,250

(2 marks)

3   B buys goods from a wholesaler, paying the price of the goods plus VAT. B sells goods in its shop to customers. The customers pay the price of the goods plus VAT.

From the perspective of B, the VAT would have

A   Effective incidence
B   Formal incidence
C   Ineffective incidence
D   Informal incidence

(2 marks)

4   CT has taxable profits of $100,000 and pays 50% as dividends.

The total tax due is calculated as:

CT's corporate income tax ($100,000 × 25%)	$25,000
CT's shareholder's personal income tax on dividends received ($50,000 × 20%)	$10,000
Total tax due	$35,000

The tax system in use here would be classified as a:

A   Imputation tax system
B   Partial imputation tax system
C   Classical tax system
D   Split rate tax system

(2 marks)

5   The International Accounting Standards Board's *Framework for the Presentation and Preparation of Financial Statements* sets out four qualitative characteristics, relevance and reliability are two, list the other two.   **(2 marks)**

6   The CIMA Code of Ethics for Professional Accountants sets out five principles that a professional accountant is required to comply with. Two principles are objectivity and professional competence/due care, list the other two.   **(2 marks)**

7   The purpose of an external audit is to:

A   Check the accounts are correct and to approve them.

B   Enable the auditor to express an opinion as to whether the financial statements give a true and fair view of the entity's affairs.

C   Search for any fraud taking place in the entity.

D   Check that all regulations have been followed in preparing the financial statements and to authorise the financial statements.   **(2 marks)**

8   Goodwill arising on acquisition is accounted for according to IFRS 3 *Business combinations*. Goodwill arising on acquisition is:

    A   Carried at cost, with an annual impairment review

    B   Written off against reserves on acquisition

    C   Amortised over its useful life

    D   Revalued to fair value at each year end   **(2 marks)**

9   IT has 300 items of product ABC2 in inventory at 31 March 20X9. The items were found to be damaged by a water leak. The items can be repaired and repackaged for a cost of $1.50 per item. Once repackaged, the items can be sold at the normal price of $3.50 each.

The original cost of the items was $2.20 each. The replacement cost at 31 March 20X9 is $2.75 each.

What value should IT put on the inventory of ABC2 in its statement of financial position at 31 March 20X9?

    A $600

    B $660

    C $810

    D $825   **(2 marks)**

10   (i)   CD is Z's main customer.

    (ii)   FE is a supplier of Z.

    (iii)   ST is Z's chairman of the board and a major shareholder of Z.

    (iv)   K is Z's banker and has provided an overdraft facility and a $1,000,000 loan.

    (v)   JT is the owner of a building entity that has just been awarded a large building contract by Z. JT is also the son of ST.

Which 2 of the above can be regarded as a related party of Z?

    A   (i) and (iii)

    B   (ii) and (iv)

    C   (iii) and (v)

    D   (iv) and (v)   **(2 marks)**

(Total = 20 marks)

49   Mixed objective test questions bank 2 (5/10)   36 mins

1   An ideal tax system should conform to certain principles. Which one of the following statements *is not* generally regarded as a principle of an ideal tax?

    A   It should be fair to different individuals and should reflect a person's ability to pay.

    B   It should not be arbitrary, it should be certain.

    C   It should raise as much money as possible for the government.

    D   It should be convenient in terms of timing and payment.   **(2 marks)**

2   Which one of the following could be said to be a progressive tax?

    A   Property sales tax at 1% of the selling price of all properties sold.

    B   Value added tax at a rate of 0%, 10% or 15% depending on the type of goods or services provided.

    C   Corporate wealth tax at 2% of total net assets up to $10 million then at 0.5% on total net assets greater than $10 million.

    D   Personal income tax at 10% on earnings up to $10,000, then at 15% from $10,001 up to $100,000 and 25% over $100,000.   **(2 marks)**

3   An item of equipment cost $60,000 on 1 April 20X6. The equipment is depreciated at 20% per annum on a reducing balance basis.

The amount of deferred tax relating to this asset that should be recognised in the statement of financial position as at 31 March 20X9 is:

A $1,781
B $3,461
C $3,975
D $13,845   **(2 marks)**

4   The International Accounting Standards Board's (IASB) *Framework for the Preparation and Presentation of Financial Statements (Framework)* is the IASB's conceptual framework. Which one of the following does the Framework not cover?

A   The format of financial statements
B   The objective of financial statements
C   Concepts of capital maintenance
D   The elements of financial statements   **(2 marks)**

5   The IASB's Framework identifies reliability as one of the four qualitative characteristics of financial information. Which one of the following is not an element of reliability?

A   Information should be timely
B   Information should be free from material error
C   Information should be free from bias
D   Information must be complete   **(2 marks)**

6   OC signed a contract to provide office cleaning services for an entity for a period of one year from 1 October 20X8 for a fee of $500 per month.

The contract required the entity to make one payment to OC covering all twelve months' service in advance. The contract cost to OC was estimated at $300 per month for wages, materials and administration costs.

OC received $6,000 on 1 October 20X8.

How much profit/loss should OC recognise in its statement of comprehensive income for the year ended 31 March 20X9?

A $600 loss
B $1,200 profit
C $2,400 profit
D $4,200 profit   **(2 marks)**

7   Which one of the following could be classified as deferred development expenditure in M's statement of financial position as at 31 March 20X9 according to IAS 38 *Intangible assets*?

A $120,000 spent on developing a prototype and testing a new type of propulsion system for trains. The project needs further work on it as the propulsion system is currently not viable.

B   A payment of $50,000 to a local university's engineering faculty to research new environmentally friendly building techniques.

C $35,000 spent on consumer testing a new type of electric bicycle. The project is near completion and the product will probably be launched in the next twelve months. As this project is the first of its kind for M it is expected to make a loss.

D $65,000 spent on developing a special type of new packaging for a new energy efficient light bulb. The packaging is expected to be used by M for many years and is expected to reduce M's distribution costs by $35,000 a year.   **(2 marks)**

8   A finance lease for 6 years has an annual payment in arrears of $24,000. The fair value of the lease at inception was $106,000. Using the sum of digits method, the liability for the lease at the end of year 2 is:

	$'000
A	58.0
B	77.9
C	86.1
D	115.9

(2 marks)

9   PQ has ceased operations overseas in the current accounting period. This resulted in the closure of a number of small retail outlets.

Which one of the following costs would be *excluded* from the loss on discontinued operations?

A   Loss on the disposal of the retail outlets
B   Redundancy costs for overseas staff
C   Cost of restructuring head office as a result of closing the overseas operations
D   Trading losses of the overseas retail outlets up to the date of closure

(2 marks)

10   The following balances were extracted from N's financial statements:

STATEMENT OF FINANCIAL POSITION (EXTRACT)

	As at 31 December 20X8 $'000	As at 31 December 20X7 $'000
Non Current liabilities		
Deferred tax	38	27
Current Liabilities		
Current tax payable	119	106

STATEMENT OF COMPREHENSIVE INCOME FOR THE YEAR ENDED 31 DECEMBER 20X8 (EXTRACT)

	$'000
Income tax expense	122

The amount of tax paid that should be included in N's statement of cash flows for the year ended 31 December 20X8 is:

	$'000
A	98
B	109
C	122
D	241

(2 marks)

(Total = 20 marks)

50   Mixed section B questions bank 1 (Specimen Paper)   54 mins

(a)   ATOZ operates in several countries as follows:

- ATOZ was incorporated in country BCD many years ago. It has curtailed operations in BCD but still has its registered office in country BCD and carries out a small proportion (less than 10%) of its trade there.

- ATOZ buys most of its products and raw materials from country FGH.

- ATOZ generates most of its revenue in country NOP and all its senior management live there and hold all the management board meetings there.

Required

(i)   Explain why determining corporate residence is important for corporate income tax.   **(2 marks)**

(ii)   Explain which country ATOZ will be deemed to be resident in for tax purposes   **(3 marks)**

(Total = 5 marks)

(b)   WX operates a retail business in country X and is registered for VAT purposes.

During the last VAT period WX had the following transactions:

Purchases of materials and services, all at standard VAT rate, $130,000 excluding VAT.

Purchase of new machinery, $345,000, inclusive of VAT.

Sales of goods in the period, all inclusive of VAT where applicable, were:

Sales of goods subject to VAT at standard rate	$230,000
Sales of goods subject to VAT at zero rate	$115,000

Assume you are WX's trainee management accountant and you have been asked to prepare the VAT return and calculate the net VAT due to/from the tax authorities at the end of the period.

Assume WX has no other transactions subject to VAT and that all VAT paid can be recovered.

Required

(i)   Explain the difference between a single stage sales tax and VAT.   **(2 marks)**

(ii)   Calculate the net VAT due to/from WX at the end of the period.   **(3 marks)**

(Total = 5 marks)

(c)   Country K uses prescriptive accounting standards. Country K's standard on intangible assets has a list of intangible assets covered by the standard and an extensive list of items that are not allowed to be recognised as assets. RS has incurred expenditure on a new product that does not appear to be specifically listed as "not allowed" by the standard. RS's management want to classify the expenditure as an intangible non-current asset in RS's statement of financial position. They argue that the type of expenditure incurred is not listed in the accounting standard as being "not allowed" therefore it is allowed to be capitalised.

RS's auditors have pointed out that the expenditure is not listed as being "allowed" and therefore should not be capitalised.

Required

Explain the possible advantages of having accounting standards based on principles rather than being prescriptive. Use the scenario above to illustrate your answer.   **(Total = 5 marks)**

(d)   BD is a well established double glazing business, manufacturing building extensions, doors and windows in its own manufacturing facility and installing them at customer properties.

BD's financial statements for the year ended 31 March 20X7 showed the manufacturing facility and installation division as separate reportable segments.

On 1 March 20X8, BD's management decided to sell its manufacturing facility and concentrate on the more profitable selling and installation side of the business.

At BD's accounting year end, 31 March 20X8, BD had not found a buyer for its manufacturing facility and was continuing to run it as a going concern. The facility was available for immediate sale; the management were committed to the sale and were actively seeking a buyer. They were quite sure that the facility would be sold before 31 March 20X9.

The manufacturing facility's fair value at 31st March 20X8 was $2.8 million, comprising total assets with a fair value of $3.6 million and liabilities with a fair value of $0.8 million. BD's management accountant calculated that the manufacturing facility had incurred a loss for the year of $0.5 million before tax and the estimated cost of selling the manufacturing facility was $0.2 million.

Required

Explain, with reasons, how BD should treat the manufacturing facility in its financial statements for the year ended 31 March 20X8. **(Total = 5 marks)**

(e) L leases office space and a range of office furniture and equipment to businesses. On 1 April 20X8 C acquired a lease for a fully furnished office space (office space plus office furniture and equipment) and a separate lease for a computer system from L.

The office space was a lease of part of a large building and the building had an expected life of 50 years. The lease was for 5 years with rental payable monthly. The first year was rent free. The $1,000 per month rental commenced on 1 April 20X9.

The computer system lease was for 3 years, the expected useful life of the system was 3 years. The $15,000 per year lease rental was due annually in arrears commencing with 31 March 20X9. The interest rate implicit in the lease is 12.5% and the cost of the leased asset at 1 April 20X8 was $35,720. C depreciates all equipment on the straight line basis.

Under the terms of the computer system lease agreement C is responsible for insuring, servicing and repairing the computers. However, L is responsible for insurance, maintenance and repair of the office.

C allocates the finance charge for finance leases using the actuarial method.

Required

Explain the accounting treatment, required by international financial reporting standards, in the financial statements of C in respect of the two leases for the year ended 31 March 20X9. **(Total = 5 marks)**

(f) PS issued 1,000,000 $1 cumulative, redeemable preferred shares on 1 April 20X8. The shares were issued at a premium of 25% and pay a dividend of 4% per year.

The issue costs incurred were $60,000. The shares are redeemable for cash of $1.50 on 31 March 20Y8. The effective interest rate is 5.18%. Ignore all tax implications.

The management accountant of PS has extracted the following amounts from the preferred shares ledger account, for the year ended 31 March 20X9:

Account – Non-current liability – Preferred shares

	$
Net amount received on issue	1,190,000
Finance cost @5.18%	61,642
Less dividend paid	(40,000)
Balance at 31 March 20X9	1,211,642

Required

(i) Explain the IAS 32 *Financial instruments – presentation* and IAS 39 *Financial instruments – recognition and measurement* requirements for the presentation and measurement of an issue of preferred shares. **(3 marks)**

(ii) Using the information provided above, explain the amounts that PS should include for the preferred shares in its statement of comprehensive income and statement of financial position for the year ended 31 March 20X9. **(2 marks)**

(Total = 5 marks)

(Total = 30 marks)

51 Mixed section B questions bank 2 (5/10) 54 mins

(a)   Cee has reduced her tax bill by taking advice from a tax expert and investing her surplus cash in government securities. The income from government securities is free of tax.

Gee works as a night security guard for a local entity and also has a job working in a supermarket during the day. Gee has reduced his tax bill by declaring only his day job income on his annual tax return.

Required

Explain the difference between tax evasion and tax avoidance, using Cee and Gee to illustrate your answer. **(5 marks)**

(b)   W is a business in Country X, that uses locally grown fruit and vegetables to make country wines. During 20X8 W paid $30,000 plus VAT for the ingredients and other running costs.

When the wine is bottled W pays $1 tax per bottle to the tax authority. During 20X8 W produced 10,000 bottles.

W sold all the wine to retailers for an average price of $8.05 per bottle, including VAT at standard rate.

Required

(i)   Explain the difference between unit taxes and ad valorem taxes, using the scenario above to illustrate your answer. **(3 marks)**

(ii)   Calculate the amounts of indirect tax payable by W for the year ended 31 December 20X8. **(2 marks)**

(Total = 5 marks)

(c)   H, an entity, carries out business in Country X, buying and selling goods.

The senior management of H meet regularly in the entity's offices in Country X.

H owns 100% of S, an entity that buys and sells goods in Country Y. The senior management of S meet regularly in the entity's offices in Country Y. S reported a profit of $500,000 for 20X8 and received an income tax bill from Country Y's tax authority for $100,000.

S has declared a dividend of $200,000 and is required to deduct tax at 10% before remitting cash to overseas investors, such as H.

Assume Country X and Country Y have a double tax agreement based on the Organisation for Economic Co-Operation and Development (OECD) – Model Tax Convention.

Required

Explain the terms "competent jurisdiction" and "withholding tax". Illustrate how each relates to the H group. **(5 marks)**

(d)   B's profits have suffered due to a slow-down in the economy of the country in which it operates. AB's draft financial statements show revenue of $35 million and profit before tax of $4 million for the year ended 31 December 20X8.

AB's external auditors have identified a significant quantity of inventory that is either obsolete or seriously impaired in value. The audit senior has calculated the inventory write-down of $1 million. AB's directors have been asked by the audit senior to record this in the financial statements for the year ended 31 December 20X8.

AB's directors are refusing to write-down the inventory at 31 December 20X8, claiming that they were not aware of any problems at that date and furthermore do not agree with the auditor that there is a problem now. The directors are proposing to carry out a stock-take at 31 May 20X9 and to calculate their own inventory adjustment, if required. If necessary the newly calculated figure will be used to adjust inventory values in the year to 31 December 20X9.

Required

(i)　Explain the objective of an external audit.　　　　　　　　　　　**(2 marks)**

(ii)　Assuming that AB's directors continue to refuse to amend the financial statements, explain the type of audit report that would be appropriate for the auditors to issue.　　**(3 marks)**

(Total = 5 marks)

(e)　On 1 April 20X7 CC started work on a three year construction contract. The fixed value of the contract is $63 million.

During the year ended 31 March 20X8 CC's contract costs escalated.

The value of work done and the cash received for the two years to 31 March 20X9 are summarised below:

	Year to 31 March 20X9	Year to 31 March 20X8
Percentage of work completed in year	40%	35%
Cost incurred in year	$26 million	$18 million
Estimated further costs after the year end to complete project	$20 million	$36 million
Progress payments received in the year	$22 million	$15 million

Amounts recognised by CC in its statement of comprehensive income for the year ended 31 March 20X8:

Revenue	$22 million
Cost of sales	$18 million

Required

Calculate the amounts to be recorded for the above contract in CC's statement of comprehensive income for the year ended 31 March 20X9 and in the statement of financial position at that date.

Show all calculated figures to the nearest $ million.　　　　　　　　**(5 marks)**

(f)　AD operates five factories in different locations in a country. Each factory produces a different product line and each product line is treated as a separate segment under IFRS 8 Operating Segments.

One factory, producing a range of shoes, had an increased annual loss of an estimated $2,000,000 for the year to 31 March 20X9. On 1 March 20X9 AD's management decided to close the factory and cease the sale of it's range of shoes. Closure costs, net of any gains on disposal of the assets, are estimated as $150,000.

On 31 March 20X9 AD's management is still negotiating payment terms with the shoe factory workforce and has not agreed an actual closure date. AD has not yet attempted to find a buyer for the factory or its assets.

AD's management wants to completely exclude the shoe factory results from AD's financial statements for the year ended 31 March 20X9. They argue that as the shoe factory is about to be closed or sold, it would mislead investors to include the results of the shoe factory in the results for the year.

Required

Assume that you are a trainee accountant with AD.

AD's finance director has asked you to draft a briefing note that she can use to prepare a response to AD's management.

Your briefing note should explain how AD should treat the shoe factory in its financial statements for the year ended 31 March 20X9.

You should make reference to any relevant International Financial Reporting Standards and to CIMA's Code of Ethics for Professional Accountants.　　　　　　　　　　**(5 marks)**

(Total = 30 marks)

ANSWERS

1 Objective test answers: The regulatory framework

1   C   Guidance on application and interpretation of IASs/IFRSs is provided by the International Financial Reporting Interpretations Committee (IFRIC).

2   A   The priority given to different user groups in different countries (eg investor groups in the US and employees in Europe) is actually a **barrier** to harmonisation.

3   B   Many of the older IASs permitted **two** accounting treatments for like transactions or events – the benchmark treatment and the allowed alternative. As these are revised allowed alternative treatments are being eliminated. This gives preparers of accounts **less** choice.

4   Expense and equity

5   C   The *Framework* cites two underlying assumptions:

The accounts have been prepared on an accruals basis (accruals).
The business is expected to continue in operation for the foreseeable future (going concern).

6   B   The elements of financial statements are assets, liabilities and equity in the statement of financial position and income and expenses in the statement of comprehensive income. Profits and losses are not elements.

7   B   The income statement measures **performance**. Financial position is measured in the statement of financial position and financial adaptability in the statement of cash flows

8   D   Accruals and going concern.

9   An asset is a resource controlled by an entity as a result of past transactions or events and from which future economic benefits are expected to flow to the entity.

10   D   Generally accepted accounting practice

11   C   International Accounting Standards Committee (IASC) Foundation Trustees

12   C   IFRIC reports to the IASB. SAC advises the IASB.

13   Decreases in economic benefits during the accounting period in the form of outflows or depletions of assets or incurrences of liabilities that result in decreases in equity, other than those relating to distributions to equity participants.

[This is the IASB definition, which contains **36** words. You can choose which words to leave out.]

14   To provide information about the financial position, performance and changes in financial position of an entity that is useful to a wide range of users in making economic decisions.

15   D   Going concern and accruals

16   D   The IASC Foundation oversees and directs the work of the IASB.

17   Reliability and understandability.

18   Going concern and accruals based accounting

19   The four stages are:

1   Establishment of Advisory Committee
2   Discussion Paper issued
3   Exposure Draft issued
4   IFRS issued

2 Objective test answers: External audit

1	D	An external audit provides reasonable assurance that the financial statements are free from material misstatements. An external audit does not **guarantee** that there are no material misstatements in the financial statements. There are inherent limitations in an audit which affect the auditor's ability to discover material misstatements that arise from the nature of financial reporting, the nature of audit procedures, time and cost limitations and the requirement for the auditor to exercise judgment.
2	B	The auditor has been prevented from obtaining sufficient appropriate audit evidence.
3	C	No qualification is needed as the directors have made full disclosure.
4	D	The auditors report covers all of these matters.
5	B	This is a limitation on scope.
6	C	The auditors will be unable to give an opinion in this case.
7	C	Even though the finance department may prepare the accounts, management have overall responsibility for the preparation of the financial statements. External auditors give an opinion on whether the financial statements give a true and fair view.
8	A	In order to state that the financial statements show a true and fair view the auditor must satisfy himself that the other three matters are valid.
9	D	The auditors will begin by trying to persuade the directors.
10		Power to require access to all books and records Power to require information and explanations from officers of the company Power to attend meetings and address shareholders
11	C	If the auditor believes that the financial statements do not show a true and fair view this should first be discussed with management. If management refuse to adjust the accounts, the auditor would give an adverse opinion in the audit report.
12	A	The external audit is carried out by external auditors who are independent of the company so that they can provide an independent opinion as to the truth and fairness of the company's financial statements.
13	A	The auditor does not report on items that are not material.
14		To enable the auditor to express an opinion as to whether the financial statements give a true and fair presentation of the entity's affairs.

3 Objective test answers: Ethics

1	B	The audit of the financial statements will be carried out by an accountant in practice.
2	B	Reliability, Morality and Efficiency are not fundamental principles.
3	A	Self-interest. If such threats are significant (ie the interest is direct and of high value), safeguards will have to be put in place.
4	B	A principles-based approach sets out principles and guidelines, rather than detailed rules to cover every specific situation. This leads to the listed advantages – but not to consistent application, since there is a high degree of discretion in applying guidelines to different cases.
5	A	The principle of due care is that, having accepted an assignment, you have an obligation to carry it out to the best of your ability, in the client's best interests, and within reasonable timescales, with proper regard for the standards expected of you as a professional. In this scenario, any answer you give on the spot would risk being incomplete, inaccurate or out-of-date, with potentially serious consequences, if the client relies and acts on your reply. Integrity is honesty, fair dealing and truthfulness; professional behaviour is upholding the reputation of your profession; and

confidentiality is not using or disclosing information given to you by employers or clients in the course of your work. (None of these issues applies directly here.)

6   B   This raises issues of professional competence and due care. You know that you do not have the knowledge to answer these questions at this time and in this situation. For your own professional safety, you should make the client clearly aware of this and not be prepared to give any opinion, as this may be relied upon by the client despite the circumstances. The most appropriate form of action would be to make an appointment with the client to discuss the matter properly after you have done some research into these specific areas, or refer them to a colleague with experience in this area.

7   Confidentiality
     Professional competence/due care.

8   C   A, B and D all describe the features of a rules-based code.

9   A   B describes integrity; C describes objectivity and D describes professional competence and due care.

10   B   Disclosure of information to advance the interests of a new client would not be permitted under the Code.

11   D   HMRC is not a source of ethical codes for accountants.

4   Section B answers: Regulation

(a)   The IASB *Framework* lays out the elements of financial statements as follows.

   (i)   Asset

        A resource controlled by an entity as a result of past events and from which future economic benefits are expected to flow to the entity.

        An example of an asset is an item of machinery used in the business.

   (ii)   Liability

        A present obligation of the entity arising from past events, the settlement of which is expected to result in an outflow of resources from the entity.

        An example of a liability is an amount due to a supplier for goods received.

   (iii) Equity
        The residual interest in the assets of the entity after deducting all its liabilities.

        Ordinary share capital is an example of equity.

   (iv)   Income

        Increases in economic benefits during the accounting period in the form of inflows or enhancements of assets or decreases of liabilities that result in increases in equity, other than those relating to contributions from equity participants.

        An example of income is income recognised on the sale of goods.

   (v)   Expenses

        Decreases in economic benefits during the accounting period in the form of outflows or depletions of assets that result in decreases in equity, other than those relating to distributions to equity participants.

        Depreciation is an example of an expense.

(b)

> **Examiner's comments.** Candidates failed to include enough detail in their answers. Many answers identified a characteristic and then the explanation added nothing to it, for example, 'Relevance – information needs to be relevant'.

The four principal qualitative characteristics of financial information are as follows.

Relevance

Information is said to be relevant when it influences the economic decisions of users by helping them to evaluate past, present and future events or by confirming, or correcting their past evaluations. So relevant information has both a predictive and confirmatory role.

Reliability

Information is reliable when it is free from material error and bias, and can be depended upon by users to represent faithfully that which it either purports to represent or could reasonably be expected to represent.

Comparability

The importance of comparability is that users must be able to compare the financial statements of an entity over time and to compare the financial statements of different entities. For this to be possible users must be informed of the accounting policies employed in the preparation of the financial statements and any changes in those policies and their effects. The financial statements must also show corresponding amounts for the previous period.

Understandability

The financial statement information should be readily understandable to users. For this purpose users are assumed to have a reasonable knowledge of business and economic activities and accounting and a willingness to study the information with reasonable diligence.

(c)

> **Examiner's comments.** Most candidates did well on this question, although some could not think of three alternatives. A common error was using bullet points or short notes to answer the question and as a result not providing sufficient detail for 5 marks.

C could pursue any of the following options:

(i) **Develop its own standards without reference to the IASB**. This would produce standards which reflected trading conditions in the country but, when it developed to the point of needing to attract foreign investment, investors may not be drawn to companies whose financial statements are not prepared under generally recognised standards.

(ii) **Adopt IFRS**. This would mean that C had adopted high-quality, generally recognised standards from the outset, and would have no future harmonisation process to undergo. However, it may find that time and expense has gone into implementing standards which may not be that relevant to its current economic situation.

(iii) **Adopt those IFRSs which are currently applicable**, such as IAS 41 *Agriculture*, and **develop additional standards of its own based on IFRS**. This would produce a set of standards which were theoretically high-quality and relevant to its own economy. However, the judgement and expertise required to carry this out may not be available and C will be resolving issues between local standards and IFRS on an ongoing basis.

(d)

> **Top tips.** We have only given five answers here as this is all that is required for five marks.
>
> **Examiner's comments.** The answers provided for this question were very weak. Many candidates did not know what the purpose of the Framework was and tried explaining the purpose of financial statements.

The purposes of the *Framework* are:

(i) To assist in the **review of existing IASs and IFRSs** and the **development of new IFRSs**

(ii) To promote **harmonisation** of accounting standards by reducing the number of allowed alternative accounting treatments

(iii) To **assist national standard-setting bodies** in developing national standards

(iv) To assist preparers of financial statements in **applying IFRSs** and dealing with topics not yet covered by an IFRS

(v) To **assist auditors** in determining whether financial statements comply with IFRS

Alternative answers

You would also have scored marks if you had identified any of the following purposes.

- To assist users of financial statements prepared under IFRS in interpreting the information contained in them

- To provide general information on the approach used in formulating IFRSs

(e)

Examiner's comments. This question was very badly answered. Those candidates that did identify the correct IAS and the correct accounting treatment often omitted to explain why the items should be treated that way, as a consequence only partial marks could be awarded.

In order to decide how to treat these items of expenditure in its financial statements, EK must decide whether the expenditure gives rise to an asset or intangible asset which can be recognised in the statement of financial position. Asset recognition criteria are dealt with in the IASB *Framework*. Intangible assets are covered by IAS 38 *Intangible assets*.

The IASB *Framework* defines an asset as **a resource controlled by an entity as a result of past events** and from which **further economic benefits are expected to flow** to the entity.

Both assets and intangible assets can only be recognised if both the following apply.

- It is probable that future economic benefits will flow to the entity.
- The cost of the asset can be measured reliably.

(i) Book publishing and film rights

These rights give access to future economic benefits and could even be resold, so the $1m cost can be recognised as an intangible asset. No amortisation is necessary until the book is actually published.

(ii) Trade fair

Since no new orders were taken as a direct result of the event and no estimate can be made of additional revenue, the cost of the trade fair cannot be recognised as an asset. Future economic benefits may not be probable. The cost of the trade fair does not meet the recognition criteria for an asset and should therefore be treated as an expense in the year incurred.

(iii) Consultant

Although the cost of the consultancy itself is known, it is virtually impossible to quantify any change in the value of the image of EK. Since the cost of the corporate image cannot be measured reliably, the consultancy fees should not be recognised as an asset and should be expensed in the year incurred.

5 Section B answers: External audit

(a)

Examiner's comments. Common errors made by candidates in this question were:

- incorrectly concluding that item 1 was material by incorrectly calculating the percentage of revenue as 500/15,000 instead of 500/15,000,000 and the percentage of profit as 500/1,500 instead of 500/1,500,000.

- suggesting that item 2 (development costs) should be written off against the previous year's profit, which is incorrect as the circumstances existing at that balance sheet date met the criteria required by IAS 38.

> – not recognising that item 3 required immediate full provision as per IAS 37.

(i) <u>Item 1</u> – the obsolete inventory is not material as $500 is 0·003% of revenue and is 0·03% of profit, therefore management's decision is acceptable. The inventory can be written off in the current year.

<u>Item 2</u> – the deferred development expenditure must be charged to profit or loss as soon as it ceases to meet the IAS 38 criteria for deferral. As the project has now been abandoned, the expenditure ceases to meet the IAS 38 criteria for deferral. Therefore the $600,000 should be charged to profit or loss in the current year.

(ii) <u>Item 3 – decommissioning costs</u>

IAS 37 *Provisions, contingent liabilities and contingent assets* requires decommissioning costs to be recognised as soon as the liability arises, which is usually when the facility starts to operate. HF should create a provision for the full $5,000,000 decommissioning costs, discounted to present value, and add it to the cost of the asset (debit asset, credit provision). This will be a material increase in the net asset value and will increase the depreciation charged to profit or loss .

<u>Audit report</u>

If the directors do not agree to change the treatment of the decommissioning costs to recognise the full provision in the financial statements, an "except for" qualified audit report will need to be issued as all matters are correct except for the treatment of the decommissioning costs.

(b) (i) **Qualified opinion** – an auditor will be unable to issue an unqualified audit report if he has disagreements with management regarding the treatment of one or more items in the accounts, or if the scope of his audit has been limited in some way, for instance certain records may not have been made available to him. When the auditor concludes that he cannot issue an unqualified report for one of these reasons, but that the effect of the disagreement or limitation of scope is not so material or pervasive as to require an adverse opinion or a disclaimer of opinion, then he will express a qualified opinion. The opinion will be expressed as being 'except for the effects of the matter to which the qualification relates'.

(ii) **Disclaimer of opinion** – where the possible effect of a limitation on scope is so material or pervasive that the auditor has not been able to obtain sufficient appropriate audit evidence and is therefore unable to express an opinion on the financial statements, a disclaimer of opinion will be expressed. This limitation may have arisen through circumstances, or may have been imposed by the client or may have arisen due to the inadequate nature of the company's accounting records. The auditor's report should give an explanation of the nature of the limitation of scope and quantify the effects on the financial statements where possible.

(iii) **Adverse opinion** – where the effect of a disagreement is so material or pervasive that the auditor concludes that a qualified opinion is insufficient to disclose the misleading or incomplete nature of the financial statements an adverse opinion will be expressed. Such a disagreement may concern the selection of accounting policies, the application of accounting standards or the inadequacy of disclosures. The report must fully describe the circumstances leading to the adverse opinion. The opinion will state that, because of the effect of these circumstances, the financial statements do not present fairly the financial position of the company and its results.

(c) <u>Right of access to records</u>

The auditor has a right of access at all times to the books, accounts and vouchers of the company.

<u>Right to require information</u>

The auditor has a right to require from the company's officers such information and explanations as he thinks necessary for the performance of his duties as auditor. It is an offence for a company's officer to make a statement to the auditor which is materially misleading, false or deceptive.

These rights make it possible for the auditor to carry out an audit. If these rights are violated, the auditor will qualify his report. If the situation is serious, for instance if the auditor believes the directors to be involved in a fraud, he has the following rights which enable him to communicate directly to the shareholders:

<u>Right to attend/receive notice of general meetings</u>

The directors cannot keep the auditor away from the AGMs by not informing him of when they are taking place.

<u>Right to speak at general meetings</u>

The auditor has a right to be heard at general meetings which he attends, on any part of the business that concerns him as auditor.

<u>Right in relation to written resolutions</u>

The auditor has the right to receive a copy of any written resolution proposed. This means that he must receive a copy of any resolution which is proposed to terminate his engagement.

In practice, an auditor would not expect to have to invoke these rights very often, but the fact that they exist establishes his status in relation to the directors and makes it possible for him to get the co-operation that he needs in order to carry out his engagement.

(d)

> **Examiner's comments**. Many answers to this question were of low quality. Many candidates clearly did not understand the objective of an audit and a large proportion of answers were unable to correctly identify the type of report or the information required.

(i) **The objective of an external audit** is to enable the auditor to express an opinion on whether the financial statements give a true and fair view (or present fairly) the financial position of the company and the results of its operations and its cash flows, in accordance with applicable Accounting Standards.

(ii) **EA & Co should issue a qualified opinion** based on disagreement on accounting policies under ISA 700. We have not been told that this issue is so material or pervasive that the financial statements are misleading or incomplete, so an adverse opinion is not indicated.

<u>They will include in their report:</u>

'Profit on long-term contracts has not been accounted for in accordance with IAS 11. Per the standard, a foreseeable loss on a long-term contract should be recognised immediately. In the financial statements for the year to 30 September 2006, only that portion of the loss which has been incurred to date has been included. $3.7m has been included in the statement of comprehensive income in respect of long-term contracts. This should be amended to $1.3m in order to recognise in full the expected loss.

In our opinion, except for the effect on the financial statements of the matter referred to in the preceding paragraph, the financial statements give a true and fair view...'

6 Section B answers: Ethics

(a) The CIMA Code requires the professional accountant to comply with five fundamental principles:

- Integrity
- Objectivity
- Professional Competence and Due Care
- Confidentiality
- Professional Behaviour

Compliance with these principles is required in order for the accountant to discharge his duty to act in the public interest.

Specific threats to his compliance with these principles can arise during the course of his work. The conceptual framework requires the accountant to identify, evaluate and address threats to compliance with the fundamental principles.

The framework sets out five categories of threat:

- Self-interest threats
- Self-review threats

- Advocacy threats
- Familiarity threats
- Intimidation threats

The accountant must recognise the threat when it arises, evaluate whether or not it is significant and put in place safeguards to deal with it. The Code gives examples of how the categories of threat can arise and examples of relevant safeguards.

There are major differences between this approach and a rules-based approach. The conceptual framework approach puts the responsibility on the accountant to ensure compliance with the principles. In this way, whatever threat arises, the accountant has to consider it. A list of rules could not encompass every possible threat and could even lead to attempts to circumvent them. Any situation not explicitly covered would be deemed to be not a threat and situations would then arise which would require the rules to be continually updated. The application of a conceptual framework avoids this.

(b) The five fundamental principles are:

Integrity – a professional accountant should be straightforward and honest in all professional and business relationships.

Objectivity – a professional accountant should not allow bias, conflict of interest or undue influence of others to override professional or business judgments.

Professional competence and due care - a professional accountant has a continuing duty to maintain professional knowledge and skill at the level required to ensure that a client or employer receives competent professional service based on current developments in practice, legislation and techniques. A professional accountant should act diligently and in accordance with applicable technical and professional standards when providing professional services.

Confidentiality – a professional accountant should respect the confidentiality of information acquired as a result of professional and business relationships and should not disclose any such information to third parties without proper and specific authority unless there is a legal or professional right or duty to disclose. Confidential information acquired as a result of professional and business relationships should not be used for the personal advantage of the professional accountant or third parties.

Professional behaviour – a professional accountant should comply with relevant laws and regulations and should avoid any action that discredits the profession.

(c) **Advantages of a code based on principles include**:

- Having principles rather than rules places the onus on the professional to **consider actively** relevant issues in a given situation, rather than just agreeing action with a checklist of forbidden items.

- Principles rather than rules prevent professionals interpreting legalistic requirements narrowly to get around the ethical requirements.

- Principles rather than rules allow for variations that are found in every individual situation.

- A principles-based code prescribes minimum standards of behaviour that are expected.

Disadvantages of a code based on principles include:

- Principles-based codes can be difficult to enforce legally, unless the breach of the code is blatant.

- International codes (such as the IFAC Code) cannot fully capture regional variations in beliefs and practice.

- Illustrative examples given in principles-based codes can be interpreted mistakenly as rules to follow in all similar circumstances.

- As ethical codes cannot include all circumstances and dilemmas, accountants need a very good understanding of the underlying principles in order to effectively apply them.

7 Objective test answers: Presentation

1	A	Members do not inspect the accounting records – the auditors do this on their behalf.
2	A	All of these items appear in the statement of changes in equity.
3	D	Authorised share capital is disclosed in the notes to the balance sheet, the other disclosures are made in the income statement or notes.
4	C	2 is a change of accounting estimate, 4 is specifically mentioned in IAS 8 as not constituting a change of accounting policy.
5	D	Material errors are treated in the same way as changes of accounting policy, by the application of retrospective restatement.
6	B	IAS 8 requires that a change in accounting policy is accounted for by retrospective application.
7	B	A change in the method of valuing inventory is a change of accounting policy
8	A	Changing the method of depreciation is a change of estimation technique not a change of accounting policy and therefore retrospective application is not required. However the current year figures must be changed to reflect the change in estimation technique and the change must be disclosed.
9	C	Provisions are covered by IAS 37.
10	D	Revenue and finance cost
11	B	This is the most commonly seen form of the statement of comprehensive income (income statement), which includes cost of sales and distribution costs.
12	D	A is a change in accounting policy, B is specifically mentioned in IAS 8 as a change in an accounting policy to be dealt with as a revaluation in accordance with IAS 16 , C is an error per IAS 8.

8 Section B answers: Presentation

(a) Companies might be expected to publish accounts using standard formats so as to ensure **complete disclosure** of material and important items and to ensure **consistency between accounting periods and comparability between companies.**

In addition, in certain European and other countries where standard formats have been in use for many years their use provides governments with **consistent information for the preparation of national accounts** and other economic statistics.

The detail shown in each of the standard income statements would enable users of accounts to calculate certain key **ratios** such as gross margins, net margins, ratio of administration costs to sales or profit and to identify the proportion of the net income arising from operations separately to that arising from financing transactions.

This information would be of use to **shareholders** and stockholders' analysts who will wish to assess the **profitability** of a company and compare it with possible alternative investments.

(b)

> **Examiner's comments.** Candidates scored high marks on this question. This question was the most popular part of question 2 and was generally the best answer.
>
> The most common error was to incorrectly adjust for the change in inventory value and some candidates ignored the requirement to make a provision for compensation.

CE
STATEMENT OF COMPREHENSIVE INCOME FOR THE YEAR ENDED 31 MARCH 20X6

	$'000
Revenue	2,000
Cost of sales (W)	(688)
Gross profit	1,312
Distribution costs	(200)
Administrative expenses (260 + 500)	(760)
Finance costs	(190)
Profit before tax	162

Working: Cost of sales

Per trial balance	480
Inventory adjustment	16
Depreciation ((1,500 – 540) × 20%)	192
	688

9   Objective test answers: Statements of cash flows

1   A   It is important to know which way round the additions and subtractions go when preparing a cash flow statement.

2   D   Profit on disposal will be included in profit, so should be deducted.

3   C   These items do not affect cash flow.

4   D   The final figure in the cash flow statement is the increase or decrease in cash and cash equivalents.

5   A

Property, plant and equipment carrying value

	$m
Balance b/d	30
Disposals (balancing figure)	(4)
Depreciation	(6)
	20
Cash paid for additions	16
Balance c/d	36

As the carrying value of the asset disposed of is $4m and there was a loss on disposal of $1m, the proceeds were $3m.

6   B   Equity investments do not generally fulfil the description of cash equivalents

7   A   All of these items involve movements of cash

8   C   Depreciation and losses on disposal are added back.

9   A

	$'000
Cash from sales	
$3,600 + $600 – $700	3,500
Cash paid for purchases	
$2,400 + $300 – $450	(2,250)
Payments for expenses	(760)
	490

10   Property, plant and equipment purchases = $105,000

	$'000
Balance b/d	180
Revaluation	20
Disposals	(5)
Depreciation	(40)
	155
Cash paid for additions (balancing figure)	105
Balance c/d	260

11   A   Interest paid = $38,000

	$
Balance b/d	12,000
Statement of comprehensive income	41,000
	53,000
Cash paid (balancing figure)	(38,000)
Balance c/d	15,000

10   Section B answer: Statement of cash flows

Examiner's comments. A very large proportion of candidates prepared a statement of cash flows according to IAS 7 indirect method rather than the direct method, thereby losing most of the marks.

FC
STATEMENT OF CASH FLOWS FOR THE YEAR ENDED 31 MARCH 20X8

Cash flows from operating activities	$'000	$'000
Cash received from customers (W1)	440	
Rents received	45	
Cash paid to suppliers (W2)	(225)	
Cash paid to and on behalf of employees	(70)	
Other operating expenses	(15)	
Cash generated from operations		175

Workings

1   *Cash received from customers*

	$'000
Opening trade receivables	45
Revenue	445
Closing trade receivables	(50)
Cash received from customers	440

2   *Cash paid to suppliers*

	$'000
Cost of sales	220
Opening inventory	(25)
Closing inventory	40
Purchases	235
Opening payables	20
Closing payables	(30)
Cash paid to suppliers	225

11   Dickson

> **Text references.** Statements of cash flows are covered in Chapter 8: IAS 7: Statement of cash flows.
>
> **Top tips.** This is a really great question to practice preparing statements of cash flows. The calculation of interest paid and income tax paid should have been fairly straightforward. It was easy to miss the amortisation on development expenditure and instead just include the cash spent during the year – be on the lookout for this in your exam. The new finance lease was tricky – make sure you understand how it affected the PPE and finance liability workings. Remember that no cash changes hands in a bonus issue of shares!

DICKSON CO

STATEMENT OF CASH FLOWS FOR THE YEAR ENDED 31 MARCH 20X6

	$'000	$'000
Cash flows from operating activities		
Profit before taxation	342	
Adjustments for:		
Depreciation	57	
Amortisation (W3)	60	
Interest expense	15	
Profit on disposal of assets	(7)	
	467	
Decrease in trade receivables (W1)	50	
Increase in inventories (W1)	(133)	
Decrease in trade payables (W1)	(78)	
Cash generated from operations	306	
Interest paid (15 – 5)	(10)	
Income taxes paid (W4)	(256)	
Net cash from operating activities		40
Cash flows from investing activities		
Development expenditure	(190)	
Purchase of property, plant & equipment (W2)	(192)	
Proceeds from sale of property, plant & equipment	110	
Net cash used in investing activities		(272)
Cash flows from financing activities		
Issue of shares (850 – 500 – (400 × 1/8)]	300	
Issue of loan notes	50	
Payment of finance lease liabilities (W5)	(31)	
Dividends paid (W6)	(156)	
Net cash from financing activities		163
Net decrease in cash and cash equivalents		(69)
Cash and cash equivalents at beginning of period		109
Cash and cash equivalents at end of period		40

NOTES TO THE STATEMENT OF CASH FLOWS

1   *Property, plant and equipment*

During the period, the company acquired property, plant and equipment with an aggregate cost of $248,000 of which $56,000 was purchased by means of finance leases. Cash payments of $192,000 were made to acquire property, plant and equipment.

2   *Cash and cash equivalents*

Cash and cash equivalents consist of cash on hand and balances with banks, and investments in government bonds. Cash and cash equivalents included in the cash flow statement comprise the following balance sheet amounts.

	20X6	20X5
	$'000	$'000
Cash on hand and balances with banks	(103)	63
Short-term investments	143	46
Cash and cash equivalents	40	109

Workings

1   *Inventories, trade receivables and trade payables*

	Inventories $'000	Trade receivables $'000	Trade payables $'000
Balance b/d	227	324	352
Increase/(decrease) (balancing figure)	133	(50)	(78)
Balance c/d	360	274	274

2   *Property, plant and equipment*

	$'000
Balance b/d	637
Revaluation (160 – 60)	100
Disposals	(103)
Finance leases	56
Depreciation	(57)
	633
Cash paid for additions (balancing figure)	192
Balance c/d	825

Alternative working:

PROPERTY, PLANT AND EQUIPMENT

	$		$
Bal b/d	637	Depreciation	57
Revaluations (160 – 60)	100	Disposals	103
Finance leases	56	Bal c/d	825
∴ Additions	192		
	985		985

3   *Development expenditure*

	$'000
Balance b/d	160
Amortisation	(60)
	100
Cash paid (balancing figure)	190
Balance c/d	290

Alternative working:

DEVELOPMENT EXPENDITURE

	$		$
Bal b/d	160		
Expenditure	190	∴ Amortisation	60
		Bal c/d	290
	350		350

4   *Income tax payable*

	$'000
Balance b/d – current tax	45
Balance b/d – deferred tax	153
Income tax charge	162
	360
Cash paid (balancing figure)	(256)
Balance c/d – current tax	56
Balance b/d – deferred tax	48

Alternative working:

INCOME TAX PAYABLE

	$		$
		Bal b/d – current	45
		– deferred	153
∴ Paid	256	Income statement	162
Bal c/d – current	56		
– deferred	48		
	360		360

5   *Finance lease liability*

	$'000
Balance b/d – > 1 year	80
Balance b/d – < 1 year	12
New finance lease	56
	148
Cash paid (balancing figure)	(31)
Balance c/d – > 1 year	100
Balance b/d – < 1 year	17

Alternative working:

FINANCE LEASE LIABILITY

	$		$
		Bal b/d – > 1 year	80
		– < 1 year	12
∴ Paid	31		
Bal c/d – > 1 year	100	New finance lease	56
– < 1 year	17		
	148		148

6   *Dividends payable*

	$'000
Balance b/d	103
Retained earnings	131
	234
Cash paid (balancing figure)	(156)
Balance c/d	78

Alternative working:

DIVDENDS PAYABLE

	$		$
		Bal b/d	103
∴ Paid	156	Retained earnings	131
Bal c/d	78		
	234		234

12 Tex

Text references. Statements of cash flows are covered in Chapter 8.

Top tips. The key to this type of question is familiarity with the format of the statements. The best way to achieve this is through practising your question technique. This question gives you practice on all three financial statements.

Easy marks. There was some calculation to do on taxes, but there were a lot of easy marks in the statement of cash flows. You should have been able to get most of the marks for the statement of cash flows and scored well on the statement of financial position as long as you proceeded methodically.

Marking scheme

		Marks	Marks
(a)	**Statement of cash flows**	1	
	Finance cost	½	
	Depreciation	1	
	Working capital charges – each	3	
	Interest paid	½	
	Income tax paid	2	
	Purchase of PPE	1	
	Proceeds of sale of PPE	1	
	Dividend paid	½	
	Repayment of borrowings	1	
	Proceeds from share issue	1½	
			13
(b)	**Statement of financial position**		
	Property, plant and equipment	1½	
	Inventory	1	
	Trade receivables	1½	
	Bank	3	
	Share capital	½	
	Retained earnings	1	
	Interest-bearing borrowing	½	
	Deferred tax	½	
	Trade payables	1½	
	Taxation	½	
	Presentation	½	
			12
			25

(a) TEX
STATEMENT OF CASH FLOWS FOR THE YEAR ENDED 30 SEPTEMBER 20X1

	$'000	$'000
Cash flows from operating activities		
Profit before taxation	3,576	
Finance cost	124	
Depreciation	2,640	
Loss on disposal (2,600 – 900 – 730)	970	
Operating profit before working capital changes	7,310	
Increase in inventory (W1)	(500)	
Increase in receivables (W1)	(700)	
Decrease in payables (W1)	(100)	
Cash generated from operations	6,010	
Interest paid	(124)	
Income taxes paid (W2)	(485)	
Net cash from operating activities		5,401
Cash flows from investing activities		
Purchase of property, plant and equipment	(8,000)	
Proceeds of sale of property, plant and equipment	730	
Net cash used in investing activities		(7,270)
Cash flows from financing activities		
Dividend paid	(1,000)	
Repayment of interest-bearing borrowings	(1,200)	
Proceeds from issue of shares (10,834 – 7,815)	3,019	
Net cash from financing activities		819
Net decrease in cash and cash equivalents (1,200 – 150)		(1,050)
Cash and cash equivalents at 1 October 20X0		1,200
Cash and cash equivalents at 30 September 20X1		150

Workings

1 Inventories, trade receivables and trade payables

	Inventories	Trade receivables	Trade payables
	$'000	$'000	$'000
Balance b/d	1,100	800	800
Increase/(decrease) (balancing figure)	500	700	(100)
Balance c/d	1,600	1,500	700

2 Income tax payable

	$'000
Balance b/d – current tax	685
Balance b/d – deferred tax	400
Income tax charge	1,040
	2,125
Cash paid (balancing figure)	(485)
Balance c/d – current tax	1,040
Balance b/d – deferred tax	600

(b) TEX
STATEMENT OF FINANCIAL POSITION AS AT 30 SEPTEMBER 20X2

	$'000	$'000
Non-current assets		
Property plant and equipment (18,160 – (5000 - 2000))		15,160
Current assets		
Inventory (W1)	1,700	
Trade receivables (W2)	2,800	
Bank (W4)	4,390	8,890
		24,050

	$'000	$'000
Equity and liabilities		
Equity		
Share capital		10,834
Retained earnings (W5)		8,216
		19,050
Non-current liabilities		
Interest-bearing borrowing		1,700
Deferred tax		600
Current liabilities		
Trade payables (W3)	1,400	
Taxation	1,300	2,700
		24,050

Workings

1 Inventory

	$'000
Balance b/d	1,600
Purchases	9,000
	10,600
Cost of sales	(8,900)
Balance c/d	1,700

2 Trade receivables

	$'000
Balance b/d	1,500
Sales	18,000
	19,500
Cash received	(16,700)
Balance c/d	2,800

3 Trade payables

	$'000
Balance b/d	700
Purchases	9,000
	9,700
Cash paid	(8,300)
Balance c/d	1,400

4 Cash

	$'000
Balance b/d	150
Cash received from customers	16,700
Cash paid to suppliers	(8,300)
Expenses paid	(2,000)
Taxes paid	(1,040)
Loan interest paid	(120)
Dividend paid	(1,000)
Balance c/d	4,390

5 Retained earnings

	$'000
Balance b/d	6,536
Profit for the year	2,680
	9,216
Dividend paid	(1,000)
Balance c/d	8,216

13 AG

AG
STATEMENT OF CASH FLOWS FOR THE YEAR ENDED 31 MARCH 20X5

	$'000	$'000
Cash flows from operating activities		
Profit before taxation	135	
Depreciation	720	
Profit on sale of non-current assets (98 – 75)	(23)	
Development expenditure amortised	80	
Goodwill written-off	100	
Increase in accrued expenses (W2)	10	
Interest expense	65	
		1,087
Increase in receivables (W1)	(95)	
Increase in inventories (W1)	(110)	
Increase in payables (W1)	130	
		(75)
Cash generated from operations		1,012
Interest paid (W3)	(140)	
Income taxes paid (W4)	(150)	
		(290)
Net cash from operating activities		722
Cash flows from investing activities		
Purchase of property, plant and equipment (W5)	(370)	
Sale of property, plant and equipment	98	
Development expenditure (W6)	(50)	
Net cash used in investing activities		(322)
Cash flows from financing activities		
Ordinary share issue (1.4m shares @ $0.75)	1,050	
Preference share issue (0.5m shares @ $1.00)	500	
Dividend paid	(100)	
Repurchase of loan notes	(1,000)	
Net cash used in financing activities		450
Net increase in cash and cash equivalents		850
Cash and cash equivalents at beginning of period		232
Cash and cash equivalents at end of period		1082

Workings

1   *Inventories, trade receivables and trade payables*

	Inventories $'000	Trade receivables $'000	Trade payables $'000
Balance b/d	575	420	350
Increase (balancing figure)	110	95	130
Balance c/d	685	515	480

2   *Accrued expenses*

	$'000	$'000
Balance at 31.3.20X4		172
Less accrued interest payable		(87)
		85
Balance at 31.3.20X5		107
less accrued interest payable		(12)
		95
Increase in non-interest accruals		10

3   *Interest paid*

	$'000
Balance b/d	87
Finance costs	65
	152
Cash paid (balancing figure)	(140)
Balance c/d	12

4   *Income tax payable*

	$'000
Balance b/d	190
Deferred tax transfer	(50)
Income tax charge	90
	230
Cash paid (balancing figure)	(150)
Balance b/d – deferred tax	80

5   *Property, plant and equipment*

	$'000
Balance b/d	3,900
Revaluation	125
Disposals	(75)
Depreciation	(720)
	3,230
Cash paid for additions (balancing figure)	370
Balance c/d	3,600

6   *Development costs*

	$'000
Balance b/d	400
Amortisation	(80)
	320
Cash paid (balancing figure)	50
Balance c/d	370

14 CJ

(a)   CJ
      STATEMENT OF CASH FLOWS FOR THE YEAR ENDED 31 MARCH 20X6

	$'000	$'000
Cash flows from operating activities		
Profit before tax	4,198	
Depreciation	4,055	
Finance cost	1,302	
Profit on sale of plant (118 – 95)	(23)	
Increase in inventory (W1)	(214)	
Increase in receivables (W1)	(306)	
Increase in payables (excluding interest) (W1)	420	
Cash generated from operations	9,432	
Interest paid (1,302 – 350 + 650)	(1,602)	
Income tax paid (1,810 + 1,900 – 1,914)	(1,796)	
Net cash from operating activities		6,034
Cash flows from investing activities		
Payment to acquire property, plant and equipment (W2)	(2,310)	
Receipt on disposal of plant	118	
Net cash used in investing activities		(2,192)
Cash flow from financing activities		
Proceeds of share issue	10,000	
Dividends paid	(800)	
Net cash flow from financing activities		9,200
Increase in cash and cash equivalents		13,042
Cash and cash equivalents at 31.3.X5		(880)
Cash and cash equivalents at 31.3.X6		12,162

Workings

1   Inventories, trade receivables and trade payables

	Inventories	Trade receivables	Trade payables
	$'000	$'000	$'000
Balance b/d	2,500	1,800	1,050
Increase (balancing figure)	214	306	420
Balance c/d	2,714	2,106	1,470

2   *Property, plant and equipment*

   Property

	$'000
Balance b/d	18,000
Revaluation	1,500
Depreciation	(2,070)
	17,430
Cash paid for additions (balancing figure)	1,730
Balance c/d	19,160

   Plant and equipment

	$'000
Balance b/d	10,000
Disposal	(95)
Depreciation	(1,985)
	7,920
Cash paid for additions (balancing figure)	580
Balance c/d	8,500

   Additions

	$'000
Property additions	1,730
Plant additions	580
Total	2,310

(b)   CJ
   STATEMENT OF FINANCIAL POSITION AT 31 MARCH 20X6

	$'000	$'000
Non-current assets		
Property, plant and equipment	27,660	
Available for sale investments	2,100	
		29,760
Current assets		
Inventory and WIP (2,714 + 560(W))	3,274	
Trade receivables (2,106 + 500(W))	2,606	
Cash at bank	11,753	
Cash in hand	409	
		18,042
Total assets		47,802
Equity and liabilities		
Ordinary shares	12,000	
Share premium	10,000	
Revaluation surplus	4,200	
Retained earnings (2,809 + 360(W))	3,169	
		29,369
Non-current liabilities		
Interest bearing borrowings	13,000	
Provision for deferred tax	999	
		13,999
Current liabilities		
Trade and other payables (1,820 + 700)	2,520	
Income tax payable	1,914	
		4,434
Total equity and liabilities		47,802

   Working

   Long-term contract

	$'000
Total expected profit (5,000 – 2,500 – 700)	1,800
Profit to date (1,800 × 20%)	360

Adjustment to retained profit

	$'000
Revenue (5,000 × 20%)	1,000
Cost of sales	(640)
Profit	360

Adjustments to statement of financial position

	$'000
Inventory – WIP	
Gross amount due from customers	
Costs to date	700
Profit to date	360
	1,060
Progress billings	(500)
Due from customers	560
Receivables – progress billings	500
Payables – due to suppliers	700

15 DN

Top tips. You need to be well organised to get the statement of financial position done in this question. Make sure you know your proformas and can set them out accurately and quickly. As with all Section C questions, it is best to concentrate on the easy marks first and make an attempt at some of the harder workings at the end of the question time.

Easy marks. Nothing here was difficult, although part (b) was time pressured. If your workings were clear, there were plenty of easy marks available.

Examiner's comments. (part a) There were some excellent answers to this question. Common errors were:

- Not using the correct IAS 7 format
- Mixing up proceeds of sale and gain on disposal
- Not allowing for property revaluation
- Incorrectly calculating proceeds of share issue

Marking scheme

	Marks	Marks
Statement of cash flows		
Cash flows from operating activities		
Profit before tax	1	
Depreciation	1	
Interest expense	1	
Profit on disposal	1	
Movement in: receivables	1	
Inventories	1	
Payables	1	
Interest paid	1½	
Tax paid	½	
		9
Cash flows from investing activities		
Proceeds of disposal	1	
Cost of additions	2	
		3

Cash flows from financing activities

Proceeds of new loan	1	
Proceeds of share issue	1	
	—	2
Movement in cash and cash equivalents		1
		15

Statement of financial position

Property, plant and equipment	½	
Inventory	½	
Receivables	1	
Cash	2½	
Share capital	½	
Share premium	½	
Revaluation surplus	½	
Retained earnings	2½	
Loan stock	½	
Trade payables	1	
	—	10
Total		25

(a) DN

STATEMENT OF CASH FLOWS FOR THE YEAR ENDED 31 OCTOBER 20X6

	$'000	$'000
Cash flows from operating activities		
Profit before tax		790
Adjustments for:		
Depreciation (230 + 100)		330
Interest expense		110
Profit on sale of plant		(5)
		1,225
Increase in receivables (W1)		(110)
Increase in inventories (W1)		(50)
Increase in payables (W1)		20
Cash generated from operations		1,085
Interest paid (75 + 110 – 55)		(130)
Income taxes paid		(120)
Net cash from operating activities		835
Cash flows from investing activities		
Proceeds from sale of plant	15	
Cost of acquiring new plant (W2)	(677)	
Net cash used in investing activities		(662)
Cash flows from financing activities		
Repayment of loan	(2,000)	
Proceeds from new loan	1,500	
Proceeds of share issue (300 + 300)	600	
Net cash from financing activities		100
Net increase in cash and cash equivalents		273
Cash and cash equivalents at beginning of period		45
Cash and cash equivalents at end of period		318

Workings

1   *Inventories, trade receivables and trade payables*

	Inventories	Trade receivables	Trade payables
	$'000	$'000	$'000
Balance b/d	140	230	85
Increase (balancing figure)	50	110	20
Balance c/d	190	340	105

2   *Plant and equipment*

	$'000
Balance b/d	1,405
Disposals	(10)
Depreciation	(230)
	1,165
Cash paid for additions (balancing figure)	677
Balance c/d	1,842

Note. There were no additions to properties, which is cost and revaluation surplus less depreciation.

(b)   DN
STATEMENT OF FINANCIAL POSITION AT 31 OCTOBER 20X7

	$'000	$'000
Net current assets		
Property, plant and equipment (4,942 – 330)		4,612
Current assets		
Inventory	190	
Receivables (340 + 3,300 – 3,100)	540	
Cash (W1)	1,043	
		3,773
Total assets		6,385
Equity and liabilities		
Equity		
Share capital	1,300	
Share premium	300	
Revaluation surplus	400	
Retained earnings (W2)	2,680	
		4,680
Non-current liabilities		
Bank loans		1,500
Current liabilities		
Trade payables (105 + 1,700 – 1,600)		205
Total equity and liabilities		6,385

Workings

1   *Cash*

	$'000
Balance b/d	318
Cash received from customers	3,100
Cash paid to suppliers	(1,600)
Expenses paid	(500)
Interest 20X6	(55)
Interest 20X7 ($1,500 × 6%)	(90)
Taxes 20X6	(70)
Taxes 20X7	(60)
Balance c/d	1,043

2 *Retained earnings*

		$'000
Balance b/d		2,060
Profit for the year		620
Balance c/d		2,680

3 *Profit to 31 October 20X7*

		$'000
Revenue		3,300
Cost of sales		(1,700)
Gross profit		1,600
Depreciation		(330)
Expenses		(500)
Finance cost		(90)
		680
Tax		(60)
Profit for year		620

16 HZ

Text references. Statements of cash flows are covered in Chapter 8.

Top tips. In the exam write out your proformas and insert the numbers that don't require calculation first. There was quite a lot to do, so work methodically and remember to tackle the parts you can confidently do before you deal with the more tricky areas.

Easy marks. This statement of cash flows contained some tricky parts, such as calculating the property, plant and equipment additions. However, there were some easy marks available in the cash flows from financing activities, such as dealing with the loan repayment and the share issues.

Marking scheme

	Marks	Marks
Statement of cash flows		
Cash flows from operating activities		
Profit before tax	1	
Finance cost	1	
Depreciation	1	
Gain on disposal	2	
Development expenditure	1	
Impairment of goodwill	1½	
Provision for legal claim	1½	
Movement in: Receivables	1	
Inventories	1	
Payables	1	
Interest paid	2	
Tax paid	2	
		16
Cash flows from investing activities		
Proceeds of disposal	1	
Cost of additions	1½	
Development expenditure	1	
		3½

	Marks	Marks
Cash flows from financing activities		
Repayment of loan	1	
Proceeds of ordinary share issue	1½	
Proceeds of preferred share issue	1	
Equity dividend paid	1	
		4½
Movement in cash and cash equivalents		1
		25

Examiners comments. Format marks were frequently lost in this part of the question as candidates included items in the wrong category in the statement of cash flows. Common mistakes made by candidates included:
– not deducting the gain on disposal
– not adding back the goodwill impairment or the provision for legal claim
– not including share premium in the funds raised from the new share issue

HZ
STATEMENT OF CASH FLOWS FOR THE YEAR ENDED 31 MARCH 20X9

	$'000	$'000
Cash flows from operating activities		
Profit before taxation	293	
Finance cost	122	
Depreciation	940	
Gain on disposal (98-128)	(30)	
Development expenditure	170	
Impairment of goodwill (350 – 217)	133	
Provision for legal claim	120	
Operating profit before working capital changes	1,748	
Increase in inventory (W1)	(140)	
Increase in receivables (W1)	(529)	
Increase in payables (W1)	179	
Cash generated from operations	1,258	
Interest paid (W2)	(206)	
Income taxes paid (W3)	(250)	
Net cash from operating activities		802
Cash flows from investing activities		
Purchase of property, plant and equipment (W4)	(480)	
Proceeds of sale of property, plant and equipment	128	
Development expenditure	(28)	
Net cash used in investing activities		(380)
Cash flows from financing activities		
Dividend paid	(290)	
Repayment of interest-bearing borrowings	(1,250)	
Proceeds from issue of equity shares (2,873-2,470) + (732 - 530)	605	
Proceeds from issue of preferred shares (1,000 – 70)	930	
Net cash used in financing activities		(5)
Net increase in cash and cash equivalents (717 – 300)		417
Cash and cash equivalents at 1 April 20X8		300
Cash and cash equivalents at 31 March 20X9		717

Workings

1   *Inventories, trade receivables and trade payables*

	Inventories $'000	Trade receivables $'000	Trade payables $'000
Balance b/d	750	545	565
Increase (balancing figure)	140	529	179
Balance c/d	890	1,074	744

2   *Interest paid*

	$'000
Preference shares issued	1,000
Less finance cost	(70)
	930
Add interest payable (6.72% × 930)	62
Less dividends paid during year	(50)
Balance per statement of financial position	942

Interest payable on loan notes:

	$'000
Balance b/d	113
Finance cost per statement of comprehensive income (excluding pref shares) (122 – 62)	60
	173
Cash paid (balancing figure)	(156)
Balance c/d	17

Total interest paid = 50,000 + 156,000 = $206,000

3   *Income taxes paid*

	$'000
Balance b/d current tax	247
Balance b/d deferred tax	250
Statement of comprehensive income	182
	679
Cash paid (balancing figure)	(250)
Balance c/d current tax	117
Balance c/d deferred tax	312

4   *Property, plant and equipment*

	$'000
Balance b/d	6,250
Revaluation (562 – 400)	162
Disposals	(98)
Statement of comprehensive income (depreciation)	(940)
	5,374
Cash paid (balancing figure)	480
Balance c/d	5,854

17 Objective test answers: Non-current assets, inventories and construction contracts I

1	C	780 + 117 + 30 + 28 + 100 = 1,055
2	D	They are all correct
3	D	Neither internally generated goodwill nor internally developed brands can be capitalised.
4	A	Goodwill on acquisition is retained in the statement of financial position and reviewed annually for impairment.
5	A	Carriage outwards is charged to distribution, abnormal costs are not included in inventory.
6	D	1 Production overheads should be included in cost on the basis of a company's normal level of activity.
		2 Trade discounts should be deducted but not settlement discounts.
		3 IAS 2 does not allow the use of LIFO.

7	C		$
		Contract revenue recognised (900 × 60%)	540,000
		Costs	(840,000)
		Expected loss (900 – 1,200)	(300,000)
		Costs incurred	720,000
		Recognised loss	(300,000)
		Progress billings	(400,000)
		Due from customer	20,000

8   C   Recoverable amount is the higher of value in use and net realisable value.

9   Revenue = $40m × 45% = $18m
     Profit   = $6m × 45%   = $2.7m

	$m
Contract price	40
Total costs (16 + 18)	(34)
Anticipated profit	6

10

	$
Carrying value (100,000 × 0.75^4)	31,640
Recoverable amount	28,000
Impairment loss	3,640

11   The contract is 70% complete. Revenue earned = $90m × 70% = $63m.

12   CN should recognise a loss of $20m (90m – 77m – 33m).

13   D   An allocation of EW's administration costs would not be included as these do not relate specifically to the non-current asset.

18   Objective test answers: Non current-assets, inventories and construction contracts II

1   C

	$
Original purchase price	50,000
Depreciation 20X1: (50,000 – 5,000)/5	(9,000)
Depreciation 20X2	(9,000)
Upgrade	15,000
	47,000
Depreciation 20X3: (47,000 – 5,000)/5	(8,400)
Net book value 1 January 20X4	38,600
Disposal proceeds	(7,000)
Loss on disposal	31,600

2   B   The impairment loss is applied first against the goodwill and then against the other non-current assets on a pro-rata basis. It will be allocated as follows:

	$m
Building	10
Plant and equipment	5
Goodwill	5
	20

The carrying value of the building will then become $10m (20 – 10)

3   A fall in the value of an asset, so that its recoverable amount is now less than its carrying value in the statement of financial position.

4   B   Low production or idle plant does *not* lead to a higher fixed overhead allocation to each unit.

5   The amount for which an asset could be exchanged between knowledgeable, willing parties in an arm's length transaction.

6   The publishing rights cannot be recognised as they have no reliable monetary value as they were a gift and had no cost. The expected future value cannot be recognised as an asset as the event has not yet occurred.

7   Value of goodwill = $130,000

	$'000	$'000
Fair value of consideration – shares (10,000 × $20)		200,000
Cash		20,000
		220,000
Fair value of net assets acquired:		
Tangible non-current assets	25,000	
Patents	15,000	
Brand name	50,000	
		(90,000)
Goodwill		130,000

8

Year ended:	Cost/valuation	Depreciation	Acc depreciation	Carrying Value
March 20X2	100,000	10,000	10,000	90,000
March 20X3	100,000	10,000	20,000	80,000
March 20X4	95,000	(20,000)	–	95,000
March 20X4	95,000	11,875 (95,000/8)	11,875	83,125
March 20X5	**95,000**	**16,625** (83,125/5)	**28,500**	**66,500**

9   Depreciable amount is asset cost or valuation less residual value.

10   A   This is replacement of a significant part of the asset. The carrying amount of the existing furnace lining must be derecognised. B, C and D refer to repairs and maintenance.

11   Carrying value of machine at 30 September 20X5 = 10,500

Remaining useful life = 2 years

Depreciation for year ended 30 September 20X6 (10,500/2) = 5,250

12   This question appears to refer to the criteria for recognising development expenditure, which are:

1   Technical feasibility of completing the intangible asset
2   Intention to complete and use or sell the asset
3   Ability to use or sell the asset
4   The asset will generate future economic benefits
5   Adequate resources exist to complete the project
6   Expenditure on the asset can be reliably measured

The answer only requires four of these.

13

	$'000
Total contract value	3,000
Total costs (1,500 + 250 + 400)	(2,150)
Expected total profit	850

Percentage completed = 1,500/2,150 % = 70%

Statement of comprehensive income amounts:

	$'000
Revenue (3,000 × 70%)	2,100
Costs	(1,500)
Profit	600

19 Section B answers: Non-current assets, inventories and construction contracts

(a) (i) **Research costs**

IAS 38 does not allow the capitalisation of research costs.

Development costs

IAS 38 lays down strict **criteria** to determine when carry forward of development costs is permissible.

- The expenditure attributable to the intangible asset during its development must be measurable.
- The technical feasibility of completing the product or process so that it will be available for sale or use can be demonstrated.
- The entity intends to complete the intangible asset and use or sell it.
- It must be able to use or sell the intangible asset.
- There must be a market for the output of the intangible asset or, if it is to be used internally rather than sold, its usefulness to the entity, can be demonstrated.
- Adequate technical, financial and other resources must exist, or their availability must be demonstrated, to complete the development and use or sell the intangible asset.

(ii) IAS 1 has three basic accounting assumptions: going concern, accruals and consistency.

Each of these concepts is relevant in considering the criteria discussed above for carrying forward development expenditure.

Going concern. The business must be in a position to continue its operations at least to the extent of generating resources sufficient to complete the development project and therefore to market the end product.

Accruals. The purpose of deferring development expenditure at all is to comply with the accruals concept by matching such expenditure with the income expected to arise from it.

Consistency. IAS 38 states that the criteria for deferral of expenditure should be consistently applied.

(b) The general principle underlying IAS 2 is that inventories should be shown in financial statements at the **lower of cost and net realisable value**. This principle accords with both the matching concept, which requires costs to be matched with the relevant revenues, and the prudence concept, which requires that profits are not anticipated and any probable losses are provided for.

The **cost** of an item of manufactured inventory can include both external and internal costs and it is important that only correctly attributable costs are included. These are direct acquisition costs, direct inventory holding costs and production overheads based on a **normal** level of activity. General overheads are excluded.

Production overheads are usually incurred on a time basis and not in relation to the quantities of inventory produced. Most businesses, however, are assumed to continue to exist in the medium term and production overheads are part of the inevitable cost of providing production facilities in the medium term. Thus, so long as the scale of the overheads is not distorted by unusual levels of activity, it is reasonable to include them in the 'cost' of inventory produced in the period to which they relate. Identifying a 'normal' level of activity is more difficult where business is seasonal.

The establishment of NRV also poses a number of practical problems. For many intermediate products, and even for finished items, there may be a limited market and the inventory volumes may represent a significant proportion of the market especially if disposed of under distress conditions. Where a well-developed and liquid market does not exist, it is usually appropriate to base NRV on an orderly disposal after allowing for the reasonable additional costs of marketing and distribution.

(c)

MEMO

To: Transport manager
From: Trainee management accountant
Subject: Useful life

IAS 16 *Property, plant and equipment* requires that the useful lives of non-current assets should be regularly reviewed and changed if appropriate.

By 31 March 20X2 the delivery vehicle will have been depreciated for two years out of the original estimate of its useful life of four years:

	$
Cost	20,000
Depreciation ($20,000 × $^2/_4$)	(10,000)
Carrying value at 31 March 20X2	10,000

The carrying value at the start of the year ending 31 March 20X3 should now be written off over the remaining, revised useful life of four years giving an annual depreciation charge of $2,500 ($10,000/4).

In the income statement for the year ended 31 March 20X3 therefore the depreciation charge will be $2,500. In the statement of financial position the delivery vehicle will appear at its carrying value of $7,500 ($10,000 – 2,500).

(d)

> **Examiner's comments**. Most candidates made a better attempt at the buildings part of the question then the brand name. Some candidates did not depreciate the buildings for enough years before revaluating. Despite the question saying that the brand name had been acquired for £500,000, many candidates treated it as internally generated.

Building

The building has previously been revalued upwards and the gain on revaluation taken to the revaluation surplus). Therefore IAS 36 *Impairment of assets* states that the impairment loss of $200,000 ($1.7m – 1.5m) should be charged against the previous revaluation surplus of $900,000 leaving a revaluation surplus of $700,000 and a carrying value for the building of $1,500,000. The building is reported under property, plant and equipment.

Revaluation surplus at 30 Sept 20X4 = $1.8m – ($1.0 – ($1.0 × 2/20))
                                   = $900,000

Carrying value of building at 30 Sept 20X5 = $1.8m – ($1.8m/18)
                                          = $1.7m

Market value at 30 Sept 20X5 = $1.5m

Brand name

IAS 36 requires the brand to be written down to its recoverable amount, which is the higher of its fair value less costs to sell and value in use. Therefore the recoverable amount is the market value of $200,000 as this is higher than its value in use of $150,000.

The impairment loss of $50,000 (250,000 – 200,000) is recognised immediately in the income statement. The brand is measured at $200,000 in the statement of financial position and reported as an intangible asset.

Carrying value = $500,000 – ($500,000 × 5/10)
              = $250,000

Recoverable amount = higher of fair value and value in use
                   = $200,000

Impairment = $50,000 ($250,000 – 200,000) charged to the income statement

Brand in statement of financial position = $200,000

(e)

Building A

	$
Cost	200,000
Depreciation to 31.8.01 (200,000/20 × 5)	(50,000)
Carrying value	150,000
Revaluation 31.8.01 – to revaluation surplus	30,000
Carrying value	180,000
Depreciation to 31.8.06 (180,000/15 × 5)	(60,000)
	120,000
Valuation 31.8.06 – impairment loss	(20,000)
Carrying value	100,000

Building A has suffered an impairment loss of $20,000 at 31 August 2006 which can be debited to revaluation surplus reversing the previous revaluation gain.

Building B

	$
Cost	120,000
Depreciation to 31.8.01 (120,000/15 × 5)	(40,000)
Carrying value	80,000
Valuation 31.8.01 – impairment loss	(5,000)
Carrying value	75,000
Depreciation to 31.8.06 (75,000/10 × 5)	(37,500)
	37,500
Valuation 31.8.06 – impairment loss	(7,500)
Carrying value	30,000

Building B has suffered impairment losses totalling $7,500 at 31 August 2006, which will be charged to the statement of comprehensive income.

(f)

HS Construction contract

	$'000
Total revenue	300
Total costs to complete (170 + 100)	(270)
Total profit	30

State of completion of contract = 165/300 × 100% = 55%

Amounts recognised in the statement of comprehensive income for the year ended 31 March 20X9

	$'000
Revenue (value of work completed)	165.0
Profit (30 x 55%)	16.5

Amounts recognised in the statement of financial position at 31 March 20X9

	$'000
Costs incurred	170.0
Profit recognised	16.5
	186.5
Less progress billings	(130.0)
Amount recognised as an asset/(liability)	56.5

Recognise an asset in statement of financial position under current assets:

Gross amount due from customer $56,500

20 Geneva

> **Top tips.** Begin by working out for each contract whether a profit or a loss is forecast. If it is a profit, calculate how much can be recognised. If it is a loss, it is all recognised immediately.
>
> **Easy marks.** Note that all of these contacts started in the current year – so any attributable profit to date belongs to the current year. This makes the calculations easier.

Treatment of construction contracts in the statement of financial position

	$'000
Contract Lausanne	
Asset (1,000 + 240 – 1,080)	
Gross amount due from customers for contract work	160
Contract Bern	
Liability (1,100 – 200 – 950)	
Gross amount due to customers for contract work	50
Contract Zurich	
Liability (640 + 70 – 800)	
Gross amount due to customers for contract work	90

Treatment of construction contracts in the statement of comprehensive income

	Lausanne	Bern	Zurich
	$'000	$'000	$'000
Revenue	1,200	1,000	700
Cost of sales	960	1,200	630
Gross profit/(loss)	240	(200)	70

21 Objective test answers: Capital transactions and financial instruments

1	C	The premium is transferred from share capital to share premium
2	C	$500,000 + $11,000 (990,000 × 50c + 10,000 × $1.60)
		Note that the forfeited shares each brought in a total of $2.60
3	D	Share capital $500,000 + $250,000 + $300,000 + $350,000
		Share premium $800,000 – $250,000 + $900,000 + $910,000
4	A	The called-up value will be debited to share capital and credited to a forfeited shares account.
5	D	All four are permitted.
6	D	If a shareholder fails to pay a call his shares are forfeited and the company is not obliged to return his money.
7	C	Cumulative and redeemable preference shares are classified as financial liabilities under IAS 32.

8	B	As a deduction from equity.
9	A	Cash received on application and allotment

$1 \times 5,000 = \$5,000$

Balance of share capital due $= \$2,500$

Cash received on reissue of shares $1 \times 5,000 = \$5,000$

Additional share premium:

INVESTMENT IN OWN SHARES ACCOUNT

	$		$
Call amount	2,500	Bank	5,000
Share premium	2,500		
	5,000		5,000

10 $3.8m

	$m
Receipt from issue ($10m - $0.5m)	9.5
Dividend payable over 4 years ($10m × 7% × 4)	(2.8)
Payable on redemption ($10m + 5%)	(10.5)
Total finance charge	(3.8)

11 $10.025m

	$m
Receipt from issue	9.5
Finance charge 10%	0.95
Dividend paid	(0.7)
Balance at 31 December 20X8	9.75
Finance charge 10%	0.975
Dividend paid	(0.7)
Balance at 31 December 20X9	10.025

12	B	Treasury shares are an entity's own shares which it has repurchased and holds in 'treasury'. Treasury shares can be re-issued or issued as part of employee share schemes in the future.

22 Objective test answers: Accounting standards I

1	A	$^3/_{10} \times \$3,000$
2	D	$^2/_6 \times \$3,000$
3	D	Adjusting events are shown in the financial statements, not the notes.
4	C	$1,800,000 - \$116,000 - \$20,000 = \$1,664,000$
5	B	Discovery of fraud, error or impairment, which will have existed at the end of the reporting period.
6	D	These have all occurred after the reporting period.
7	C	1 Contingent liability that is possible, therefore disclose. 2 Contingent liability but remote, therefore no disclosure. 3 Non-adjusting event after the reporting period, material therefore disclose.
8	B	IAS 37 excludes retraining and relocation of continuing staff from restructuring provisions.
9	A	All three criteria must be present.
10	D	This does not affect the position as at the year end.
11	D	The dividend will not be shown in the statement of comprehensive income or appear as a liability in the statement of financial position.

12	1	An entity has a present obligation as a result of a past event.
	2	It is probable that an outflow of resources embodying economic benefits will be required to settle the obligation.
	3	A reliable estimate can be made of the amount of the obligation.
13	C	
14		An **operating segment** is a component of an entity:
	(a)	that engages in business activities from which it may earn revenues and incur expenses
	(b)	whose operating results are regularly reviewed by the entity's chief operating decision maker to make decisions about resources to be allocated to the segment and assess its performance, and
	(c)	for which discrete financial information is available
15	B	Revenue must be 10% or more of the total revenue of all segments.
16	B	This does not affect the position as at the year end.
17	D	

23 Objective test answers: Accounting standards II

1	C	Item 1 is not correct – if it is probable and the amount can be estimated reliably, then it must be provided for.
2	C	Customers, suppliers and providers of finance are not related parties.
3	C	In a finance lease, the risks and rewards of ownership are transferred.

4   A

	$
Deposit	30,000
Instalments (8 × $20,000)	160,000
	190,000
Fair value	154,000
Interest	36,000

$$\text{Sum of the digits} = \frac{8 \times 9}{2} = 36$$

6 months to	June X1	$^8/_{36}$ × $36,000		
	Dec X1	$^7/_{36}$ × $36,000		
	June X2	$^6/_{36}$ × $36,000		
	Dec X2	$^5/_{36}$ × $36,000		
	June X3	$^4/_{36}$ × $36,000	=	$4,000
	Dec X3	$^3/_{36}$ × $36,000	=	$3,000
				$7,000

5	D	The fire is non-adjusting as it does not clarify the 31 December value of the building. It is therefore only disclosed if it threatens the company's going concern status.
		Again the customer is assumed to be insolvent at 31 December. We simply did not know this and therefore it is an adjusting event and it should be adjusted for.
		The answer would be B if the customer had become insolvent after the year end.

6	C	1	As the board decision had not been communicated to customers and employees there is assumed to be no legal or constructive obligation therefore no provision should be made.
		2	As refunds have been made in the past to all customers there is a valid expectation from customers that the refunds will be made therefore the amount should be provided for.
		3	There is no present obligation to carry out the refurbishment therefore no provision should be made under IAS 37.

7   B   Members of the close family of any key management of an entity are presumed to be related parties.

8   An entity has a present obligation (legal or constructive) as a result of a past event.

It is probable that an outflow of resources embodying economic benefits will be required to settle the obligation.

A reliable estimate can be made of the amount of the obligation.

9   C   A provision should be made for the claim against AP.

10 B   Customers, suppliers and bankers are not normally related parties.

11 Finance cost = $2,160

		$
Total finance cost		
Total payments 12,000 × 5		60,000
Fair value		51,900
Finance cost		8,100

Payments being made over five year period:

To 30 Sept 20X4   5/15 × 8,100
To 30 Sept 20X5   4/15 × 8,100 $2,160

12 C   BW must provide for customer refunds.

13 Any four of the following:

- the seller has transferred to the buyer the significant risks and rewards of ownership
- the seller retains neither continuing managerial involvement to the degree usually associated with ownership nor effective control over the goods sold
- the amount of revenue can be measured reliably
- it is probable that the economic benefits associated with the transaction will flow to the seller
- the costs incurred or to be incurred in respect of the transaction can be measured reliably

14

	$
Cost 1.1.X4	80,000
Interest 7.93%	6,344
Instalment	(20,000)
Balance 31.12.X4	66,344
Interest 7.93%	5,261
Instalment	(20,000)
Balance 31.12.X5	51,605
Interest 7.93%	4,092
Instalment	(20,000)
Balance 31.12.X6	35,697
Current liability (51,605 – 35,697) =	15,908
Non-current liability	35,697
Total balance at 31.12.X5	51,605

15

	$
Original cost	80,000
Depreciation 2004/2005 (80,000/12,000 × (2,600 + 2,350))	(33,000)
Net book value	47,000

16 D   No sale has taken place, so DT must show that it is holding $90,000 which belongs to XX.

17 D   Fair value less costs to sell ($740,000 - $10,000) is lower than carrying value ($750,000).

Note that non-current assets held for sale are not depreciated.

18 B   Non-current assets held for sale are shown separately under the 'current assets' heading.

19 C Share transactions after the reporting period do not require adjustment.

20 A Large customers are *not necessarily* related parties of the entity.

21 Operating lease – spread the rent-free period over the term of the lease

Total rent payable = 4 x $12,000 = $48,000

Over five years = $48,000/5 = $9,600 per annum

$9,600 charged to profit or loss in each of 30 April 20X8 and 30 April 20X9.

24 Section B answers: Accounting standards I

(a) Asset

IAS 17 is an example of economic substance triumphing over legal form. In legal terms, with a finance lease, the lessor may be the owner of the asset, but the lessee enjoys all the **risks and rewards** which ownership of the asset would convey. This is the key element to IAS 17. The lessee is deemed to have an asset as they must maintain and run the asset through its useful life.

Liability

The lessee enjoys the future economic benefits of the asset as a result of entering into the lease. There is a corresponding liability which is the obligation to pay the instalments on the lease until it expires. Assets and liabilities cannot be netted off. If finance leases were treated in a similar manner to the existing treatment of operating leases then no asset would be recognised and lease payments would be expensed through the statement of comprehensive income as they were incurred. This is 'off balance sheet finance'. The company has assets in use and liabilities to lessors which are not recorded in the financial statements. This would be misleading to the user of the accounts and make it appear as though the assets which were recorded were more efficient in producing returns than was actually the case.

(b)   **MEMO**
To: Production manager
From: Trainee management accountant
Subject: De-commissioning costs

Provision

The accounting question regarding the de-commissioning costs is whether or not a provision should now be set up in the accounts for the eventual costs. According to IAS 37 any future obligations arising out of past events should be recognised immediately. The de-commissioning costs are a future obligation and the past event is the granting of the licence and the drilling of the site.

Therefore a provision should be recognised immediately in the accounts for the year ended 31 March 20X3. This will be $20million discounted to present value.

Discounting

As this cost gives access to future economic benefits in terms of oil reserves for the next 20 years then the discounted present value of the de-commissioning costs can be capitalised and treated as part of the cost of the oil well in the balance sheet. However this total cost, including the discounted de-commissioning costs should be reviewed to ensure that the net book value does not exceed the recoverable amount. If there is no impairment then the total cost of the oil well and discounted de-commissioning costs should be depreciated for the next 20 years and a charge made to the statement of comprehensive income.

(c) Because the airline operation was sold before the year end and was a distinguishable component of the entity it is a **discontinued operation** as defined by IFRS 5 *Non-current assets held for sale and discontinued operations.* A separate line in the statement of comprehensive income for discontinued operations should be included after the profit after tax for continuing operations. IFRS 5 states that this should be made up of the post-tax profit or loss of the discontinued operation and the post-tax gain or loss on disposal of the airline assets. The loss on sale of the fleet of aircraft of $250m and the provision for severance payments of $20m will both be reported in this line.

	$m
Discontinued operations	(270)

IFRS 5 also requires an **analysis** of the amount into:

(i)   the revenue, expenses and pre-tax profit of discontinued operations (to include the loss made by the airline for the year and the provision for the $20m severance payments); and

(ii) the gain or loss recognised on the disposal of the assets (the $250m loss on the sale of the fleet of aircraft).

This can be presented either on the face of the statement of comprehensive income or in the notes.

The **cash flows** attributable to the operating, investing and financing activities of the airline should also be disclosed, either in the notes to the financial statements or in the statement of cash flows itself.

As the restructuring has been agreed and active steps have been taken to implement it a **provision** is required for $10m (because the entity has a constructive obligation to carry out the plan). This will be reported as part of the continuing activities, probably as part of administrative expenses.

(d)

> **Examiner's comments.** Most candidates correctly identified that the customer was not a related party. Most candidates correctly identified that George was a related party but did not give sufficient explanation.
>
> Some candidates correctly identified the provider of finance as not being a related party, but did not go on to identify that Arnold was a related party.

XC

XC is not a related party of CB. The discount represents no more than a normal commercial arrangement with a favoured customer.

Property

George is one of the key management personnel of the company and thus a related party, and the sale of the property to him at a discount of $250,000 must be disclosed in the financial statements.

FC

As a provider of finance, FC is not itself a related party. However, Arnold is close family of George and therefore a related party to CB, and the loan does not appear to have been advanced at normal commercial terms. The loan and the involvement of Arnold will need to be disclosed.

(e)

> **Examiner's comments.** Few candidates did well on this question. Most candidates failed to include all three elements of the finance cost in the total cost. Some candidates used the straight line or sum of digits method to allocate the finance cost instead of the actuarial method, despite the discount rate of 10% being given.

(a)

	$
Receipt (2,000,000 – 192,800)	1,807,200
Costs:	
Dividends (100,000 × 5)	500,000
Redemption	2,300,000
	(2,800,000)
Finance cost	(992,800)

(b)

	Balance	Interest 10%	Dividend	Balance
20X6	1,807,200	180,720	(100,000)	1,887,920
20X7	1,887,920	188,792	(100,000)	1,976,712
20X8	1,976,712	197,671	(100,000)	2,074,383
20X9	2,074,383	207,438	(100,000)	2,181,821
20Y0	2,181,821	218,179	(100,000)	2,300,000

The balance at 31 March 20Y0 is $2,300,000, which is the amount needed to redeem the shares.

(f)

> **Examiner's comments**. A large proportion of candidates seemed to have problems with the dates in this question. They said that the 20X5 accounts should be changed, despite the fact that the fraud was discovered more than 6 months after the year end and the accounts had been signed off by the directors two months earlier.

Fraud

The discovery of the fraud in April 20X6 would be an adjusting event after the reporting period if it had occurred before the financial statements were authorised for issue. If the accounts were approved on 1 March, they would probably have been issued by April. So it is unlikely that this can be accounted for in the September 20X5 financial statements.

In the September 20X6 financial statements the overstatement of profit for the year ended 30 September 20X5 must be accounted for as a prior year adjustment. This will be shown in the Statement of Changes in Equity. The profit for the year ended 30 September will be reduced to $555,000. This will affect the retained earnings for the current year but not the current year profit.

Payment from new customer

The payment received in advance in September 20X6 cannot be treated as income because DF has not yet done anything to earn that income. It should be posted to current liabilities as 'deferred income' and released to the statement of comprehensive income when the goods are despatched.

(g)

> **Examiner's comments**. Most candidates correctly identified the factory closure as a discontinued activity but did not give sufficient explanation to gain more than a mark. Few candidates were able to explain how to deal with assets 'held for sale'.

The factory will be treated as a *discontinued operation* under IFRS 5 at 31 March 20X7, as all operations have ceased and sale of the land and buildings is 'highly probable'.

In the statement of comprehensive income **one figure** will be shown under *discontinued operations*, being the trading loss for the period from the discontinued operation (we are not told what this is), plus the loss on disposal of the plant and equipment ($70,000), plus the closure costs ($620,000), less any tax allowances. This single figure should then be analysed in the notes.

In the statement of financial position, the carrying value of the land and buildings ($750,000) should be moved out of non-current assets and shown under current assets as 'non-current assets held for sale'. The fair value less costs to sell would be higher, so the property is left at its carrying value. It is not depreciated.

(h)　(i)

> **Examiner's comments**. A large proportion of answers did not refer to the asset values and costs given in the question. If a question asks for an explanation of the treatment in financial statements and provides figures it should be fairly obvious that the answer must include reference to costs and asset values given.

EK can treat the sale of its retailing division as a discontinued operation under IFRS 5 for the following reasons:

- It is classified as held for sale.
- It represents a separate major line of business, with clearly distinguishable cash flows.

The retailing division can be classified as 'held for sale' because it is available for immediate sale, the company expects to dispose of it within one year and negotiations are already proceeding with a buyer.

(ii)　Statement of comprehensive income

EK should disclose a single amount on the face of the statement of comprehensive income comprising:

(a)　The post-tax profit or loss of the retailing division up to 31 October 20X7; and

(b)　The post tax gain or loss on measurement to fair value less costs to sell. A disposal group held for sale should be measured at the lower of its carrying amount and fair value less costs to sell. For EK this is the lower of $443,000 and $398,000 ($423,000 – $25,000). The impairment loss of $45,000 should be recognised.

Statement of financial position

The assets of the retailing division should be removed from non-current assets and shown at their fair value under current assets, classified as 'non-current assets held for sale'. The impairment should all be deducted from the goodwill balance.

25　Section B answers: Accounting standards II

(a)　IAS 37 defines a provision as a liability of uncertain timing or amount. It goes on further to state that a provision should only be recognised when:

(a)　There is a present obligation, either legal or constructive, arising as a result of a past event.

(b)　It is probable that an outflow of resources embodying economic benefits will be required in order to settle the obligation.

(c)　A reliable estimate of the amount of the obligation can be made.

This can be compared to the IASB's definition of a liability in its Framework for *Preparation and Presentation of Financial Statements:*

A liability is a present obligation of the entity arising from past events, the settlement of which is expected to result in an outflow of resources from the entity.

The key elements from the liability definition are all encompassed in the rules for recognising a provision.

(a)　**Obligation.** A liability is a present obligation and a provision is only recognised if there is an obligation. This obligation can either be a legal or a constructive obligation. A constructive obligation arises out of past practice or as a result of actions which have previously taken place which have created an expectation that the organisation will act in such a way.

(b)　**Past event.** A provision must arise out of a past event so the event must already have happened at the balance sheet date. If the event has not yet occurred then there is no provision as the entity may be able to avoid it.

(c)　**Outflow of resources.** A provision will only be recognised if it is probably that there will be an outflow of resources to settle the obligation which ties in with the IASB's definition of a liability.

(b)　STATEMENT OF COMPREHENSIVE INCOME (EXTRACTS)

	Year 1	Year 2
	$'000	$'000
Finance charge (W1)	5,567	4,453
Depreciation charge (W3)	17,660	17,660

STATEMENT OF FINANCIAL POSITION (EXTRACTS)

	Year 1 $'000	Year 2 $'000
Non– current assets		
Property, plant and equipment (W3)	70,640	52,980
Non-current liabilities		
Amounts due under leases (W2)	56,320	38,660
Current liabilities		
Amounts due under leases		
(72,867 – 56,320) (W2)	16,547	
(56,320 – 38,660) (W2)		17,660

Workings

1   *Finance charge*

	$'000
Total lease payments (5 × $21,000)	105,000
Fair value of asset	(88,300)
Total finance charge	16,700

Finance charge allocation

		$
Year 1	5/15 × 16,700	5,567
Year 2	4/15 × 16,700	4,453
Year 3	3/15 × 16,700	3,340
Year 4	2/15 × 16,700	2,227
Year 5	1/15 × 16,700	1,113
		16,700

2   *Lease liabilities*

	$
Fair trade value	88,300
Finance charge	5,567
Repayment	(21,000)
Balance end year one	72,867
Finance charge	4,453
Repayment	(21,000)
Balance end year two	56,320
Finance charge	3,340
Repayment	(21,000)
Balance end year three	38,660

3   *Non-current assets*

$$\text{Annual depreciation charge} = \frac{\$88,300}{5} = \$17,660$$

	$
Year 1	
Cost	88,300
Depreciation	(17,660)
Carrying value	70,640
Year 2	
Depreciation	(17,660)
Carrying value	52,980

(c)

Examiner's comments. Few candidate were able to produce a correct answer. Errors included:

- Not calculating overall profitability of the contract
- Ignoring the work in progress inventory

INCOME STATEMENT

	$'000
Sales revenue (W)	30,000
Cost of sales (balancing figure)	21,500
Recognised profit (W)	8,500

STATEMENT OF FINANCIAL POSITION	$,000
Total costs to date	24,000
Recognised profit	8,500
Progress billings	(25,000)
Gross amount due from customer	7,500

Working

Revenue	60,000
Costs to date	(24,000)
Costs to completion	(19,000)
Total expected profit	17,000
Profit to date: 17,000 × 50%	8,500
Revenue to date: 60,000 × 50%	30,000

(d)

> **Examiner's comments.** Most candidates were able to calculate the finance cost and the outstanding balances at each year end, but many were unable to produce correct statement of comprehensive income and statement of financial position extracts.
>
> Common errors included:
>
> - Basing the calculation on 4 years instead of 5
> - Applying the digit weightings in reverse order
> - Applying the sum of the digits to the annual repayment instead of the finance charge

(i) The amount of finance cost charged to the income statement for the year ended 31 March 20X5 is $9,067.

Working

	$
Total lease payments	150,000
Fair value of asset	116,000
Finance charge	34,000

Using sum of the digits:

31.3.X4	34,000 × 5/15 =	11,333
31.3.X5	34,000 × 4/15 =	9,067
31.3.X6	34,000 × 3/15 =	6,800
31.3.X7	34,000 × 2/15 =	4,533
31.3.X8	34,000 × 1/15 =	2,267
		34,000

(ii) *Statement of financial position extracts*

	$
Property, plant and equipment	
Held under finance lease	116,000
Depreciation (2/5)	46,400
	69,600
Non-current liabilities	
Amounts due under finance leases	53,200
Current liabilities	
Amounts due under finance leases (76,400 – 53,200)	23,200

Working

	$
1.4.X3 Fair value of asset	116,000
Finance charge	11,333
Repayment	(30,000)
Balance 31.3.X4	97,333
Finance charge	9,067
Repayment	(30,000)
Balance 31.3.X5	76,400
Finance charge	6,800
Repayment	(30,000)
Balance 31.3.X6	53,200

(e)

> **Examiner's comment.** Most candidates were able to score good marks on this question. Many had learnt a mnemonic to aid their recall of the six criteria. In Part (ii) some candidates failed to explain why the development costs should be treated as recommended.

(i) Under IAS 38 development costs will normally be recognised as an expense in the accounting period in which they are incurred. However, they may be capitalised if they meet *all* of the following criteria:

- It is **technically feasible** to complete the asset so that it is available for use or sale.
- The **intention** is to **complete** the asset so that it can be used or sold.
- The business is able to **use** or **sell** the asset
- It can be demonstrated that the asset will **generate future economic benefits**. For instance, a market must exist for the product.
- **Adequate technical, financial and other resources exist** to complete the development.
- The development expenditure can be **reliably measured**.

(ii) CD's development costs meet all of the above criteria. The development is complete, testing has confirmed the future economic benefits and the costs involved have been reliably measured. CD should capitalise $180,000 development costs at 30 April 20X6. Amortisation should begin on 1 May 20X6 and continue over the expected life of the process.

(f)

> **Examiner's comments.** Most candidates were able to correctly calculate the finance charges and balances for each of the three years, but many candidates could not select the correct figures from their workings to answer the question.

(i) Finance charge for the year ended 31 March 20X7: $72,000

(ii) Current liability: $228,000
Non-current liability: $378,000

Working

	$'000
Purchase price	900
Payment 1 April 20X5	(228)
	672
Interest 13.44%	90
Payment 1 April 20X6	(228)
	534
Interest 13.44%	72
Balance at 31 March 20X7	606
Payment due 1 April 20X7 (current liability)	228
Balance due (non-current liability)	378
	606

Note. As payments are made in advance, the payment due on 1 April 20X7 includes no interest relating to future periods.

(g) **Related party** – under the terms of IAS 24 a party is related to an entity if:

(i) directly or indirectly the party

- controls, is controlled by, or is under common control with, the entity
- has an interest in the entity that gives it significant interest over the entity; or
- has joint control over the entity

(ii) the party is a member of the key management personnel of the entity or its parent, such as a director

(iii) the party is a close member of the family of any individual referred to in (i) or (ii) above

(iv) the party is an entity that is controlled, jointly controlled or significantly influenced by, or a significant proportion of whose voting rights are held by, any individual referred to in (ii) or (iii)

Related party transaction – a transfer of resources, services or obligations between related parties, regardless of whether a price is charged.

(h)

> **Examiner's comments**. Most candidates were able to give most of the IAS 18 criteria but few were able to apply the criteria correctly to the scenario.

(i) The criteria in IAS 18 for income recognition are as follows.

- The **risks** and **rewards** of ownership of the goods have been **transferred to the buyer**.
- The entity **retains neither managerial involvement nor effective control** over the goods.
- The amount of **revenue** can be **measured reliably**.
- It is **probable** that the **economic benefits** associated with the transaction will **flow** to the entity.
- The **costs** incurred in respect of the transaction can be measured reliably.
- The **stage of completion** of the transaction at the balance sheet date can be measured reliably (rendering of services).

(ii) The $150,000 received on 1 September 20X7 cannot be recognised as income at that point because the risks and rewards of ownership have not yet been transferred.

The $150,000 should be credited to deferred income in the statement of financial position and $25,000 should be released to income each month as the magazines are supplied. The estimated $20,000 each month cost of making the supply will be recognised as it arises – at which point it can be measured reliably.

Therefore at 31 October two months revenue can be taken into account and two months costs will be set against that as follows:

	$
Revenue	50,000
Cost of sales	(40,000)
Gross profit	10,000

26 AZ

> **Text references.** Leases are covered in Chapter 7: *IAS 17 Leases*. Prior year adjustments are covered in Chapter 4: *Reporting financial performance*.
>
> **Top tips.** Make sure that you approach this type of question methodically. Numerical questions can be time pressured so get as much practice as you can to perfect your technique. Always read the question carefully and then set out your proformas. Tackle the parts you can do first to secure the easy marks before moving on to the more difficult areas. You can use the reading time at the start of the exam to decide in which order to attempt the adjustments.

> **Easy marks**. A number of the adjustments will affect more than one figure. Once you have done the statement of financial position, the statement of changes in equity is very easy. The complications here are the lease and the prior year adjustments. Do the lease calculations first, but don't spend too long on them.

Marking scheme

	Marks	Marks
Statement of comprehensive income		
Revenue	½	
Cost of sales	2	
Administrative expenses	1	
Distribution costs	1	
Finance cost	2	
Taxation expense	½	
Loss for the year	1	
		8
Statement of changes in equity		
Share capital	½	
Retained earnings	2	
Total	1	
		3½
Statement of financial position		
Property, plant and equipment	2½	
Inventory	1½	
Receivables	½	
Share capital	½	
Retained earnings	2½	
Loan stock	½	
Amounts due under finance lease	3	
Trade payables	½	
Tax payable	½	
Accruals	1½	
		13½
		25

AZ
STATEMENT OF COMPREHENSIVE INCOME FOR THE YEAR ENDING 31 MARCH 20X3

	$'000	$'000
Revenue		124,900
Cost of sales (W1)		(100,835)
Gross profit		24,065
Distribution costs (9,060 + 513 (W2))	(9,573)	
Administrative expenses (W3)	(15,420)	
Other operating expenses	(121)	
		(25,114)
		(1,049)
Income from investments	1,200	
Finance cost (W8)	(1,432)	
		(232)
Loss before tax		(1,281)
Income tax expense		(15)
Net loss for the year		(1,296)

AZ
STATEMENT OF CHANGES IN EQUITY FOR THE YEAR ENDED 31 MARCH 20X3

	Share capital $'000	Retained earnings $'000	Total $'000
Balance at 1 April 20X2	19,000	14,677	33,677
Prior year adjustment	–	500	500
Total comprehensive income for the year	–	(1,296)	(1,296)
Balance at 31 March 20X3	19,000	13,881	32,881

AZ
STATEMENT OF FINANCIAL POSITION AS AT 31 MARCH 20X3

	$'000	$'000
Non-current assets		
Property, plant and equipment (W4)		21,229
Current assets		
Inventory (W6)	5,080	
Trade receivables (9,930 – 600)	9,330	
Bank and cash	25,820	
		40,230
		61,459
Equity		
Share capital		19,000
Retained earnings (W5)		13,881
		32,881
Non-current liabilities		
7% loan notes	18,250	
Amount due under finance lease (W7)	1,074	
		19,324
Current liabilities		
Trade payables	8,120	
Amount due under finance lease (W7)	480	
Tax payable	15	
Accruals (18,250 × 7% – 639)	639	
		9,254
		61,459

Workings

1 Cost of sales

	$'000
Opening inventory (4,852 + 500)	5,352
Manufacturing cost	94,000
Depreciation of plant and equipment (W2)	6,563
Less closing inventory (W6)	(5,080)
	100,835

2 Depreciation

	$'000
Plant and equipment (20% × 30,315)	6,063
Leased equipment (2m/4)	500
Vehicles ((3,720 – 1,670) × 25%)	513

3 Administrative expenses

	$'000
Per trial balance	16,020
Less leasing cost	(600)
	15,420

4   Property, plant and equipment

	Plant and equipment $'000	Vehicles $'000	Total $'000
Cost (30,315 + 2,000)	32,315	3,720	36,035
Accumulated depreciation			
(6,060 + 6,563) (W2)	(12,623)		
(1,670 + 513) (W2)		(2,183)	(14,806)
Carrying value	19,692	1,537	21,229

5   Retained earnings

	$'000
Per trial balance	14,677
Prior year adjustment – inventory	500
Net loss for the year	(1,296)
	13,881

6   Closing inventory

	$'000
As stated	5,180
Cost of damaged goods	(1,200)
NRV of damaged goods	1,100
	5,080

7   Finance lease

	$'000
Original cost	2,000
Interest 7.7%	154
Payment	(600)
Balance 31.3.X3	1,554
Interest 7.7%	120
Payment	(600)
Balance 31.3.X4	1,074
Due within 1 year (600 – 120)	480
Due after 1 year	1,074
	1,554

8   Finance cost

Interest payable on finance lease	154
Loan note interest (18,250 × 7%)	1,278
	1,432

27   AF

Text references. Operating leases are covered in Chapter 7: *IAS 7 Leases*.

Top tips. Begin by setting out the pro-formas for the statement of comprehensive income and statement of financial position, then go methodically through the workings, making sure they are neat and easy for the marker to read and understand. You must show workings.

Easy marks. The property, plant and equipment calculations were straightforward and would have been worth a few marks, especially if you charged the depreciation to cost of sales as instructed. You may not have known how to deal with the operating lease, but the statement of comprehensive income was otherwise relatively simple. With a correct statement of financial position format in place, you could have slotted in those figures which needed no calculation, plus your plant and equipment figure. The only tricky part was probably the accruals, for which you needed to have worked out the loan interest and the charge for the operating lease.

Examiner's comments. Many candidates achieved almost full marks on this question, but very few were able to correctly deal with the operating lease. Errors were also made in dealing with the investment, tax, loan interest, and dividends.

Marking scheme

	Marks	Marks
Statement of comprehensive income		
Revenue	½	
Cost of sales	1½	
Other income	½	
Administrative expenses	½	
Distribution costs	½	
Finance costs	1	
Taxation expenses	1½	
Other comprehensive income	2	
		8
Statement of changes in equity		
Share capital	1	
Share premium	1	
Retained earnings	1½	
Revaluation surplus	1½	
		5
Statement of financial position		
Property, plant and equipment	2	
Available – for sales investment	1	
Inventory	½	
Receivables	½	
Cash	½	
Share capital	½	
Share premium	½	
Revaluation surplus	1	
Retained earnings	1	
Loan stock	½	
Deferred tax	1	
Trade payables	½	
Accruals	1½	
Tax payable	1	
		12
		25

AF

STATEMENT OF COMPREHENSIVE INCOME FOR THE YEAR ENDED 31 MARCH 20X5

	$'000
Sales revenue	8,210
Cost of sales (W2)	(3,957)
Gross profit	4,253
Other income	68
Distribution costs	(1,590)
Administrative expenses	(1,540)
Finance costs (1,500 × 6%)	(90)
Profit before tax	1,101
Income tax expense (W4)	(350)
Profit for the year	751
Other comprehensive income:	
Gain on available-for-sale investments	110
Total comprehensive income for the year	861

AF
STATEMENT OF CHANGES IN EQUITY FOR THE YEAR ENDED 31 MARCH 20X5

	Share capital $'000	Share premium $'000	Retained earnings $'000	Revaluation surplus $'000	Total $'000
Balance at 1 April 20X4	4,500	1,380	388	330	6,598
Total comp income for the year			751	110	861
Dividend paid			(275)		(275)
Balance at 31 March 20X5	4,500	1,380	864	440	7,184

AF: STATEMENT OF FINANCIAL POSITION AS AT 31 MARCH 20X5

	$'000	$'000
Non-current assets		
Property, plant and equipment (W1)		4,987
Available-for-sale investment		1,750
Current assets		
Inventory	1,320	
Receivables	1,480	
Bank and cash	822	
		3,622
Total assets		10,359
Equity and liabilities		
Equity		
Share capital		4,500
Share premium		1,380
Revaluation surplus (330 + 110)		440
Retained earnings		864
		7,184
Non-current liabilities		
6% loan notes	1,500	
Deferred tax (710 + 100)	810	
		2,310
Current liabilities		
Payables	520	
Accruals (W5)	95	
Taxation payable	250	
		865
Total equity and liabilities		10,359

Workings

1   Property, plant and equipment

	Property $'000	Plant and equipment $'000	Total $'000
Cost	5,190	3,400	8,590
Depreciation b/f	(1,500)	(1,659)	(3,159)
Charge for year:			
(5,190 – 2,000) × 3%	(96)		(96)
(3,400 – 1,659) × 20%		(348)	(348)
Carrying value	3,594	1,393	4,987

2   Cost of sales

	$'000
Per trial balance	3,463
Depreciation (96 + 348)	444
Operating lease (W3)	50
	3,957

3   *Operating lease*

Four years @ 62,500 = 250,000
Spread over five years = 50,000 pa

4   *Income tax expense*

	$'000
Tax charge for year	250
Transfer to deferred tax ((2,700 × 30%) – 710)	100
	350

5   *Accruals*

	$'000
Interest payable (90 – 45)	45
Operating lease (W3)	50
	95

28 BG

> **Text references.** Deferred tax is covered in Chapter 14: *IAS 12 Income taxes*. Finance leases are covered in Chapter 7: *IAS 17 Leases*.
>
> **Top tips.** This is a straightforward set of financial statements. Set out the proformas and then go through the workings tackling the parts that you find easy first. Part (b) is easier than it looks. Note that the first instalment is a deposit. You must be able to deal with deferred tax.
>
> **Easy marks.** The statement of comprehensive income down to tax is easy marks. You should have included the reversal of the provision. The assets section of the statement of financial position should have been no problem.
>
> **Examiner's comments.** Few candidates could correctly deal with the release of the provision. Many candidates are still following the old UK format, including the dividend paid as a deduction from the statement of comprehensive income. Errors were made in calculating deferred and current tax.

Marking scheme

		Marks	Marks
(a)	**Statement of comprehensive income**		
	Revenue	½	
	Cost of sales	1½	
	Distribution costs	½	
	Administrative expenses	½	
	Reversal of provision	1	
	Finance costs	½	
	Taxation expenses	1½	
			6
	Statement of financial position		
	Property, plant and equipment	2	
	Inventory	½	
	Receivables	½	
	Cash	½	
	Share capital	½	
	Share premium	½	
	Retained earnings	1½	
	Loan stock	½	
	Deferred tax	1	
	Trade payables	1	
	Tax payable	½	
			9
			15

	Marks	Marks
(b) **Redraft retained earnings**		
Add back rental payments	2	
Deduct finance lease interest	4	
Deduct depreciation	3	
Restated retained equipment	1	
		10
		25

(a) BG

STATEMENT OF COMPREHENSIVE INCOME FOR THE YEAR ENDED 30 SEPTEMBER 20X5

	$'000
Revenue	1,017
Cost of sales (W1)	(799)
Gross profit	218
Distribution costs	(61)
Administrative expenses	(239)
Reversal of provision	190
Finance costs (net) (15 – 11)	(4)
Profit before tax	104
Income tax expense (W2)	(88)
Profit for the year	16

BG

STATEMENT OF FINANCIAL POSITION AS AT 30 SEPTEMBER 20X5

	$'000	$'000
Assets		
Non-current assets		
Property, plant and equipment (W3)		232
Current assets		
Inventories	37	
Trade receivables	346	
Bank and cash	147	
		530
Total assets		762
Equity and liabilities		
Equity		
Share capital		200
Share premium		40
Retained earnings (W5)		212
		452
Non-current liabilities		
Long-term borrowings	150	
Deferred tax (50 + 15)	65	215
Current liabilities		
Trade and other payables (W4)	31	
Current tax payable	64	95
Total equity and liabilities		762

Workings

1   Cost of sales

	$'000
Cost of cleaning materials consumed	101
Direct operating expenses	548
Depreciation – equipment and fixtures (20% x 752)	150
	799

2   *Income tax expense*

	$'000
Tax due for year	64
Underprovision in previous year	9
Deferred tax	15
	88

3   *Equipment and fittings*

	$'000
Cost	752
Accumulated depreciation (370 + 150 (W1))	520
Carrying value	232

4   *Trade and other payables*

	$'000
Trade payables	24
Accrued bond interest (15 – 8)	7
	31

5   *Retained earnings*

	$'000
Opening balance at 30 September 20X4	256
Total comprehensive income for the year	16
Dividends paid	(60)
	212

(b)

	$'000
Retained earnings as stated	212
Add back rental payments (61 × 2)	122
Deduct finance lease interest (W)	(36)
Deduct depreciation (180,000 × 40%)	(72)
Retained earnings if finance lease option used	226

Working

	$
Original cost	180,000
Deposit (8,000 × 9) 1.10.X3	(72,000)
	108,000
Interest to 30.9.X4 @ 21.53%	23,252
Instalment 1.10.X4	(72,000)
	59,252
Interest to 30.9.X5 (rounded)	12,748
Instalment 1.10.X5	(72,000)
	–

29 DZ

Text references. Chapter 3 and 5.

Top tips. Non-current assets (tangible and intangible) figured heavily in this question and it was important to organise the material clearly. A good answer to part (a) makes part (b) much easier. But do not spend too long on part (a). Time management is vital. The best way to pass is to make a good attempt at all parts of the exam and not spend too long on certain parts of a question.

Easy marks. There were quite a few marks available for the financial statements and any errors on non-current assets would only be penalised once, so if your workings were clear you could still have scored well.

Examiner's comments. Very few gained full marks as they were unable to correctly prepare a property, plant and equipment note. A significant number still have problems calculating basic depreciation and dealing with development expenditure.

Marking scheme

	Marks	Marks
Property, plant and equipment		
Land	1½	
Buildings	2	
Plant	2½	
		6
Statement of comprehensive income		
Revenue	½	
Cost of sales	2½	
Distribution costs	½	
Administrative expenses	1	
Gain on disposal of land	1	
Taxation expense	½	
Other comprehensive income	2½	
		8½
Statement of changes in equity		
Share capital	½	
Retained earnings	1½	
Revaluation surplus	1½	
Total	½	
		4
Statement of financial position		
Capitalised development costs	2	
Inventory	½	
Receivables	½	
Cash	½	
Share capital	½	
Revaluation surplus	½	
Retained earnings	½	
Trade payables	½	
Accruals	½	
Tax payable	½	
		6½
		25

(a) Property, plant and equipment

Cost	Land at valuation $'000	Land at cost $'000	Buildings $'000	Plant $'000	Total $'000
Balance 1 April 20X6	1,250	3,500	7,700	4,180	16,630
Disposal	(1,250)			(620)	(1,870)
Revaluation	–	600	(2,000)	–	(1,400)
	–	4,100	5,700	3,560	13,360
Depreciation					
Balance at 1 April 20X6	–	–	1,900	2,840	4,740
Disposals	–	–	-	(600)	(600)
			1,900	2,240	4,140
Charge for year:	–	–	385 *	330**	715
			2,285	2,570	4,855
Revaluation adjustment	–	–	(2,285)	–	(2,285)
	–	–	–	2,570	2,570
Balance 31 March 20X7	–	4,100	5,700	990	10,790
Balance 31 March 20X6	1,250	3,500	5,800	1,340	11,890

* 7,700 × 5%
** 3,560 – 2,240 × 25%

Depreciation charge:

	Cost of sales	Admin
Buildings	308	77
Plant	330	
	638	

(b) DZ

STATEMENT OF COMPREHENSIVE INCOME FOR THE YEAR ENDED 31 MARCH 20X7

	$'000
Revenue	8,772
Cost of sales (W1)	(4,457)
Gross profit	4,315
Distribution costs	(462)
Administration costs (891 + 77)	(968)
Gain on disposal of land (1,500 – 1,250)	250
Profit before taxation	3,135
Income tax expense	(811)
Profit for the year	2,324
Other comprehensive income:	
Gain on property revaluation (9,800 – (11,200 – 1,900 – 385))	885
Total comprehensive income for the year	3,209

DZ

STATEMENT OF CHANGES IN EQUITY FOR THE YEAR ENDED 31 MARCH 20X7

	Share capital $'000	Retained earnings $'000	Revaluation surplus $'000	Total $'000
Balance at 1 April 20X6	1,000	4,797	2,100	7,897
Transfer to retained earnings*		750	(750)	–
Total comprehensive income for the year	–	2,324	885	3,209
Balance at 31 March 20X7	1,000	7,871	2,235	11,106

* The land which was sold had previously been revalued from $500,000 to $1,250,000. Upon sale, this revaluation gain can be recognised and so is transferred to retained earnings.

DZ

STATEMENT OF FINANCIAL POSITION AT 31 MARCH 20X7

	$'000	$'000
Non-current assets		
Capitalised development costs (W2)		198
Property, plant and equipment (see (a))		10,790
		10,988
Current assets		
Inventory	435	
Receivables	1,059	
Cash	208	
		1,702
Total assets		12,690
Equity and liabilities		
Equity		
Share capital		1,000
Revaluation surplus		2,235
Retained earnings		7,871
		11,106
Current liabilities		
Payables	748	
Accruals	25	
Tax payable	811	
		1,584
Total equity and liabilities		12,690

Workings

1   *Cost of sales*

	$'000
Opening inventory (240 + 132)	372
Purchases	2,020
Production labour cost	912
Production overheads	633
Depreciation	638
Research costs	119
Amortisation of development costs ((867 + 48) × 20%)	183
Loss on disposal of plant (5 – (620-600))	15
Closing inventory (165 + 270)	(435)
	4,457

2   *Capitalised development costs*

	$'000
Balance per trial balance	500
Deduct research costs	(119)
Less current year amortisation (W1)	(183)
Balance at 31 March 20X7	198

30   FZ

Text references. Assets held for sale are dealt with in Chapter 4: *Reporting financial performance*. Provisions are covered in Chapter 9: *Miscellaneous standards.*

Top tips. In this question it is important to recognise that you are required to present financial statements under IFRS 5 *Non-current assets held for sale and discontinued operations*. Always read the question carefully so that you do not miss anything important. Make sure you know how to show discontinued operations in the statement of comprehensive income.

Easy marks. Write out the proforma statement of comprehensive income and statement of financial position and slot in figures from the trial balance for some easy marks.

Examiner's comments. A disappointing number of candidates were unable to correctly identify the sale of shops as a discontinued operation. Most candidates that correctly identified the discontinued operation did not apply their answer in part (a) to their workings in part (b).

A disappointing number of candidates wanted to create a provision for the reorganisation package, even though the items constituting the package were all disallowed by IAS 37.

Very few students provided for a discontinued operation in calculating the profit for the year.

Marking scheme

		Marks	Marks
(a)			
	Newsagents' shops	3	
	Reorganisation costs	2	
			5
(b)	**Statement of comprehensive income**		
	Revenue	½	
	Cost of sales	1½	
	Distribution costs	2	
	Administrative expenses	1	
	Finance costs	1½	
	Income tax expense	1	
	Loss from discontinued operation	2	
			9½
	Statement of financial position		
	Property, plant and equipment	2	
	Trade receivables	1	
	Non-current assets held for sale	1½	
	Inventory	½	
	Cash and cash equivalents	½	
	Share capital	½	
	Share premium	½	
	Revaluation surplus	½	
	Retained earnings	½	
	5% loan notes	½	
	Deferred tax	½	
	Trade payables	½	
	Tax payable	½	
	Interest payable	1	
			10½
	Total		25

(a) (i) The newsagents' shops meet the criteria of an **asset held for sale** under IFRS 5 *Non-current assets held for sale and discontinued operations*.

- The shops are available for immediate sale in their present condition.
- The sale is highly probable.

Non-current assets held for sale should be **measured at the lower of carrying amount and fair value less costs to sell**. For the newsagents' shops this is the $5,000,000 fair value less $200,000 selling costs or $4,800,000. The carrying amount is the higher amount of $5,260,000.

Under IFRS 5, an **impairment loss** should be recognised when fair value less costs to sell is lower than carrying amount. Thus, the difference between the carrying amount and the fair value less costs to sell of $460,000 should be written off, with $300,000 being allocated to goodwill and the remaining $160,000 to the newsagents' shops.

The newsagents' shops should be **presented separately** from other assets in the balance sheet under the heading 'non-current assets classified as held for sale'. A single amount should be presented on the face of the statement of comprehensive income as 'loss for the year from discontinued operation'. This amount should be the total of:

- The post-tax profit or loss of discontinued operations and
- The post-tax gain or loss recognised on the measurement to fair value less costs to sell.

(ii)   IAS 37 Provisions, *contingent liabilities and contingent assets* deals with the accounting treatment necessary for this item.

When a **restructuring** involves a sale of an operation, as is the case with the newsagents' shops, IAS 37 states that no obligation arises until the entity has entered into a binding sale agreement. Since at year-end the sale of the shops had not been concluded, a provision cannot be made.

It is worth noting that even if the sale was binding at year-end, a provision would still be prohibited under IAS 37. This is because staff retraining, staff relocation and development of new computer systems are **specifically excluded**.

(b)   FZ: STATEMENT OF COMPREHENSIVE INCOME FOR THE YEAR ENDED 31 MARCH 20X8

Continuing operations

	$'000
Revenue (10,170 – 772)	9,398
Cost of sales (W1)	(4,363)
Gross profit	5,035
Distribution costs (W3)	(384)
Administrative expenses (W5)	(406)
Profit from operations	4,245
Finance cost (1,000 × 5%)	(50)
Profit before tax	4,195
Income tax expense (W6)	(1,080)
Profit for the year from continuing operations	3,115
Discontinued operation	
Loss for the year from discontinued operation (W7)	(301)
Profit for the year	2,814

FZ
STATEMENT OF FINANCIAL POSITION AT 31 MARCH 20X8

	$'000	$000
Assets		
Non-current assets		
Property, plant and equipment (W8)		11,516
Current assets		
Inventory	900	
Trade receivables (929 – 62)	867	
Cash and cash equivalents	853	
		2,620
Non-current assets classified as held for sale		4,800
Total assets		18,936
Equity and liabilities		
Equity		
Share capital (4,000 + 1,000)	5,000	
Share premium account (2,500 + 500)	3,000	
Revaluation surplus	190	
Retained earnings (5,808 + 2,814 – 500)	8,122	
		16,312
Non-current liabilities		
5% Loan notes		1,000
Deferred tax		237
Current liabilities		
Trade payables	417	
Tax payable	920	
Interest payable	50	
		1,387
Total equity and liabilities		18,936

Workings

1   *Cost of sales continuing operations*

	$'000
Cost of goods sold (4,120 – 580)	3,540
Depreciation (W2)	823
Cost of sales	4,363

2   *Depreciation continuing operations*

	$'000
Factory buildings (12,000 × 3%)	360
Plant and equipment (2,313 × 20%)	463
Depreciation	823

3   *Distribution costs continuing operations*

	$'000
Distribution costs (432 – 57)	375
Vehicles depreciation ((147 – 67 – 57 + 52) × 25%)	19
Gain on disposal vehicles (W4)	(10)
	384

4   *Gain on disposal*

	$'000
Disposed vehicle cost	(57)
Disposed vehicle depreciation	52
Cash received	15
Gain on disposal	10

5   *Administrative expenses continuing operations*

	$'000
Administrative expenses (440 – 96)	344
Bad debt from customer X	62
Administrative expenses	406

6   *Income tax expense continuing operations*

	$'000
Taxation due for year (920 + 120)	1,040
Increase in deferred tax provision (237 – 197)	40
Income tax expense	1,080

7   *Loss for the year on discontinued operation*

	$'000
Revenue	772
Cost of sales	(580)
Impairment of goodwill	(300)
Impairment of shops	(160)
Administrative expenses	(96)
Distribution costs	(57)
Tax credit	120
Loss for the year	(301)

Note that IFRS 5 allows the analysis of the discontinued operation to be provided in the statement of comprehensive income rather than in the notes. The answer did not take this approach as note (k) of the question stated that FZ wants to disclose the minimum information allowed by IFRSs.

8   Property, plant and equipment

	Buildings $'000	Plant and equipment $'000	Vehicles $'000	Total $'000
Cost (147 – 57)	12,000	2,313	147	14,460
Disposal			(57)	(57)
Accumulated depreciation b/f	(720)	(1,310)	(67)	(2,097)
Depreciation disposal			52	52
Depreciation charge for the year	(360)	(463)	(19)	(842)
Carrying value	10,920	540	56	11,516

31 GZ

Text references. Chapter 3, 5, 7 and 9.

Top tips. Write out your proformas first making sure you space these out. Next, slot the trial balance figures which are unaffected by any adjustments into your proforma. Then tackle the information in the order you find easiest to complete the requirements.

Examiner's comments. Few candidates realised that the question included a discontinued activity so there were few answers with discontinued activities correctly treated in the statement of comprehensive income or the non-current assets held for sale correctly treated in the statement of financial position.

Common mistakes made by candidates were:

– not including leased plant as a non-current asset
– not treating the government licence as an intangible non-current asset. Most candidates charged it as an expense during the year.
– not grouping the discontinued activities together as an item in the income statement

Marking scheme

Property, plant and equipment	Marks	Marks
Mine property	3	
Plant	2	
Leased plant	1	
		6
Statement of comprehensive income		
Revenue	½	
Cost of sales	2	
Investment income	½	
Distribution costs	½	
Administrative expenses	½	
Finance costs	1	
Taxation expense	1½	
Loss from discounted operations	2	
		8½
Statement of changes in equity		
Share capital	1	
Retained earnings	1	
		2

Statement of financial position

	Marks	Marks
Intangible assets	1	
Inventory	½	
Receivables	½	
Cash	½	
Non-current asset held	1½	
Deferred Tax	½	
Provision	1	
Trade payables	½	
Tax payable	½	
Amounts due under finance lease	2	
		8½
		25

(a) Plant and equipment

	Mine property $'000	Plant $'000	Leased plant $'000	Total $'000
Cost				
Balance at 1 November 20X7	6,719	3,025	0	9,744
Leased plant			900	900
Disposal		(200)		(200)
Decommissioning costs	3,230			3,230
Transfer to non-current assets held for sale	(2,623)			(2,623)
	7,326	2,825	900	11,051
Depreciation				
Balance at 1 November 20X7	2,123	370	0	2,493
Disposal		(195)		(195)
Transfer to non-current assets held for sale	(2,123)			(2,123)
Charge for year (W2)	366	663	225	1,254
	366	838	225	1,429
Carrying value 31 October 20X8	6,960	1,987	675	9,622

(b) GZ

STATEMENT OF COMPREHENSIVE INCOME FOR THE PERIOD ENDING 31 OCTOBER 20X8

	$'000
Revenue	9,600
Cost of sales (W3)	(6,504)
Gross profit	3,096
Investment income	218
Distribution costs	(719)
Administrative expenses	(1,131)
Profit from operations	1,464
Finance cost	(55)
Profit before tax	1,409
Income tax expense (W5)	(328)
Profit for the year from continuing operations	1,081
Loss for the year from discontinued operations (W9)	(68)
Profit for the year	1,013

GZ

STATEMENT OF CHANGES IN EQUITY FOR THE PERIOD ENDED 31 OCTOBER 20X8

	Share capital $'000	Share premium $'000	Retained earnings $'000	Total $'000
Balance at 1 Nov 20X7	5,000	0	1,790	6,790
Total comprehensive income for the period			1,013	1,013
Dividends			(550)	(550)
Issue of share capital (W6)	1,400	420		1,820
Balance at 31 Oct 20X8	6,400	420	2,253	9,073

GZ
STATEMENT OF FINANCIAL POSITION AT 31 OCTOBER 20X8

	$'000	$000
Assets		
Non-current assets		
Property, plant and equipment (see a)		9,622
Intangible assets (W7)		95
		9,717
Current assets		
Inventory	2,410	
Trade receivables	2,715	
Cash and cash equivalents	1,240	
Non-current assets classified as held for sale (W1)	493	
		6,858
Total assets		16,575
Equity and liabilities		
Equity		
Share capital (W6)		6,400
Share premium account (W6)		420
Retained earnings		2,253
		9,073
Non-current liabilities		
Deferred tax (731-60)	671	
Finance lease (W4)	682	
Provision (W8)	3,230	
		4,583
Current liabilities		
Trade payables	2,431	
Tax payable	375	
Finance lease (W4)	113	
		2,919
Total equity and liabilities		16,575

Workings

			$'000
1	*Non-current asset held for sale*		
	Carrying amount		500
	Fair value less costs to sell (520-27)		(493)
	Loss on revaluation		7
2	*Depreciation*		
	Mines (7,326 × 5%)		366
	Property, plant and equipment (2,825 – 370 + 195) × 25%		663
	Leased plant (900 × 25%)		225
			1,254
3	*Cost of sales*		
	Per trial balance		5,245
	Amortisation operating licence (100/20)		5
	Depreciation (W2)		1,254
			6,504
4	*Finance lease*		
	Total lease payments (7 × 160)		1,120
	Fair value of asset		(900)
	Total finance charge		220

Using sum of digits method:

31.10.X8   220 × 7/28 = 55 (finance charge)

	$'000
1 November 20X7	900
Finance charge	55
Payment	(160)
Balance at 31 October 20X8	795
Finance charge	47
Payment	(160)
Balance at 31 October 20X9	682

	$'000
Due within one year (795 – 682)	113
Due after one year	682
	795

5   *Income tax expense*

	$'000
Per trial balance	13
Reduction in deferred tax provision	(60)
Charge for year	375
	328

6   *Share issue*

	$'000
Share capital (1,400 x 1)	1,400
Share premium ((1,400 x 1.3) -1400)	420
	1,820

Share capital after issue = 5,000 + 1,400 = 6,400

7   *Intangible assets*

	$'000
Licence	100
Amortisation – (100/20)	(5)
Total	95

8   *Provision*

	$'000
As per trial balance	950
Gold mine closed	(950)
Decommissioning costs	3,230
	3,230

9   *Discontinued operation*

	$'000
Decommissioning expenditure	1,008
Less provision	(950)
	58
Loss on non-current asset held for sale (W1)	7
Loss on disposal of non-current asset (5 – 2)	3
Loss on discontinued operation	68

32 XY

Text references. Deferred tax is covered in Chapter 19. Preparation of single company financial accounts is covered in Chapters 4 to 12.

Top tips. Don't be put off by part (a), the deferred tax is not too difficult to calculate. Don't forget that you need to calculate the movement on the deferred tax provision for the statement of comprehensive income. For part (b) the key to success is familiarity with the format of the statements. The best way to achieve this is through practising your question technique. Easy errors to make are:

- Not accounting for the impairment of the land
- Not recording interest payable on the long term loan in both the SOCI and the SOFP
- Ignoring the underprovision for tax in the previous year
- Not including the gain on available-for-sale investments in the revaluation reserve.

Easy marks. There were easy marks to be gained by inserting all the numbers that didn't require calculation into the proformas – eg revenue, trade payables, trade receivables, cash, share capital, share premium.

(a)   *Deferred tax at 31 March 20X9*

	$'000
Accounting value	
Cost (630 – 378)	252
Accounting depreciation (630 × 20%)	(126)
Carrying value	126
Tax WDV	
Cost (630 – 453)	177
Tax depreciation @ 25%	(44)
Tax written down value	133
Temporary difference	(7)
Deferred tax @ 25%	(2)

Change in deferred tax balance

	$'000
Deferred tax liability at 31.03.X8	(19)
Less deferred tax asset at 31.08.X9	(2)
Credit to income tax expense	(21)

XY STATEMENT OF COMPREHENSIVE INCOME FOR YEAR ENDING 31 MARCH 20X9 (extract)

	$'000
Income tax expense – reduction in deferred tax	21

XY STATEMENT OF FINANCIAL POSITION AT 31 MARCH 20X9 (extract)

	$'000
Non-current assets	
Deferred tax asset	2

(b)   XY STATEMENT OF COMPREHENSIVE INCOME FOR THE YEAR ENDING 31 MARCH 20X9

	$'000
Revenue	1,770
Cost of sales (908 + 126 (part a))	(1,034)
Gross profit	736
Profit on disposal of non-current assets (W2)	9
Distribution costs	(176)
Administrative expenses (303 + 14 (W1))	(317)
Profit from operations	252
Finance cost (5% × 280)	(14)
Profit before tax	238
Income tax expense (W3)	(87)
Profit for the year	151

	$'000
Other comprehensive income:	
Gain on available for sale investments	44
Total comprehensive income for the year	195

XY STATEMENT OF FINANCIAL POSITION AS AT 31 MARCH 20X9

	$'000	$'000
Assets		
Non-current assets		
Land	729	
Property, plant and equipment	126	
Available for sale investments	608	
Deferred tax asset	2	
		1,465
Current assets		
Inventory	76	
Trade receivables	210	
Cash and cash equivalents	21	
		307
Total assets		1,772
Equity and liabilities		
Equity		
Share capital	500	
Share premium	200	
Revaluation surplus (160 + 44)	204	
Retained earnings	422	
		1,326
Non-current liabilities		
Long-term borrowings		280
Current liabilities		
Trade payables	56	
Tax payable	96	
Interest payable	14	
		166
Total liabilities and equity		1,772

XY STATEMENT OF CHANGES IN EQUITY FOR THE YEAR ENDING 31 MARCH 20X9

	Share capital $'000	*Share premium* $'000	*Revaluation surplus* $'000	*Retained earnings* $'000	*Total* $'000
Balance at 1 April 20X8	400 (bal.fig)	150 (bal.fig)	160	321	1,031
Issue of share capital	100	50	–	–	150
Dividends	–	–	–	(50)	(50)
Total comprehensive income for the year	–	–	44	151	195
Balance at 31 March 20X9	500	200	204	422	1,326

Workings

1   *Impairment of land*

	$'000
Cost at 31 March 20X8	782
Less disposal	(39)
Cost at 31 March 20X9	743
Fair value at 31 March 20X9	729
Impairment of land	(14)

Charge to administrative expenses

2 *Profit on disposal of land*

	$'000
Proceeds	48
NBV of land	(39)
Profit on disposal	9

3 *Income tax expense*

	$'000
Under provision from prior year	12
Current year charge	96
Reduction in deferred tax	(21)
	87

33 EZ

Text references. Preparation of single company financial accounts is covered in Chapters 4 to 12.

Top tips. This question is relatively straightforward if you know your proformas – the best way to get to grips with the proformas is through question practice. These errors were easy to make:

- Incorrectly accounting for the land revaluation
- Not recording interest payable on the long term loan in both the SOCI and the SOFP
- Incorrectly accounting for the operating lease charge and forgetting to include the operating lease payable.

Easy marks. There were plenty of easy marks to be gained in this question by inserting all the numbers that didn't require calculation into the proformas. The property, plant and equipment calculation was also fairly straightforward. Don't be put off by the mention of deferred tax – all you had to do was deduct 10 from the deferred tax provision and from the income statement tax charge!

EZ STATEMENT OF COMPREHENSIVE INCOME FOR THE YEAR ENDING 31 MARCH 20X9

	$'000
Revenue	720
Cost of sales (418 + 44 (W1))	(462)
Gross profit	258
Loss on disposal of non-current assets (2 – 7)	(5)
Distribution costs	(69)
Administrative expenses (86 + 125)	(211)
Impairment of land (675 – 700 + 10)	(15)
Operating lease (W2)	(24)
Loss from operations	(66)
Finance cost (4% × 250)	(10)
Loss before tax	(76)
Income tax expense (18 – 10)	(8)
Loss for the year	(84)
Other comprehensive income:	
Loss on revaluation of land	(10)
Total comprehensive loss for the year	(94)

EZ STATEMENT OF FINANCIAL POSITION AS AT 31 MARCH 20X9

	$'000	$'000
Assets		
Non-current assets		
Land	675	
Property, plant and equipment (W1)	285	
		960
Current assets		
Inventory	112	
Trade receivables	150	
Cash and cash equivalents	22	
		284
Total assets		1,244

	$'000	$'000
Equity and liabilities		
Equity		
Share capital	600	
Share premium	300	
Retained earnings	5	
		905
Non-current liabilities		
Long-term borrowings	250	
Deferred tax	20	
Current liabilities		
Trade payables	32	
Operating lease payable	9	
Tax payable	18	
Interest payable	10	
		69
Total liabilities and equity		1,244

EZ STATEMENT OF CHANGES IN EQUITY FOR THE YEAR ENDING 31 MARCH 20X9

	Share capital $'000	Share premium $'000	Revaluation surplus $'000	Retained earnings $'000	Total $'000
Balance at 1 April 20X8	400 (bal.fig)	200 (bal.fig)	10	181	791
Issue of share capital	200	100	–	–	300
Dividends	–	–	–	(92)	(92)
Total comprehensive income for the year	–	–	(10)	(84)	(94)
Balance at 31 March 20X9	600	300	0	5	905

Workings

1   *Property, plant and equipment*

	$'000
Cost at 31 March 20X8	480
Less disposal	(37)
Cost at 31 March 20X9	443
Accumulated depreciation at 31 March 20X8	(144)
Disposal	30
Charge for year (443 x 10%)	(44)
	(158)

Depreciation charged to administrative expenses

2   *Operating lease*

	$'000
Total charge over 30 months (2.5 x 24)	60
Charge per month (60/30)	2
Charge for year (2 x 12)	24

34 Objective test answers: Group financial statements

1   D

	$'000
Fair value of net assets acquired:	
Ordinary shares	400
Retained earnings at 1 January 20X7	100
Retained for 9 months to acquisition date (80 × 9/12)	60
	560
Add goodwill	30
	590

2   D

	$
Consolidated retained earnings	560,000
Less Mercedes plc	(450,000)
Add back unrealised profit (50,000 × 25/125)	10,000
	120,000

3   C

	$
Cost of investment	50,000
Share of post-acquisition retained earnings (20 × 35%)	7,000
Less dividend received (10 × 35%)	(3,500)
Less impairment	(6,000)
	47,500

4   B

	$'000
Profit on sale (160,000/4)	40,000
Unrealised profit (40,000 × 25%)	10,000
Group share (10,000 × 30%)	3,000

5   A

	Colossal plc	Enormous Ltd
	$	$
Retained earnings per question	275,000	177,000
Less pre-acquisition		(156,000)
Depreciation on FV adjustment (20,000/4)		(5,000)
		16,000
Goodwill impairment (W)	(12,000)	
Enormous Ltd	16,000	
Group retained earnings	279,000	

Working

	$	$
Consideration transferred		300,000
Share capital	100,000	
Retained earnings	156,000	
Fair value adjustment	20,000	
		(276,000)
Goodwill at acquisition		24,000
Impairment (50%)		12,000

6   C

	$
Consideration transferred	120,000
Share of post-acquisition retained earnings ((140 – 80) × 40%)	24,000
Unrealised profit (30,000 × 25% × 40%)	(3,000)
	141,000

7   C

	$	$
Consideration transferred		210,000
Net assets acquired:		
Share capital	100,000	
Retained earnings	90,000	
		(190,000)
Goodwill at acquisition		20,000
Impairment		(10,000)
Goodwill at 31 December 20X9		10,000

8   A

	$
A – Retained earnings	210,000
B – Post-acquisition retained earnings (160,000 – 90,000)	70,000
Goodwill impairment	(10,000)
Group retained earnings	270,000

9   B

	$	$
Consideration transferred		350,000
Net assets acquired:		
Share capital	140,000	
Share premium	50,000	
Retained earnings	60,000	
		(250,000)
Goodwill at 31 December 20X9		100,000

10   A $140,000 + $80,000 + $40,000 = $260,000

35 Goose and Gander

> **Text reference.** Consolidated financial statements are covered in Chapters 13-16.
>
> **Top tips.** Don't forget **Part (b).** There are five marks here for explaining the purpose of consolidated financial statements. Do it first, before getting tied up with Part (a).

(a)   GOOSE GROUP

DRAFT CONSOLIDATED STATEMENT OF COMPREHENSIVE INCOME
FOR THE YEAR ENDED 31 DECEMBER 20X8

	$'000
Revenue (5,000 + 1,000 – 100)	5,900
Cost of sales (2,900 + 600 – 100 +20)	3,420
Gross profit	2,480
Other expenses (1,700 + 320)	2,020
Net profit	460
Tax (130 + 25)	155
Profit for the year	305
Other comprehensive income:	
Gain on property revaluation	100
Total comprehensive income	405

DRAFT CONSOLIDATED STATEMENT OF FINANCIAL POSITION AS AT 31 DECEMBER 20X8

	$'000	$'000
Non-current assets		
Property, plant and equipment (2,000 + 200 + 100)	2,300	
Goodwill (W2)	155	
		2,455
Current assets		
Inventory (500 + 120 + 100* – 20)	700	
Trade receivables (650 – 100 + 40)	590	
Bank and cash (390 + 35)	425	
		1,715
		4,170
Equity and liabilities		
Share capital (500 + 80)		580
Share premium (1500 + 360)		1,860
Revaluation surplus (50 + 100)		150
Retained earnings (W5)		345
		2,935
Current liabilities		
Trade payables (1,010 + 70 + 100* – 100)	1,080	
Tax (130 + 25)	155	
		1,235
Total equity and liabilities		4,170

Workings

1   *Group structure*

Goose

|
100%, 1 Jan 20X8

Gander

2   *Investment in Gander*

		$'000
Share capital	100,000 x 4/5 x 1 =	80
Share premium	100,000 x 4/5 x 4.5 =	360
		440

3   *Goodwill*

	$'000
Consideration paid	440
Less net assets acquired:	
Retained earnings	(185)
Share capital	(100)
	155

4   *Unrealised profit*

	$'000
Sale price	100
Cost price	(80)
Unrealised profit	20

Dr retained earnings, Cr group inventory

*To record the goods in transit Dr inventory, Cr payables $100,000

5   *Group retained earnings*

	Goose $'000	Gander $'000
Per individual statements	350	200
Less pre-acquisition reserves	–	(185)
	350	15
Less unrealised profit	(20)	
Gander (100% × 15)	15	
	345	

(b)   *Usefulness of consolidated financial statements*

The main reason for preparing consolidated accounts is that groups operate as a single economic unit, and it is not possible to understand the affairs of the parent company without taking into account the financial position and performance of all the companies that it controls. The directors of the parent company should be held fully accountable for all the money they have invested on their shareholders behalf, whether that has been done directly by the parent or via a subsidiary.

There are also practical reasons why parent company accounts cannot show the full picture. The parent company's own financial statements only show the original cost of the investment and the dividends received from the subsidiary. As explained below, this hides the true value and nature of the investment in the subsidiary, and, without consolidation, could be used to manipulate the reported results of the parent.

- The cost of the investment will include a premium for goodwill, but this is only quantified and reported if consolidated accounts are prepared.

- Without consolidation, the assets and liabilities of the subsidiary are disguised.

    – A subsidiary could be very highly geared, making its liquidity and profitability volatile.

    – A subsidiary's assets might consist of intangible assets, or other assets with highly subjective values.

- The parent company controls the dividend policy of the subsidiary, enabling it to smooth out profit fluctuations with a steady dividend. Consolidation reveals the underlying profits of the group.

- Over time the net assets of the subsidiary should increase, but the cost of the investment will stay fixed and will soon bear no relation to the true value of the subsidiary.

36 Molecule

Text references. The consolidated statement of financial position is covered in Chapter 14. Associates are covered in Chapter 16.

Top Tips. Note that you are specifically asked for a working for retained earnings. The adjustments for intra-group trading may be on the face of the consolidated statement of financial position or in a separate working.

(a)   *Calculation of goodwill on the acquisition of Atom*

	$'000	$'000
Consideration transferred		4,545
Share of net assets acquired		
Share capital	4,000	
Retained earnings	60	
		4,060
Goodwill		485

NOTE. Goodwill is fully written off and will not appear in the statement of financial position. The impairment will be deducted from retained earnings.

(b) MOLECULE GROUP
CONSOLIDATED STATEMENT OF FINANCIAL POSITION AS AT 31 OCTOBER 20X7

	$'000	$'000
Non-current assets		
Property, plant and equipment (3,000 + 3,300)		6,300
Investment in associate (W4)		790
Current assets		
Inventory (1,500 + 800 – 20 (W3))	2,280	
Receivables (1,800 + 750 – 30 – 450)	2,070	
Bank (600 + 350)	950	
		5,300
		12,390
Equity and liabilities		
Equity		
$1 Ordinary shares		9,000
Retained earnings (W2)		500
		9,500
Current liabilities		
Payables (1,220 + 200 – 30)	1,390	
Tax (700 + 800)	1,500	
		2,890
Total equity and liabilities		12,390

Workings

1   *Group structure*

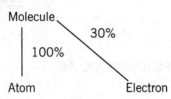

2   *Unrealised profit on intra-group sale*

Profit on intra-group sale is $240,000 \times \dfrac{20}{120} = \$40,000$

∴ Unrealised profit is $40,000 × 50% = $20,000

Dr retained earnings, Cr group inventory

3   *Investment in associate*

	$'000
Cost of investment	800
Share of post-acquisition retained earnings ((600-300) x 30%)	90
Less impairment	(100)
	790

4   *Retained earnings*

	Molecule $'000	Atom $'000	Electron $'000
Per question	1,325	200	600
Unrealised profit (W3)	(20)		
Less pre-acquisition		(60)	(300)
		140	300
Impairment of goodwill/investment in associate (485+100)	(585)		
Correction of error (write off of receivable from prior year)	(450)		
Atom	140		
Electron (300 x 30%)	90		
	500		

(c) **Significant influence** can usually be determined by the holding of **voting rights** in the entity, generally in the form of shares.

Significant influence may take various forms:

(i)   Participation in the policy making process
(ii)   Material transactions between investee and investor
(iii) Board representation
(iv) Provision of technical advice
(v)   An interchange of personnel between the companies

37 Parsley

> **Text references**. Consolidated financial statements are covered in Chapters 13-16.
>
> **Top tips**. Points to watch in this question are:
>
> (a)   Correct consolidation technique – not proportionate consolidation
> (b)   Elimination of intra-group transactions
> (c)   Adjustments to inventory, receivables and cash

(a) *Goodwill arising on acquisition of Sage*

	$'000	$'000
Consideration transferred		30,000
Net assets acquired:		
Share capital	25,000	
Retained earnings	2,000	
		27,000
Goodwill		3,000

(b) (i) PARSLEY
CONSOLIDATED STATEMENT OF COMPREHENSIVE INCOME
FOR THE YEAR ENDED 31 DECEMBER 20X9

	$'000
Revenue (135m + 74m – 12m)	197,000
Cost of sales (W1)	(89,000)
Gross profit	108,000
Distribution costs	(13,700)
Administrative expenses	(26,784)
Impairment of goodwill (3,000 – 2,250)	(750)
Finance charges (W2)	(12)
Profit before taxation	66,754
Taxation	(19,000)
Profit for the year	47,754

(ii) PARSLEY
CONSOLIDATED STATEMENT OF FINANCIAL POSITION AS AT 31 DECEMBER 20X9

	$'000	$'000
Non-current assets		
Intangible: goodwill		2,250
Property, plant and equipment (net book value):		
$(74,000,000 + 39,050,000)		113,050
		115,300
Current assets		
Inventory (10,630,000 + 4,498,000 – 1,000,000 (W1))	14,128	
Receivables (W3)	20,886	
Bank	14,744	
		49,758
		165,058

	$'000	$'000
Equity and liabilities		
Share capital		80,000
Retained earnings (W5)		48,790
		128,790
	$'000	$'000
Current liabilities		
Payables (W4)	6,118	
Taxation	18,000	
Dividends: Parsley	12,000	
		36,118
Non-current liabilities		
8% loan notes		150
		165,058

Workings

1   *Cost of sales*

	$'000
Parsley	70,000
Sage	30,000
	100,000
Less intra-group	(12,000)
	88,000
Add back unrealised profit in inventory $(12m – 8m) × 25\%$	1,000
	89,000

2   *Finance charges*

	$'000
Per question – Sage	16
Less loan interest payable to Parsley: $50,000 × 8\%$	(4)
	12

3   *Receivables*

	$'000	$'000
Parsley		18,460
Sage		12,230
Dividends	8,000	
Loan interest	4	
Intra-group	1,800	
		(9,804)
		20,886

4   *Payables*

	$'000	$'000
Parsley		6,000
Sage		1,922
Loan interest (W2)	4	
Intra-group	1,800	
		(1,804)
		6,118

5   *Retained earnings*

	Parsley	*Sage*
	$'000	$'000
Per question	37,540	15,000
Less provision for unrealised profit (W1)	(1,000)	
Pre-acquisition		(2,000)
		13,000
Goodwill impairment (W6)	(750)	
	35,790	
Share of Sage	13,000	
	48,790	

6   *Impairment of goodwill*

	$'000
Goodwill at acquisition (part (a))	3,000
Goodwill at 31 December 20X9	2,250
Impairment	750

(c)   The purpose of consolidated accounts is to present the financial position of connected companies as that of a **single entity, the group.** This means that, **in the consolidated statement of financial position, the only profits recognised should be those earned by the group in providing services to outsiders.** Similarly, **inventory should be valued at the cost to the group.**

When a company sells goods to another company in the same group, it will recognised revenue and profit in its own books. However, **from the point of view of the group, no sale has taken place**, because the goods have not been sold outside the group. The sale must therefore be eliminated from revenue and **the unrealised profit** (that is profit on inventory not sold outside the group) **must be eliminated from inventory.**

38   Tom, Dick and Harry

Text references. The consolidated statement of financial position is covered in Chapter 14. Associates are covered in Chapter 16.

Top tips. Calculating the goodwill value in part (a) is tricky, however, you should be able to explain the treatment of negative goodwill under IFRS 3 to gain some easy marks. Watch out for the extra depreciation charge created when the fair value exceeds the book value of non-current assets. In this question you have been given the extra depreciation charge, but in your exam you might be asked to calculate it. Remember that to calculate the extra depreciation charge, you need to divide the fair value adjustment by the remaining useful life.

In part (b), don't forget to set out your proforma and insert the easy numbers first.

(a)   (i)   *Goodwill on acquisition of Dick*

	$
Consideration paid	200,000
Less net assets acquired represented by:	
Share capital	(100,000)
Retained earnings	(90,000)
Plus fair value adjustment	(50,000)
	(240,000)
Goodwill	(40,000)

(ii)   *Treatment of negative goodwill under IFRS 3*

If goodwill calculated is negative it means that the aggregate value of the net assets acquired may exceed what the parent company paid for them. Under IFRS 3, this is referred to as a 'bargain purchase'. In this situation, IFRS 3 requires that:

(a)   The group should first re-assess the amounts at which it has measured both the cost of the combination and the acquired net assets. This is to identify any errors in the calculation and to check that a 'bargain purchase' really has occurred.

(b)   Any negative goodwill remaining after this exercise should be recognised immediately in profit or loss.

(b)   TOM GROUP
CONSOLIDATED STATEMENT OF FINANCIAL POSITION AS AT 31 OCTOBER 20X1

	$'000	$'000
Non-current assets		
Property, plant and equipment (W2)		373
Investment in associate (W5)		117
		490
Current assets		
Inventory (100 + 70 – 2 (W3))	168	
Receivables (170 + 40)	210	
Bank (190 + 30)	220	
		598
		1,088
Equity and liabilities		
Share capital		500
Retained earnings (W6)		448
		948
Current liabilities (110 + 30)		140
		1,088

Workings

1   *Group structure*

	Tom	
100%		30%
Dick		Harry

2   *Property, plant and equipment*

	$'000
Tom	205
Dick	120
Fair value adjustment	50
Depreciation adjustment	(2)
	373

3   *Unrealised Profit*

Total profit – 25,000/5 = 5,000

Profit on goods left in stock = 5,000 x 40% = 2,000

DR Retained earnings, CR Group inventory

4   *Investment in associate*

	$'000
Cost of investment	115
Share of post-acquisition retained earnings ((150 – 130) × 30%)	6
Impairment	(4)
	117

5   *Retained earnings*

	Tom	Dick	Harry
	$'000	$'000	$'000
Per individual statements	370	130	150
Less pre-acquisition		(90)	(130)
		40	20
Unrealised profit (W2)	(2)		
Negative goodwill (part (a))	40		
Depreciation adjustment	(2)		
Impairment of investment in associate	(4)		
Dick (40 × 100%)	40		
Harry (20 × 30%)	6		
	448		

39   PSA

Text references. Accounting for associates is covered in Chapter 16. Preparation of the consolidated statement of financial position is covered in Chapter 14.

Top tips. Don't get carried away with part (a), stick to the time allocation and then move on to part (b). Don't forget to include a short discussion on the relevant ethical issues in your answer to part (a).

The consolidated statement of financial position was fairly straightforward, but did contain a couple of tricky parts. Easy errors to make are:

• Not including the fair value uplift in your goodwill calculation

• Not including the depreciation on the fair value uplift in your retained earnings working

• Incorrectly calculating the investment in associate balance due to the loss made by the associate in the year

Easy marks. There were easy marks to be gained in part (a) for explaining equity accounting. In part (b), there were easy marks for calculating trade payables and receivables and cash, and for inserting the figures for P's share capital and long-term borrowings straight from the question onto your answer.

(a)   DRAFT MEMO

To: The Directors of P

From: A Management Accountant

Treatment of A in the consolidated financial statements

A is classified as an **associate** under IAS 28 because P can exercise **significant influence** (but not control) over A's strategic and operating decisions.

IAS 28 requires associates to be accounted for in the consolidated financial statements using the **equity method**.

Under the equity method, P will take account of its **share of the earnings** of A, whether or not A distributes the earnings as dividends. This is achieved by adding P's share of A's profit after tax to the consolidated profit of P. In the statement of financial position, the investment in A is recorded initially at cost and then each year will increase (or decrease) by the amount of P's share of A's change in retained reserves.

A will not be consolidated as a subsidiary as P does not exercise control over it.

It would not be in line with IAS 28 to include A as a simple investment of $13,000 in the consolidated financial statements. Including A as a simple investment would suggest that P did not have influence over the strategic and operating decisions of A. This would be potentially misleading to users of the financial statements.

The CIMA code of Ethics states that professional accountants should behave with integrity. Producing potentially misleading information is a breach of integrity and therefore is unethical.

(b)   P CONSOLIDATED STATEMENT OF FINANCIAL POSITION AS AT 31 MARCH 20X9

	$'000	$'000
Assets		
Non-current assets		
Property, plant and equipment (W2)	88,950	
Goodwill (W4)	12,600	
Investment in associate (W5)	7,720	
		109,270
Current assets		
Inventory (8,000 + 12,000 – 1,000)	19,000	
Trade receivables (17,000 + 11,000 – 250 – 4000)	23,750	
Cash and cash equivalents (1,000 + 3,000 + 2,000)	6,000	
		48,750
Total assets		158,020
Equity and liabilities		
Equity attributable to owners of the parent		
Share capital	100,000	
Retained earnings (W6)	21,270	
Total equity		121,270
Non-current liabilities		
Long-term borrowings		26,000
Current liabilities		
Trade payables (10,000 + 5,000 – 250 – 4,000)		10,750
Total liabilities and equity		158,020

Workings

1   *Group structure*

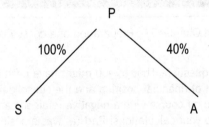

2   *Property, plant and equipment*

	$'000
P carrying value of PPE	40,000
S carrying value of PPE	48,000
Fair value uplift	1,000
Less additional depreciation*	(50)
	88,950

* Additional depreciation for fair value uplift = 1,000,000/20 = $50,000 per annum

3   *Unrealised profit*

	$'000
Sale price (cost plus 1/3)	4,000
Cost price (sales price × 3/4)	(3,000)
Unrealised profit	1,000

DR   Group retained earnings
CR   Group inventory

4   *Goodwill*

	$'000	$'000
Consideration transferred		60,000
Net assets acquired as represented by:		
Ordinary share capital	40,000	
Retained earnings on acquisition	6,400	
Fair value adjustment on buildings	1,000	
		(47,400)
Goodwill		12,600

5   *Investment in associate*

	$'000
Cost	13,000
Share of loss for the year (40% × (7,800 – 21,000))	(5,280)
	7,720

6   *Retained earnings*

	P	S	A
	$'000	$'000	$'000
Per Question	21,000	13,000	7,800
Less pre-acquisition	–	(6,400)	(21,000)
Unrealised profit (W3)	(1,000)	–	–
Depreciation on FV adjustment	–	(50)	–
	20,000	6,550	(13,200)
S × 100%	6,550		
A × 40%	(5,280)		
	21,270		

40   AX

Text references. Accounting for associates is covered in Chapter 16. Preparation of a consolidated statement of financial position is covered in Chapter 14.

Top tips. This is a pretty straightforward consolidation question. Though you might have been pushed for time because you had to do both the consolidated statement of financial position and the consolidated statement of comprehensive income. The question tried to throw you off course with a negative retained earnings balance in the subsidiary – but don't worry about it, just put it into your calculations! Part (a) was a basic corporate tax calculation that you should have found easy – the question even supplied the tax depreciation amount to use. Calculating the change in the deferred tax provision required a bit more thought.

Working methodically through part (b) using our recommended approach is the best way to make sure you have included all the balances and get the most marks.

Easy errors to make were:

- Not adjusting retained earnings for the tax calculated in part (a)
- Not including the fair value uplift in your goodwill calculation
- Incorrectly calculating goodwill due to the negative retained earnings figure
- Forgetting to remove the intra-group sales figures from revenue and cost of sales

Easy marks. There were easy marks to be gained in part (a) for calculating the corporate income tax. In part (b), there were easy marks for doing the basic adding across procedure for consolidation, filling in your proforma as you go.

(a)   AX CORPORATE INCOME TAX FOR YEAR ENDED 31 MARCH 20X9

	$'000	$'000
Accounting profit		264
Add back: entertaining expenses	4	
Accounting depreciation	31	
		35
Less: tax depreciation		(49)
Taxable profit		250
Tax charge @ 25%		63

Deferred tax provision

Difference between carrying amount and tax base increased by 49,000 – 31,000 = $18,000

Increase in deferred tax provision = 25% x 18,000 = $4,500 (round to $5,000)

(b)   AX CONSOLIDATED STATEMENT OF COMPREHENSIVE INCOME
FOR THE YEAR ENDED 31 MARCH 20X9

	$'000
Revenue (820 + 285 – 55)	1,050
Cost of sales (406 + 119 – 55 +5 (W2))	(475)
Gross profit	575
Administrative expenses (84 + 36)	(120)
Distribution costs (48 + 22)	(70)
	385
Income from associate (51 × 22%)	11
Finance cost (18 + 5)	(23)
Profit before tax	373
Taxation (16 + 63 + 5)	(84)
Profit for the year/Total consolidated income for the year	289

AX CONSOLIDATED STATEMENT OF FINANCIAL POSITION AS AT 31 MARCH 20X9

	$'000	$'000
Assets		
Non-current assets		
Property, plant and equipment (1,120 + 700 + 75)	1,895	
Goodwill (W3)	137	
Investment in associate (W4)	156	
		2,188
Current assets		
Inventory (205 + 30 – 5(W2))	230	
Trade receivables (350 + 46)	396	
Cash and cash equivalents	30	
		656
Total assets		2,844
Equity and liabilities		
Equity attributable to owners of the parent		
Share capital	1,500	
Retained earnings (W5)	543	
Total equity		2,043
Non-current liabilities		
Long-term borrowings		440
Deferred tax (120 + 16 +5)		141
Current liabilities		
Trade payables (92 + 29)	121	
Tax payable (16 + 63)	79	
Bank overdraft	20	
		220
Total liabilities and equity		2,844

Workings

1   *Group structure*

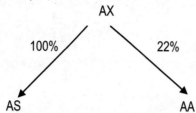

2   *Unrealised profit/Intra-group sales*

	$'000
Sale price (125%)	25
Cost price (100%)	(20)
Unrealised profit	5

DR	Group retained earnings	$5,000
CR	Group inventory	$5,000

DR	Revenue	$55,000
CR	Cost of sales	$55,000

3   *Goodwill*

	$'000	$'000
Consideration transferred		740
Net assets acquired as represented by:		
Ordinary share capital	600	
Retained earnings on acquisition	(72)	
Fair value adjustment on land	75	
		(603)
Goodwill		137

4   *Investment in associate*

	$'000
Cost	145
Share of profit for the year (22% x 51)	11
	156

5   *Retained earnings*

	AX	AS	AA
	$'000	$'000	$'000
Per Question	518	15	100
Less current tax charge (a)	(63)	–	–
Less increase in DT provision (a)	(5)	–	–
Less pre-acquisition	–	72	(49)
	450	87	51
Unrealised profit (W2)	(5)		
AS × 100%	87		
AA × 22%	11		
	543		

41 Objective test answers: General principles of taxation

1　B　The tax authorities do not have the power to detain company officials. Their powers relate to documents and information (eg information held on computer).

2　Direct taxation is charged directly on the **person** or **entity** that is intended to pay the tax.

3　C　Equity

4　Tax evasion is manipulation of the tax system by illegal means to avoid paying taxes.

5
- Domestic legislation and legal decisions
- Tax authority practice
- International treaties
- Supranational bodies

6　B　The person or entity that finally bears the cost of the tax.

7　The tax authority whose tax laws apply to an entity or person.

8　A　Power of arrest.

9　C　Effective incidence

10　Any three of the following:

(1)　To give a date from which penalties and/or interest can accrue

(2)　To get funds in as quickly as possible for use by central government

(3)　To reduce backlogs and extra work for the tax department

(4)　To prevent entities deducting tax at source, eg employers collecting payroll tax, from spending it before it reaches the tax authority

11　A　An example of hypothecation is the 'congestion charge' levied on London motorists that can only be spent on London transport.

12　**Equity**: the tax burden should be fairly distributed

Efficiency: tax should be easy and cheap to collect

Economic effects: the government must consider the effect of taxation policy on various sectors of the economy

13　A

14　A　Formal incidence

15　C　Naturally, tax authorities like to minimise the tax gap.

16　C　International tax treaties (eg double taxation treaties) are a source of tax rules.

The other options are all sources of accounting rules.

42 Objective test answers: Types of taxation I

1　(a)　Tax is deducted at source, so non-payment is not an issue
　(b)　The costs of collection are borne by employers
　(c)　The funds are received at the same time each month, which helps financial planning

2　C　The company acts as a tax collector on behalf of the tax authority. Therefore any tax deducted is put in a payable account until the money is actually paid to the tax authority. The balance on the payable account represents the amount collected but not yet paid over.

3　Accounting profit + disallowable expenditure – non-taxable income – tax allowable expenditure = taxable profit

4　C　Tax deducted at source before payment of interest or dividends.

5	A	A progressive tax

6   (a)   Under group loss relief, it is possible to set the losses of a group member against the profits of another group member. If the profit-making group member pays tax at a higher rate than the one making the loss, the total tax liability of the group for the year can be reduced.

     (b)   Claiming group loss relief can help improve group cash flows as the loss is relieved more quickly.

7   A   The classical system

	$'000
Company income tax (400,000 × 25%)	100
Personal income tax (250,000 × 30%)	75
	175

8   B   The company income tax that has already been paid on the distribution is **imputed** to the shareholder as a tax credit.

9   D   The head office is located, and all board meetings take place in, the Cayman Islands. Therefore the place of management is in the Cayman Islands.

10   The EU issues rules on sales taxes, which must be applied by all member states.

11
- Interest payments
- Dividends
- Royalties
- Capital gains accruing to non-residents

12
- Full deduction
- Exemption
- Credit

13   B   Double taxable treaties deal with **overseas** income.

14   D   The country where most of the entity's products are sold.

15   B

	$
50,000 × 12%	6,000
Less already paid	(5,000)
Balance due:	1,000

16   B   Corporate income tax is due on all profits of the branch, not just those remitted.

17   C   EA will be deemed resident in Country C, which is its place of management.

18   D   A construction project is only a permanent establishment if it lasts more than 12 months.

19   Net assets and consumption

20   C   Under the OECD model, an entity is considered to have residence in the country in which it has a permanent establishment, which includes a place of management.

21    $20,000

	$
Net dividend	90,000
Withholding tax	10,000
Gross dividend	100,000
Underlying tax (100,000 × 200,000/1,000,000)	$20,000

43   Objective test answers: Types of taxation II

1   A suitable commodity would have the following characteristics:

- A limited number of large producers
- Products that are easily defined
- A commodity produced in large volume

2   C   Sales tax is an indirect tax, all the others are direct taxes.

3   B   As long as they are registered for sales tax, options A, C and D merely act as tax collectors, it is the end consumer who suffers the tax.

4

			$
DA	Input tax (200 × 15%)		(30)
	Output tax (500 × 15%)		75
	Total due		45
DB	Input tax		(75)
	Output tax (1,000 × 15%)		150
	Total due		75
	Total		120

5

	$
Sale by DA (500 × 7%)	35
Sale by DB (1,000 × 7%)	70
Total paid	105

6   D   Sales taxes such as VAT are indirect

7   B $1,450

	$
VAT output tax (200 × 50 × 15%)	1,500
VAT input tax (200 × 35 × 15%)	(1,050)
VAT payable	450
Excise duty payable (200 × 5)	1,000
Total payable	1,450

8   Amount paid = $14,000

	$
Output VAT 120,000 × 20%	24,000
Input VAT 100,000 × 10%	(10,000)
Amount paid	14,000

9

		$			$
CU:	Output tax	37.5	CZ:	Output tax	90.0
	Input tax	(15.0)		Input tax	(37.5)
	Payable	22.5		Payable	52.5

10   VAT paid $15,000

Gross profit $100,000

	$
Output VAT (183,000 × 22/122)	33,000
Input VAT (138,000 × 15/115)	(18,000)
Amount paid	15,000
Revenue (183,000 × 100/122) + 70,000	220,000
Cost of sales (138,000 × 100/115)	(120,000)
Gross profit	100,000

11   C $5,550

Workings	$
Cost	14,000
Excise duty	3,000
	17,000
VAT @ 15%	2,550
	19,550

Taxes paid = $3,000 + $2,500 = $5,550

12

		$'000
Output tax (18,400 × 15/115)		2,400
Input tax (10,000 + 4,000 × 15%)		(2,100)
VAT due from FE		300

Note that VAT is deductible on purchases relating to zero-rated outputs, but not on purchases relating to exempt outputs

13　B

	$	$
Accounting profit		350,000
Add: depreciation	30,000	
disallowed expenses	15,000	
		45,000
		395,000
Less: non-taxable income	25,000	
tax allowable depreciation	32,000	
		(57,000)
Taxable profit		338,000

14　D

	$	$
Taxable profit		350,000
Less: depreciation	30,000	
disallowed expenses	15,000	
		(45,000)
		305,000
Add: non-taxable income	25,000	
tax allowable depreciation	32,000	
		57,000
Accounting profit		362,000

15　A

	$	$
Accounting loss		(350,000)
Add: depreciation	30,000	
disallowed expenses	400,000	
		430,000
		80,000
Less: non-taxable income	25,000	
tax allowable depreciation	32,000	
		(57,000)
Taxable profit		23,000

16　B

	$m	$m
Taxable profit		50
Less: depreciation	15	
disallowed expenses	1	
		(16)
		34
Add: non-taxable income	3	
tax allowable depreciation	4	
		7
Accounting profit		41

17　D

	$	$
Accounting profit		250,000
Add: depreciation	45,000	
disallowed expenses	20,000	
		65,000
		315,000
Less: tax allowable depreciation		(30,000)
Taxable profit		285,000

Tax payable = $285,000 × 30% = $85,500.

18 C

	$	$
Accounting profit		360,000
Add: depreciation	40,000	
disallowed expenses	10,000	
		50,000
		410,000
Less: non-taxable income	35,000	
tax allowable depreciation	30,000	
		(65,000)
Taxable profit		345,000

Tax payable = $345,000 x 20% = $69,000.

19 B

	$	$
Accounting profit		500,000
Add: depreciation	50,000	
disallowed expenses	5,000	
		55,000
		555,000
Less: non-taxable income	25,000	
tax allowable depreciation	60,000	
		(85,000)
Taxable profit		470,000

Tax payable = $470,000 × 25% = $117,500.

20 D

	$	$
Accounting profit		250,000
Add: depreciation	40,000	
disallowed expenses	2,000	
		42,000
		292,000
Less: tax allowable depreciation		(30,000)
Taxable profit		262,000

Tax payable = $262,000 × 30% = $78,600.

21 D   Direct tax and earnings tax. (This is the examiner's answer.)

22 Tax due = $22,500

	$
Accounting profit	95,000
Less non-taxable income	(15,000)
Add non– allowable expenditure	10,000
Taxable profit	90,000

Tax = $90,000 × 25%
     = $22,500

23 $4,000

	$'000
Revenue	45
Operating costs	(23)
Finance costs	(4)
Taxable allowance	(2)
Taxable amount	16
Tax @ 25%	4

24

		$
30 September 20X3	Tax on trading profits = 200 × 20%=	40,000
30 September 20X4	Tax on trading profit = (150 – 120) × 20% =	6,000
30 September 20X5	Tax on capital gains = (130 – 100) × 20% =	6,000
		12,000

25 A $320,000 less prior year over-provision ($290,000 – $280,000)

26

	Accounting book value $	Tax basis $	Difference $	Deferred tax balance $
Cost 1.4.X4	500,000	500,000		
Depreciation to 31.3.X5	(100,000)			
Capital allowance 50%	-	(250,000)	-	-
	400,000	250,000	150,000	45,000
Depreciation to 31.3.X6	(100,000)			
Capital allowance 20%	-	(50,000)	-	-
	300,000	200,000	100,000	30,000
Revaluation 1.4.X6	120,000			
	420,000			
Depreciation (42,000/3)	(140,000)			
Capital allowance 20%	-	40,000	-	-
	280,000	160,000	120,000	36,000

		$
Deferred tax balance 31.3.X6		30,000
Deferred tax balance 31.3.X7		36,000
Income statement charge X6/X7		6,000

44 Objective test answers: Deferred tax

1 A

	$
Over provision for prior period	(2,000)
Provision for current period	50,000
Increase in deferred tax charge	5,000
Charge to income statement	53,000

2 C

	$
Under provision for prior period	200
Provision for current period	30,000
Decrease in deferred tax charge	(5,000)
Charge to income statement	25,200

3 A Item 2 consists of permanent differences, all the rest are temporary differences.

4 D All four items have a carrying amount equal to their tax base.

5 B IAS 12 states that deferred tax assets and liabilities should not be discounted.

6 D

	$
Taxable temporary differences b/f	850,000
Depreciation for tax purposes	500,000
Depreciation charged in the financial statements	(450,000)
Revaluation surplus	250,000
Taxable temporary differences c/f	1,150,000
Deferred tax at 30%	345,000

7 D

	$
Over provision for prior period	(27,500)
Provision for current period	30,000
Decrease in deferred tax charge	(10,000)
Credit to income statement	(7,500)

8 It is an imputation system.

9   D

		$
	Under provision for prior period	2,800
	Provision for current period	28,000
	Increase in deferred tax charge	5,000
	Charge to income statement	35,800

10   Deferred tax balance = $66,750

Tax written down value:

	$
1 Oct 20X3 cost	900,000
20X4 tax allowance – 50% × 900,000	(450,000)
30 Sept 20X4 tax written down value	450,000
20X5 tax allowance – 25% × 450,000	(112,500)
30 Sept 20X5 tax written down value	337,500

Accounting carrying value:

	$
Cost	900,000
Depreciation 2 × (900-50)/5	(340,000)
30 Sept 20X5 accounting carrying value	560,000

Temporary difference = $560,000 – 337,500
                     = $222,500

Deferred tax balance = $222,500 × 30%
                     = $66,750

11

	$
Taxable profit for the year	946,000
Tax at 22%	208,120
Prior year over-provision	(31,000)
Increase in deferred tax provision	117,000
Charge to income statement	294,120

12   Deferred tax balance at 31 March 20X7 = $34
     Deferred tax balance at 31 March 20X8 = ($2)

Tax written down value:

	$ '000
1 Apr 20X5 cost	600
20X6 tax allowance (50% × 600,000)	(300)
31 Mar 20X6 tax written down value	300
20X7 tax allowance (25% × 300,000)	(75)
31 Mar 20X7 tax written down value	225
20X8 tax allowance (25% × 225,000)	(56)
31 Mar 20X8 tax written down value	169

Accounting carrying value:

	$
Cost	600
Depreciation (2 × (600/5))	(240)
31 Mar 20X7 carrying value	360
1 Apr 20X7 impairment review	(120)
1 Apr 20X7 carrying value	240
Depreciation X7/X8 (240/3)	(80)
31 Mar 20X8 carrying value	160

31 March 20X7
Temporary difference = $360 – $225 = $135
Deferred tax balance = $135 × 25% = $34

31 March 20X8
Temporary difference = $160– $169 = ($9)
Deferred tax balance = ($9) × 25% = ($2)

Note. The question specifies working to the nearest $1,000.

13    $200,250

	$
Accounting profits	822,000
Entertaining expenses	32,000
Political donation	50,000
	904,000
Government grant	(103,000)
Taxable profit	801,000
Tax at 25%	200,250

14    $49,500

	Carrying value	Tax base
	$	$
1 October 20X5	400,000	400,000
Depreciation 25%	(100,000)	–
First year allowance	–	(400,000)
Balance 30 Sept 20X6	300,000	–
Depreciation 25%	(75,000)	–
Balance 30 Sept 20X7	225,000	–

Difference between carrying value and tax base = $225,000

Deferred tax at 22% = $49,500

15

	Carrying value	Tax base	Difference
	$	$	$
1 April 20X7	220,000	220,000	
Depreciation (220,000/8)	(27,500)	–	
First year allowance 30%	–	(66,000)	
Balance 30 March 20X8	192,500	154,000	38,500
Revaluation	50,000	–	
	242,500	154,000	
Depreciation (242,500/7)	(34,643)	–	
Writing down allowance 20%	–	(30,800)	
Balance 30 March 20X9	207,857	123,200	84,657

Deferred tax balance at 30 March 20X9 = 84,657 x 25% = $21,164

Deferred tax balance at 30 March 20X8 = 38,500 x 25% = $9,625

Movement on deferred tax balance at 30 March 20X9 = 21,164- 9,625 = $11,539

16

	Temporary difference
B/f (12,500 – 5,000)	7,500
20X3 (2,120 – 1,630)	490
20X4 (1,860 – 1,590)	270
20X5 (1,320 – 1,530)	(210)
Balance at 31 December 20X5	8,050 × 25% = 2,012.50

45 Section B answers: Taxation I

(a)   (i)   Jurisdiction relates to the power of a tax authority to charge and collect tax. Competent jurisdiction refers to the authority whose tax laws apply to an entity or person.

(ii)   Hypothecation is the ring-fencing of revenue from certain types of tax for certain types of expenditure only, eg revenue raised from road taxes can only be spent on road improvements.

(iii) A taxable person is a person liable to pay tax. In this context, person refers to individuals but also to companies and other entities that are liable to pay tax.

(iv)   Regressive tax structure – a tax structure whereby the rate of tax falls as income rises.

(v) The tax gap is the gap between the tax theoretically collectable and the amount actually collected.

(b) (i) **Indirect taxation** is charged indirectly on the final consumer of the goods or services and is a tax on consumption or expenditure. An example is a sales tax (eg VAT in the UK; TVA in France). As value is added, the tax increases cumulatively.

Indirect taxes are not actually paid by the business. Instead, the business acts as a tax collector on behalf of the tax authorities. For example, a business charges sales tax on its sales (output tax) and it pays sales tax on its purchases (input tax). The difference between output tax and input tax is paid over to the tax authorities.

(ii) **Unit taxes** are based on the number or weight of items, eg excise duties on the number of cigarettes or on the weight of tobacco.

Ad valorem taxes are based on the value of the items, eg a sales tax or value added tax.

(c)

	$'000
INCOME STATEMENT (EXTRACT)	
Income tax expense (W1)	1,145
STATEMENT OF FINANCIAL POSITION (EXTRACT)	
Non-current liabilities	
Deferred tax (W2)	1,750
Current liabilities	
Income tax	1,000

Workings

1 *Income statement*

	$
Income tax for year	1,000,000
Over-provision in previous year	(5,000)
Increase in deferred tax	150,000
Income tax expense	1,145,000

2 *Deferred tax*

	$
Opening balance	1,600,000
Increase in year	150,000
Closing balance	1,750,000

(d)

> **Examiner's comments.** Most candidates could define withholding tax whilst many candidates found difficulty defining underlying tax. A common error Part (ii) was not grossing up the amount received before calculating withholding tax. As many candidates did not know what underlying tax was they could not calculate it.

(i) **Withholding tax** is deducted at source by the tax authority before a payment is made. This occurs most commonly when dividends are paid to non-residents. The tax authority has no power to tax the non-resident, so it taxes the dividend at source.

Underlying tax is the tax which has already been suffered by the profits from which a dividend is paid. When the recipient pays tax on his dividend income, this means that the dividend has effectively been taxed twice. To mitigate this, some tax authorities operate an imputation system, by which the recipient obtains relief for the underlying tax.

(ii) $45,000 represents 9/10 of the amount prior to withholding tax, so withholding tax is therefore $45,000/9 = $5,000.

(iii) The amount of dividend prior to withholding tax was $50,000. This has already been taxed at 20% (100/500). Therefore $50,000 is 80% and the other 20% is the underlying tax - $12,500.

(e)

> **Examiner's comments**. It was surprising how many candidates could not correctly calculate VAT when the figure inclusive of VAT was given.

(i)

		$
Revenue (40,250 × 100/115)		35,000
Cost of sales:		
Purchases plus excise duty	12,000	
Repackaging (6,900 × 100/115)	6,000	
		(18,000)
Net profit		17,000

(ii)

	$
VAT output tax (35,000 × 15%)	5,250
VAT input tax (18,000 × 15%)	(2,700)
Due to VAT authorities	2,550

46 Section B answers: Taxation II

(a) (i) Governments might apply specific excise duties:

- to discourage people from consuming too much of a substance which is harmful to health – such as alcohol and tobacco

- to raise funds to pay for the consequences of the consumption of these harmful substances – for example, the additional health care required for patients with smoking-related illnesses

- to discourage the excessive use of products which damage the environment, such as the use of petrol or diesel in vehicles and aircraft

- to raise maximum revenue by targeting goods which are widely used and relatively expensive.

(ii) A single stage sales tax is chargeable at a single point in the supply chain, usually at the point of sale to the final customer. An example of a single stage sales tax is the retail sales tax applied in the USA.

A multi stage sales tax is chargeable and deductible at different points in the supply chain, such as VAT in the UK. As value is added the tax increases cumulatively. However with VAT, the business deducts the VAT it pays and pays over the balance to the government. The incidence of the tax is therefore on the final consumer of the goods or services. A multi-stage sales tax can also be cumulative, where no credit is received for tax paid in the previous stage.

(b) Power to review and query filed returns

The tax authorities usually have the power to ask for further information if they are not satisfied with a filed return. These queries must be answered or there may be legal penalties.

Power to request special reports or returns

The special report may take the form of asking for details of pay and tax deducted from an individual employee, where there are indications that the tax rules have been broken. There have been instances of casual employees having a number of jobs but using a number of false names, so that the tax authority has been defrauded.

Power to examine records

Most tax authorities have the power to inspect business records to ensure compliance. If mistakes in returns have been made, the tax authority may be able to re-open earlier years and collect back taxes owed.

Powers of entry and search

Where the tax authority believes fraud has occurred, it can obtain warrants to enter a business's premises and seize the records.

Exchange of information with tax authorities in other jurisdictions

This has become very important as a counter-terrorism measure in recent years. One tax authority may become aware of funds being moved to another country in suspicious circumstances. It will then warn the tax authority in that other jurisdiction. Exchange of information is also useful in dealing with drug smuggling and money laundering.

(c)   If a company makes payments to an individual or another company resident in a different tax jurisdiction, it may have to pay **withholding tax** to the tax authority of its own jurisdiction.

The reason for this is to stop companies paying all their earnings abroad and then stopping trading without paying any tax to the tax authorities of the country where they are resident. Therefore the local tax authority will take a payment on account of the final tax liability by deducting at source a withholding tax from all payments sent abroad. The withholding tax can be as low as 5% or as high as 40%.

Payments affected are usually interest payments or dividends.

> **Alternative answers**. You would also have scored marks for stating royalties or capital gains accruing to non-residents.

(d)   Double taxation agreements

A company is taxed in the country it is resident in for tax purposes. Tax residency can be determined in different ways in different jurisdictions, so that a company may find itself deemed to be resident in two different countries. For example if a company is legally incorporated in one country, but has its place of effective management in another country, it may be deemed resident in both countries and its income may be taxed in both countries – ie it may suffer double taxation.

Countries need double taxation agreements to determine which country such tax a company's income in this kind of situation. Double taxation agreements also specify what kind of reliefs are available to companies who have a taxable presence in more than one country.

Methods of giving relief

One way is to give full **deduction** for foreign taxes paid. However this is not always appropriate, particularly if the country where the tax is paid has a high tax rate and the other has a low rate.

Relief may be given by **exemption**. In this case, if income is taxed in Country A, then it will not be taxed in Country B.

Another way of giving relief is by **credit**. This usually occurs where the tax rate in Country A is higher than that in Country B. Instead of deducting the full amount of tax paid in Country A, Country B credits the amount it would have paid in Country B. For example, the income is $10,000 and the tax rate in Country A is 30%, while that in Country B is 20%. The tax paid in Country A will be $3,000 but the double tax relief allowed in Country B will be $2,000 (20% × $10,000).

(e)

> **Examiner's comments.** Most candidates were able to explain the meaning of avoidance and evasion, with fewer highlighting the difference between them. Some candidates gave odd examples of tax avoidance, such as 'claiming capital allowances' or 'claiming loss relief'. These are not examples of tax avoidance, they are proper application of the tax legislation and are not 'loopholes'.
>
> Several candidates stated that giving double taxation relief on overseas profits was a means of preventing tax avoidance, which is incorrect.
>
> Many candidates did not give enough examples or sufficient detail within the examples to earn full marks.

(i)   **Tax avoidance** is successful tax planning. It is arranging the financial affairs of an individual or an entity in such a manner as to minimise tax liability. It is perfectly legal.

Tax evasion is the use of illegal means to avoid paying tax, such as not declaring income, claiming deduction for non-deductible expense, or contravening tax legislation.

(ii)   Although only evasion is illegal, avoidance is just as much of a problem for government. Methods that governments can use to reduce avoidance and evasion are:

- Anti-avoidance legislation. This outlaws specific avoidance schemes.
- Deducting tax at source such as the PAYE system in the UK.
- Keeping the tax system as simple as possible to minimise the number of factors that can be manipulated.
- Making sure that penalties for evasion are high enough to act as a deterrent.
- Increasing the efficiency of the tax collection and investigation machinery.
- Having a tax system which is not generally perceived as unfair. An unfair system makes people feel justified in avoiding tax.

47   Section B answers: Taxation III

(a)   **Deferred tax – disclosure and note**

	$m
Temporary differences on non-current assets	0.56
Provision at 30 April 20X3	0.69
Deferred tax credit in income statement	(0.13)
Provision at 30 April 20X4	0.56

Working

Deferred tax

	$m
Temporary difference at 30 April 20X3	2.30
Temporary difference at 30 April 20X4	2.00
Deferred tax at 30 April 20X3 (2.30 × 30%)	0.69
Deferred tax at 30 April 20X4 (2.00 × 28%)	0.56
Reduction in deferred tax provision	0.13

Alternative approach

The reduction in provision is made up of two elements.

	$m
Reversal of temporary differences ((2.30 – 2.00) × 30%)	0.09
Change in tax rate (2.00 × (30% – 28%))	0.04
	0.13

(b)   **Tax on profit on ordinary activities – note to income statement**

	$m
Current tax	
Tax on profit for the period	1.40
Overprovision for previous period ($750,000 – $720,000)	(0.03)
Deferred tax	
Increase in provision ($300,000 – $250,000)	0.05
Total tax charge	1.42

Statement of financial position

	$m
Payables	
Current tax	1.40
Deferred tax	0.30

(c)

	Accounting value $	Tax value $
Cost	200,000	200,000
Depreciation 20X3 – 20X5	(120,000)	(131,400)*
Balance 30 September 20X5	80,000	68,600
Disposal proceeds	(60,000)	(60,000)
Loss	20,000	8,600

(i)   Timing difference at 30 September 20X5 (80,000 – 68,600) = 11,400

Tax at 20% = 2,280

(ii)   The carrying value of the asset at 30 September 20X6 is $80,000. Disposal at $60,000 will give rise to an accounting loss of $20,000.

(iii)   At the date of disposal the tax WDV of the asset is $68,600. Disposal at $60,000 gives rise to a balancing allowance of $8,600.

* (60,000 + 42,000 + 29,400)

(d)

Year ended	Cost	Depreciation	Tax allowance
31.3.X4	250,000	50,000	125,000
31.3.X5	250,000	50,000	31,250
		100,000	156,250

(i)   Deferred tax balance: 31.3.X4: (125,000 – 50,000) × 30% = $22,500
(ii)   Deferred tax balance: 31.3.X5: (156,250 – 100,000) × 30% = $16,875
(iii)   Income statement credit: year ended 31.3.X5 = (22,500 – 16,875) = $5,625

(e)

	$
Profit before tax	29,800
Gain on disposal	(4,000)
Depreciation	14,200
	40,000
Capital allowances:	
Buildings (80,000 × 5%)	(4,000)
Plant and equipment – first year (30,000 × 50%)	(15,000)
– disposal balancing allowance (11,812 – 5,000)	(6,812)
Taxable profit	14,188
Tax due for year ended 30 April 20X8 at 20%	2,838

48 Mixed objective test questions bank 1

1   D   Tax evasion is a way of paying less tax by illegal methods

             Tax avoidance is a way of arranging your affairs to take advantage of the tax rules to pay as little tax as possible, and is legal.

2   D

	$
Accounting profit	72,000
Add: disallowable expenditure: entertaining	15,000
book depreciation	12,000
	99,000
Less: tax allowable depreciation (40,000 × 25%)	(10,000)
	89,000

             Tax at 25% × $89,000 = $22,250

3   B   The effective incidence is on B's customers.

4   C   This is a classical system of taxation as company income tax is charged on all the profits of the entity, whether distributed or not. This leads to double taxation of dividends as dividends are paid out of taxed profits and are then chargeable to personal income tax in the hands of the shareholder. Under an imputation system the shareholder would receive a tax credit for some or all of the underlying tax.

5   Understandability and Comparability

6   Any two of: Confidentiality, Integrity, Professional behaviour

7   B   The purpose of an external audit is to enable the auditor to express an opinion on whether the financial statements are prepared, in all material respects, in accordance with an identified financial reporting framework. The auditor will express this opinion using the phrases 'give a true and fair view' or 'present fairly, in all material respects'.

8   A   In accordance with IFRS 3, goodwill arising on acquisition is recognised at cost and then reviewed annually for impairment.

9   A   Per IAS 2, inventories should be measured at the lower of cost and net realisable value.

	$
Cost	2.20
Net realisable value:	
Selling price	3.50
Less additional costs for repair and sale	(1.50)
	2.00

             Therefore, inventories held at $2.00 each

             Total value 300 × $2.00 = $600

10   C   ST is a related party of Z as he is a member of key management personnel of Z

             JT is related part of Z as he is a close family member of ST.

49 Mixed objective test questions bank 2

1   C   A 'good tax' should be **convenient**, **equitable**, **certain** and **efficient** according to Adam Smith's canons of taxation.

2   D   In a progressive tax structure, the rate of tax rises as income rises.

3   B $3,461

	Carrying amount	Tax base
	$	$
Cost	60,000	60,000
Depreciation/Tax-depreciation	(12,000)	(30,000)
Balance at 31.3.X7	48,000	30,000
Depreciation/Tax-depreciation	(9,600)	(7,500)
Balance at 31.3.X8	38,400	22,500
Depreciation/Tax-depreciation	(7,680)	(5,625)
Balance at 31.3.X9	30,720	16,875

Deferred tax = 25% × (30,720 − 16,875) = $3,461

4   A   IAS 1 deals with the format of financial statements.

5   A   Timeliness is a element of relevance.

6   B   (500 x 12) − (300 x 12) = 2400 x 6/12 = $1,200 profit

7   D   A: project is not yet viable, costs are therefore research costs and cannot be capitalised

B: payment is for research and therefore cannot be capitalised

C: project is not expected to generate future economic benefits therefore costs cannot be capitalised

8   B   Interest = (24 × 6) − 106 = $38k

Sum of the digits = 6(6+1)/2 = 21

	$
Fair value	106.00
Interest (6/21 x 38)	10.86
Repayment	(24.00)
Capital balance at end of year 1	92.86
Interest (5/21 x 38)	9.05
Repayment	(24.00)
Capital balance at end of year 2	77.91

9   C   The costs of restructuring the head office do not form part of the post-tax profit or loss of the discontinued operation, or of the post-tax gain or loss recognised on the measurement to fair value less costs to sell or on the disposal of the foreign operations.

10   A $98,000

DEFERRED TAX

	$'000		$'000
Bal c/f	38	Bal b/f	27
		I/S (bal fig)	11
	38		38

CURRENT TAX

	$'000		$'000
Cash paid (bal fig)	98	Bal b/f	106
Bal c/f	119	I/S (122-11)	111
	217		217

50   Mixed Section A questions bank 1

(a)   (i)   Determining corporate residence is important as corporate income tax is usually **residency-based**.

If an entity is deemed to be resident in a country, it will usually have to pay corporate income tax in that country.

(ii)   Determining the corporate residence of ATOZ will depend on the tax rules of the countries ATOZ is connected with. For example, if a company is incorporated in the UK, it is usually deemed to be resident in the UK for tax purposes. However, if a company is incorporated overseas but its main place of management is the UK, it could also be deemed to be resident in the UK.

If a company has a presence in more than one country, it could be deemed by local law to be resident in all of those countries, and therefore it could be taxed more than once on the same income.

Where this is the case, the OECD's model tax convention suggests that the company will be deemed to be resident in the country in which it has its place of effective management.

Therefore ATOZ will be deemed to be resident in NOP according to the OECD's model.

(b) (i) A single stage sales tax is chargeable once in the supply chain, usually at the point of sale to the end customer. The tax paid is not recoverable.

However, VAT is chargeable and deductible at different points in the supply chain. Tax paid by an entity at one point in the supply chain is usually recoverable by deducting it from the tax charged at the next point in the supply chain. The end consumer therefore bears all the VAT.

(ii) Net VAT due = output VAT – input VAT

	$'000
Output VAT	
Standard rate ($230k × 15/115)	30
Zero rate ($115k @ 0%)	0
	30
Input VAT	
Purchases ($130 × 15%)	(19.5)
Equipment ($345k × 15/115)	(45.0)
	(64.5)
Net VAT due to WX	(34.5)

(c) The possible advantages of having accounting standards based on principles are as follows.

- Standards based on principles **don't go out of date** in the same way as those based on rules. For instance, the expenditure RS is concerned with may be a new type of expenditure that wasn't often incurred when the prescriptive standard was originally drafted, and therefore wasn't included. In a principles based standard, this wouldn't be a problem as the spirit of the standard would need to be applied to see if the expenditure should be recognised as an asset.

- It is more difficult for a company to **manipulate information** to avoid applying a standard based on principles than it is for a standard based on rules. For example, if the standard included a specific value that had to be reached in order to be recognised as an asset, then the company could manipulate its expenditure to fall just below this value to avoid recognition.

- Standards based on principles have **broader application** than those based on rules. For example RS's expenditure was not included in the list of items in the rules-based standard and so it is not clear whether the item should be capitalised or not. This would not be the case in principles-based standards as professional judgment would be applied to determine how the expenditure should be treated.

- Standards based on principles are **less likely to contradict each other** than those based on rules as they are all based on the same basic principles. For example, a rules-based standard may require revenues and expenditures to be matched in an entirely different manner depending on which industry they were generated in.

- Standards based on rules require that many detailed standards covering all possible situations have to be produced. This can result in **complexity in financial reporting** as there are a considerable number of standards to be followed. Having standards based on principles avoids this.

(d) *Held for sale*

Provided that the manufacturing facility is being marketed for a reasonable price and it is unlikely that the plan to sell should change, the manufacturing facility should be classified as **'held for sale'** in the financial statements because it meets the criteria detailed in IFRS 5:

(i)   The facility is available for immediate sale

(ii)   The sale is highly probable (ie management are committed to the plan, are actively engaged in finding a purchaser and expect the sale to take place within one year)

In the statement of financial position, the manufacturing facility should be **measured at the lower of its carrying value and fair value less costs to sell**.

It should be presented **separately from other assets**, and the assets and liabilities should not be offset:

	$m
Non-current assets held for sale ($3.6m – $0.2m)	3.4
Liabilities associated with non-current assets held for sale	0.8

Discontinued Operation

As the manufacturing facility is held for sale and represents a separate major line of business (apparent as it is classified as a reportable segment per IFRS 8), it should be classified as a **discontinued operation** per IFRS 5.

BD should disclose a **single amount in the statement of comprehensive income** for the discontinued operation, which is the total of:

(i)   The loss for the year of ($0.5m)

(ii)   The post-tax gain or loss recognised on the measurement to fair value less costs to sell of the manufacturing facility.

BD should give detailed analysis of this figure either in the notes to the accounts or on the face of the statement of comprehensive income.

Additionally, net operating, investing and financing cash flows associated with the manufacturing facility should be disclosed separately in the statement of cash flows or in the notes.

(e)   *Office lease*

The office lease should be treated as an **operating lease** under IAS 17 because substantially all the risks and rewards of ownership are not passed to C under the lease. For example, the length of the lease is significantly less than the useful life of the office, and the minimum lease payments are significantly less than the fair value of the office at the inception of the lease.

The lease rentals should be recognised on a **straight line basis** over the lease term. The rent free period should be recognised as a discount over the whole lease term.

Expense at 31 March 20X9:   (4 × 12,000)/5 = $9,600

No asset is recognised for the office.

Computer system lease

The computer system lease should be treated as a **finance lease** under IAS 17 because substantially all the risks and rewards of ownership are passed to C under the lease. For example, the computer system is leased for the whole of its useful life and the minimum lease payments are equivalent to the cost of the assets on inception of the lease.

The finance costs associated with the lease will be accounted for under the actuarial method:

		$
1.4.X8	Cost	35,720
	Interest at 12.5%	4,465
	Lease payment	(15,000)
31.3.X9		25,185
	Interest at 12.5%	3,148
	Lease payment	(15,000)
31.3.Y0		13,333
	Interest at 12.5%	1,666
	Lease payment	(15,000)
31.3.Y1		0

At 31 March 20X9, C will have the following entries in its financial statements:

STATEMENT OF COMPREHENSIVE INCOME (extract) $
Administrative expenses
    Office lease rental   9,600
    Depreciation – computer system (35,720/3)   11,907
Finance costs
    Interest on finance lease   4,465

STATEMENT OF FINANCIAL POSITION (extract) $
Assets
Computer systems (35,720 – 35,720/3)   23,813

Non-current liabilities
Finance lease   13,333

Current liabilities
Finance lease (25,185 – 13,333)   11,852
Rent payable   9,600

(f)   (i)   The treatment of preference shares under IAS 32 and IAS 39 depends on the contractual terms of the preference share.

        If the terms of the preference share mean that the issuer has an **obligation** to deliver cash or other financial assets in the future, the preference share is classified as a **financial liability** under IAS 32. Under IAS 39, the finance cost of the preference shares, which includes any dividends payable and any redemption amount payable, should be calculated and then allocated over the life of the preference shares using the effective interest method.

        If the terms of the preference share mean that the issuer does not have an obligation to deliver cash or other financial assets in the future, the preference share is classified as equity under IAS 32.

   (ii)   The preference shares are redeemable and cumulative so PS has an **obligation** to deliver cash in the future. Therefore the preference shares should be classified as a **financial liability**. The finance cost associated with the preference shares (ie the outstanding balance multiplied by the effective interest rate) should be shown in the statement of comprehensive income.

        STATEMENT OF FINANCIAL POSITION AS AT 31 MARCH 20X9
                                        $

        Non-current liabilities
        Preference shares   1,211,642

        STATEMENT OF COMPREHENSIVE INCOME FOR YEAR ENDED 31 MARCH 20X9
                                          $
        Finance cost   61,642

51 Mixed Section B questions bank 2

(a)   Tax avoidance is a way of arranging your affairs to take advantage of the tax rules to pay as little tax as possible. It is perfectly legal. Cee has avoided tax by taking expert tax advice and investing her money in a tax efficient way in order to pay less tax.

      Tax evasion is a way of paying less tax by illegal methods, eg not declaring the income or money laundering. Gee has evaded tax by not declaring all the income he earns on his annual tax return and so reducing his tax bill.

(b)   (i)   Unit taxes are taxes based on the number or weight of items, eg excise duties on cigarettes or tobacco. W pays a unit tax of $1 per bottle when the wine is bottled.

        Ad valorem taxes are taxes based on the value of the items, eg a sales tax or value added tax and are usually expressed as a percentage of the value. For example, W charges VAT at 15% on each bottle of wine sold for $8.05, therefore each bottle costs $7 plus VAT at 15% = $1.05.

(ii)   Net VAT due = output VAT – input VAT

	$'000
Output VAT	
Standard rate ($1.05 × 10,000)	10.5
Input VAT	
Purchases ($30,000 × 15%)	(4.5)
	6.0
Unit tax (10,000 x $1)	10.0
Total indirect tax due	16.0

(c)   **Jurisdiction** relates to the power of a tax authority to charge and collect tax. **Competent jurisdiction** is the authority whose tax laws apply to an entity or person. The competent jurisdiction is usually the tax authority in the country where the entity is deemed to be resident for tax purposes.

The OCED Model Tax Convention suggests that a company is deemed resident in the place of its effective management. As the senior management of H meet regularly in Country X, H will be deemed to be resident in Country X and will be subject to the tax laws of the tax authority in Country X. Similarly, S will be deemed resident in Country Y and will be subject to the tax laws of the tax authority in Country Y.

A **withholding tax** is a tax that is deducted by the local tax authorities when an entity resident in that country pays funds overseas, for example when a subsidiary pays a dividend to a foreign parent. The 10% tax charged by Country Y on the dividend declared by S is a withholding tax.

The dividend will be taxed twice because it will be included in the worldwide income of H and so taxed in Country X. However, because Country Y and Country X have a **double taxation agreement**, it is likely that H will be able to get **tax relief** for the withholding tax suffered.

(d)   (i)   The objective of an audit of financial statements is to enable the auditor to express an opinion on whether the financial statements are prepared, in all material respects, in accordance with an identified financial reporting framework.

        (ii)   Inventory is overstated by $1m. The required adjustment is:

DR	Profit before tax	$1m
CR	Inventory (SOFP)	$1m

The adjustment represents 25% of profit and therefore is a material misstatement.

If the directors refuse to amend the financial statements for this misstatement, then the auditors should issue a **qualified opinion**. An adverse opinion is not required as the misstatement is not pervasive.

The qualified opinion paragraph should state that the financial statements give a true and fair view except for the identified misstatement relating to the overstatement of closing inventory.

(e)   **Year to 31.3.X8 – 35% complete**

Expected profit/(loss) on contract:

	As at 31.03.X8	As at 31.03.X9
	$'000	$'000
Total revenue	63	63
Costs to date	(18)	(44)
Costs to complete	(36)	(20)
Expected profit/(loss)	9	(1)

As at 31.03.X9, 75% (35% + 40%) complete:

	Total to 31.03.X9
	$'000
Revenue (63 x 75%)	47.3
Costs (64 x 75%)	(48.0)
Expected loss (bal fig)	(0.3)
Profit/(loss)	(1.0)

Amounts to be included in statement of comprehensive income for year to 31.03.X9:

	Year to 31.03.X9
	$'000
Revenue (47.3 – 22)	25.3
Costs (48 – 18)	(30.0)
Expected loss	(0.3)
Profit/(loss) ((1) – 4)	(5.0)

Amounts to be included in statement of financial position at 31.03.X9:

Current assets

Gross amount due from customer

	31.03.X9
	$'000
Costs incurred to date (26 + 18)	44
Less: recognised profits less recognised losses (4 – (5))	(1)
	43
Less: progress billings to date (22 + 15)	(37)
Amount due from customer	6

(f)   **Briefing note – treatment of shoe factory**

Exclusion of factory results

It would not be in line with IFRSs to completely exclude from the financials statements the results of the factory for the year. To do so would distort the overall results of the company, making it look more profitable than it currently is and thereby **misleading** users of the accounts. This would be **unethical**. Completely excluding the results of the factory would breach the fundamental principles of the CIMA Code of Ethics for accountants to demonstrate **professional behaviour** in complying with the relevant laws and standards, and also to act with **integrity** (ie honesty) in their work.

Appropriate treatment of the factory

If the factory is classified as a discontinued operation per IFRS 5, then the loss made by the factory in the year is separately disclosed in the statement of comprehensive income, after profit from continuing operations. This would make it clear to users that the factory, although loss making, will not be part of future operations.

To be classified as a discontinued operation, the factory must firstly have either been disposed of or classified as **held for sale** under IFRS 5. To be classified as held for sale, the factory must be available for sale in its present condition and the sale must be **highly probable**. Because management have not yet committed to a plan to find a buyer for the factory, the sale is not highly probable. Therefore, the factory cannot be classified as held for sale or as a discontinued operation.

As such, management must disclose the full loss made by the factory within **continuing operations** in the statement of comprehensive income.

MOCK EXAMS

CIMA

Financial Pillar

F1 – Financial Operations

Mock Exam 1

Question Paper
You are allowed three hours to answer this question paper.
You are allowed 20 minutes reading time *before the examination begins* during which you should read the question paper and, if you wish, highlight and/or make notes on the question paper.
You are strongly advised to carefully read ALL the question requirements before attempting the question concerned (that is all parts and/or sub-questions).
You should show all working as marks are available for the method you use.
ALL QUESTIONS ARE COMPULSORY
Section A comprises of 10 sub-questions.
Section B comprises of 6 sub-questions.
Section C comprises of 2 questions.
The country 'Tax Regime' for the paper is provided on the next page.

DO NOT OPEN THIS PAPER UNTIL YOU ARE READY TO START UNDER EXAMINATION CONDITIONS

Country X – Tax regime for use throughout the examination paper

Relevant tax rules

Corporate Profits

Unless otherwise specified, only the following rules for taxation of corporate profits will be relevant, other taxes can be ignored:

(a)   Accounting rules on recognition and measurement are followed for tax purposes.

(b)   All expenses other than depreciation, amortisation, entertaining, taxes paid to other public bodies and donations to political parties are tax deductible.

(c)   Tax depreciation is deductible as follows:

- 50% of additions to property, plant and equipment in the accounting period in which they are recorded

- 25% per year of the written-down value (i.e. cost minus previous allowances) in subsequent accounting periods except that in which the asset is disposed of

- No tax depreciation is allowed on land

(d)   The corporate tax on profits is at a rate of 25%.

Value Added Tax

Country X has a VAT system which allows entities to reclaim input tax paid. In country X the VAT rates are:

Zero rated	0%
Standard rated	15%

SECTION A – 20 marks

Answer ALL sub-questions in this section

Question 1

1.1 A has a taxable profit of $100,000. The book depreciation was $10,000 and the tax allowable depreciation was $25,000. What was the accounting profit? **(2 marks)**

1.2 Company W is resident in country X and makes an accounting profit of $300,000 during the year. This includes non-taxable income of $10,000 and depreciation of $35,000. In addition, $5,000 of the expenses are for entertaining. If the tax allowable depreciation totals $30,000, what is the taxable profit?

    A $290,000
    B $295,000
    C $300,000
    D $310,000   **(2 marks)**

1.3 Which of the following is a source of tax rules?

    A   International accounting standards
    B   Supranational tax agreements
    C   Local company legislation
    D   Domestic accounting practice   **(2 marks)**

1.4 Company E is resident in Country X and has sales of $230,000, excluding sales tax, in a period. Its purchases total $113,000, including sales tax. Purchases of $10,000 are zero rated. What is the sales tax payable for the period?

    A $14,550
    B $17,550
    C $19,050
    D $21,065   **(2 marks)**

1.5 A company is resident in Country X. It has a branch in Country Y. The branch has taxable profits of $100,000, on which tax of $15,000 is paid. There is a double taxation treaty between Countries X and Y that allows tax relief on the credit basis. If the company has total taxable profits, including those of the branch, of $150,000, how much tax will it pay in Country X?

    A $12,500
    B $22,500
    C $25,000
    D $37,500   **(2 marks)**

1.6 IAS 10 *Events after the reporting period* distinguishes between adjusting and non-adjusting events.

Which of the following is an adjusting event?

    A   One month after the year end, a customer lodged a claim for $1,000,000 compensation. The customer claimed to have suffered permanent mental damage as a result of the fright she had when one of the entity's products malfunctioned and exploded. The outcome of the court case cannot be predicted at this stage.

    B   There was a dispute with the workers and all production ceased one week after the year end.

    C   A fire destroyed all of the entity's inventory in its furnished goods warehouse two weeks after the year end.

    D   Inventory valued at the year end at $20,000 was sold one month later for $15,000.   **(2 marks)**

1.7   X signed a finance lease agreement on 1 October 20X2. The lease provided for five annual payments, in arrears, of $20,000. The fair value of the asset was agreed at $80,000.

Using the sum of digits method, how much should be charged to the statement of comprehensive income for the finance cost in the year to 30 September 20X3?

A $4,000
B $6,667
C $8,000
D $20,000   (2 marks)

1.8   D purchased an item of plant on 1 April 20X0 for $200,000. The plant attracted writing down tax allowances and depreciation was 10% on the straight-line basis.

The deferred tax balance for this item of plant at 31 March 20X3 is:

A $7,500
B $20,938
C $22,500
D $83,750   (2 marks)

1.9   C started work on a contract to build a dam for a hydro-electric scheme. The work commenced on 24 October 20X1 and is scheduled to take four years to complete. C recognises profit on the basis of the certified percentage of work completed. The contract price is $10 million.

An analysis of C's records provided the following information:

Year to 30 September	20X2	20X3
Percentage of work completed and certified in year	30%	25%
	$'000	$'000
Total cost incurred during the year	2,900	1,700
Estimated cost of remaining work to complete contract	6,000	3,900
Total payments made for the cost incurred during the year	2,500	2,000

How much profit should C recognise in its statement of comprehensive income for the years ended:

	30 September 20X2	30 September 20X3
	$'000	$'000
A	100	375
B	330	375
C	330	495
D	500	825

(2 marks)

1.10   S announced a rights issue of 1 for every 5 shares currently held, at a price of $2 each. S currently has 2,000,000 $1 ordinary shares with a quoted market price of $2.50 each. Directly attributable issue costs amounted to $25,000.

Assuming all rights are taken up and all money paid in full, how much will be credited to the share premium account for the rights issue?

A $200,000
B $308,333
C $375,000
D $400,000   (2 marks)

(Total for Section A = 20 marks)

SECTION B – 30 marks

Answer ALL six sub-questions

Question 2

(a) At the beginning of the accounting period, D had a credit balance of $40,000 on its current tax account, which was paid during the period. The opening balance on the deferred tax account was $250,000 credit.

The provision for tax for the current period is $50,000 and the balance on the deferred tax account is to be reduced to $225,000.

Required

Prepare extracts from the statement of comprehensive income, statement of financial position and notes to the accounts showing these tax related items

(Total for sub-question (a) = 5 marks)

(b) IAS 12 *Income taxes* requires entities to publish an explanation of the relationship between taxable income and accounting profit. This can take the form of a numerical reconciliation between the tax expense and the product of the accounting profit and the applicable tax rate. Explain why this explanation is helpful to the readers of financial statements.

(Total for sub-question (b) = 5 marks)

(c) Discuss the usefulness of the audit report to a potential investor.

(Total for sub-question (c) = 5 marks)

The following data are to be used to answer questions (d) and (e)

The financial statements of GK for the year to 31 October 20X8 were as follows:

STATEMENT OF FINANCIAL POSITION AT	31 October 20X8		31 October 20X7	
	$'000	$'000	$'000	$'000
Assets				
Non-current tangible assets				
Property	10,000		10,500	
Plant and equipment	5,000	15,000	4,550	15,050
Current assets				
Inventory	1,750		1,500	
Trade receivables	1,050		900	
Cash and cash equivalents	310		150	
		3,110		2,550
Total assets		18,110		17,600

Equity and liabilities

Ordinary shares @ $.050 each	6,000		3,000	
Share premium	2,500		1,000	
Revaluation reserve	3,000		3,000	
Retained earnings	1,701		1,000	
		13,201		8,000

Non-current liabilities

Interest-bearing borrowings	2,400		7,000	
Deferred tax	540	2,940	450	7,450

Current liabilities

Trade and other payables	1,060		1,400	
Tax payable	909		750	
		1,969		2,150
		18,110		17,600

STATEMENT OF COMPREHENSIVE INCOME FOR THE YEAR 31 OCTOBER 20X8

	$'000	$'000
Revenue		16,000
Cost of sales		10,000
Gross profit		6,000
Administrative expenses	(2,000)	
Distribution costs	(1,200)	(3,200)
		2,800
Finance cost		(600)
Profit		2,200
Income tax expense		(999)
Profit for the year		(1,201)

Additional information:

1   Trade and other payables comprise:

	31 October 20X8	31 October 20X7
	$'000	$'000
Trade payables	730	800
Interest payable	330	600
	1,060	1,400

2   Plant disposed of in the year had a net book value of $35,000; cash received on disposal was $60,000.

3   GK's statement of comprehensive income includes depreciation for the year of $1,110,000 for properties and $882,000 for plant and equipment.

4   Dividends paid during the year were $500,000.

(d)   Using the data relating to GK above, calculate the cash generated from operations that would appear in GK's statement of cash flows, using the indirect method, for the year ended 31 October 20X8, in accordance with IAS 7 *Statement of cash flows*

(Total for sub-question (d) = 5 marks)

(e)   Using the data relating to GK above, calculate the cash flow from investing activities and cash flows from financing activities sections of GK's statement of cash flows for the year ended 31 October 20X8, in accordance with IAS 7 *Statement of cash flows* .

(Total for sub-question (e) = 5 marks)

(f)   IAS 8 *Accounting policies, changes in accounting estimates and errors* distinguishes between accounting policies and accounting estimates. Explain the distinction between accounting policies and accounting estimates, give an example of each and explain their treatment under IAS 8.

(Total for sub-question (f) = 5 marks)

(Total for Section B = 30 marks)

SECTION C – 50 marks

Answer BOTH of these questions

Question 3

HI, listed on its local stock exchange, is a retail organisation operating several retail outlets. A reorganisation of the entity was started in 20X2 because of a significant reduction in profits. This reorganisation was completed during the current financial year.

The trial balance for HI at 30 September 20X3 was as follows:

	$'000	$'000
Retained earnings at 30 September 20X2		1,890
Administrative expenses	715	
Bank and cash	1,409	
Buildings	11,200	
Cash received on disposal of equipment		11
Cost of goods sold	3,591	
Distribution costs	314	
Equipment and fixtures	2,625	
Interim ordinary dividend paid	800	
Inventory at 30 September 20X3	822	
Investment income received		37
Available-for-sale investments at market value 30 September 20X2	492	
Ordinary shares of $1 each, fully paid		5,000
Provision for deferred tax		256
Provision for reorganisation expenses at 30 September 20X2		1,010
Allowances for depreciation at 30 September 20X2		
Buildings		1,404
Equipment and fixtures		1,741
Reorganisation expenses	900	
Revaluation surplus		172
Sales revenue		9,415
Share premium		2,388
Trade payables		396
Trade receivables	852	
	23,720	23,720

Additional information provided

(a) The reorganisation expenses relate to a comprehensive restructuring and reorganisation of the entity that began in 20X2. HI's financial statements for 20X2 included a provision for reorganisation expenses of $1,010,000. All costs had been incurred by the year end, but an invoice for $65,000, received on 2 October 20X3, remained unpaid and is not included in the trial balance figures. No further restructuring and reorganisation costs are expected to occur and the provision is no longer required.

(b) Available-for-sale investments are carried in the financial statements at market value. The market value of the available-for-sale investments at 30 September 20X3 was $522,000. There were no movements in the investments held during the year.

(c) On 1 November 20X3, HI was informed that one of its customers, X, had ceased trading. The liquidators advised HI that it was very unlikely to receive payment of any of the $45,000 due from X at 30 September 20X3.

(d) Another customer is suing for damages as a consequence of a faulty product. Legal advisers are currently advising that the probability of HI being found liable is 75%. The amount payable is estimated to be the full amount claimed of $100,000.

(e) The income tax due for the year ended 30 September 20X3 is estimated at $1,180,000 and the deferred tax provision needs to be increased to $281,000.

(f) During the year, HI disposed of old equipment for $11,000. The original cost of this equipment was $210,000 and accumulated depreciation at 30 September 20X2 was $205,000. HI's accounting policy is to charge no depreciation in the year of the disposal.

(g) Depreciation is charged using the straight-line basis on non-current assets as follows.

Buildings	3%
Equipment and fixtures	20%

Depreciation is regarded as a cost of sales.

Required

Prepare the statement of comprehensive income for HI for the year to 30 September 20X3 and a statement of financial position at that date, in a form suitable for presentation to the shareholders, in accordance with the requirements of IFRS.

Notes to the financial statements are **not** required.   **(25 marks)**

Question 4

The draft statements of financial position of Hornet, its subsidiary company Wasp and its associate Ant at 31 October 20X5 are as follows.

	Hornet	*Wasp*	*Ant*
	$'000	*$'000*	*$'000*
Assets			
Non-current assets			
Land and buildings	315,000	278,000	145,000
Plant	145,000	220,000	55,000
	460,000	498,000	200,000
Investment			
Shares in Ant at cost	100,000		
Current assets			
Inventory	357,000	252,000	52,000
Receivables	375,000	126,000	78,000
Bank	208,000	30,000	10,000
	940,000	408,000	140,000
	1,500,000	906,000	340,000
Equity and liabilities			
Equity			
$1 ordinary shares	700,000	600,000	200,000
Retained earnings	580,000	212,000	80,000
	1,280,000	82,000	280,000
Current liabilities			
Payables	220,000	94,000	60,000
Total equity and liabilities	1,500,000	906,000	340,000

The following information is also available.

(a) Hornet purchased all 600 million shares in Wasp on 1 November 20X4 for a consideration of $0.25 per share plus 1 new $1 share issued in Hornet for every 2 shares in Wasp. At the date of acquisition, Wasp had a credit balance of $150 million in retained earnings. The acquisition has not been reflected in the books of Hornet as at 31 October 20X5.

(b) Each $1 share in Hornet had a fair value of $2.5 on 1 November 20X4.

(c) Hornet purchased 30% of the shares in Ant some time ago for $100 million. The retained earnings of Ant at that date were $60 million. Hornet's investment in Ant is deemed to be impaired by $10 million at 31 October 20X5.

(d)   At the date of acquisition, the property, plant and equipment of Wasp was valued at $70 million in excess of its carrying value. The valuation was attributable to:

   –   freehold land, valued at $40 million in excess of carrying value.

   –   freehold properties, valued at $30 million in excess of carrying value. The properties had a useful life of 20 years from the date of acquisition of Wasp and are measured at depreciated cost in Wasp's own financial statements at 31 October 20X5.

   The revaluations were not recorded in the accounts of Wasp.

(e)   Wasp's inventory includes goods purchased from Hornet at a price that includes a profit to Hornet of $12 million.

(f)   At 31 October 20X5 Wasp owes Hornet $25 million for goods purchased during the year.

Required

(a)   Calculate the goodwill on acquisition of Wasp.   **(5 marks)**

(b)   Prepare the consolidated statement of financial position for Hornet as at 31 October 20X5.   **(20 marks)** (Show clearly any workings.)

(Total = 25 marks)

(Total for Section C = 50 marks)

Answers

DO NOT TURN THIS PAGE UNTIL YOU HAVE
COMPLETED MOCK EXAM 1

A plan of attack

As you turned the page to start this exam any one of a number of things could have been going through your mind. Some of them may have been quite sensible, some of them may not.

The main thing to do is take a deep breath and do not panic. It's best to sort out a plan of attack before the actual exam so that when the invigilator tells you that you can begin and the adrenaline kicks in you are using every minute of the three hours wisely.

Your approach

This paper has three sections. The first section contains 10 multiple choice questions which are compulsory. The second has six short compulsory questions. The third has two compulsory questions totalling 50 marks.

OTs first again

However you find the paper, chances are you should **start with the objective test questions**. You should be able to do at least a few and answering them will give you a boost. **Don't even look at the other questions before doing Section A**. Remember how long to allocate to the OTs? That's right, 36 minutes.

You then have a **choice**.

- Read through and answer Section B before moving on to Section C
- Read the questions in Section C, answer them and then go back to Section B

Time spent at the start of each Section B and the Section C questions confirming the requirements and producing a plan for the answers is time well spent.

Doing the exam

Actually doing the exam is a personal experience. There is not a single *right way.* As long as you submit complete answers to the MCQs in Section A, the six Section B questions and the questions in Section C, your approach obviously works.

One approach

Having done or guessed at the MCQs, I would work straight through Section B. The possible pitfall would be getting sucked too deeply into Section B and leaving insufficient time for Section C.

So lets look at the Section B questions in the paper:

- Question (a) is a straightforward calculation of income tax liability. It would be a good idea to begin by putting the information into T accounts. Then the information just needs to be correctly presented. This can easily be done in 9 minutes.

- Question (b) is a discussion question on the relationship of accounting profit to taxable profit. Make a few notes before you start.

- Question (c) is a trap. You can probably think of lots of things to say about this and the worst thing you can do is to start writing them all down. You have 9 minutes for this, no more. Your plan (and you must have one) should be something like: 1. Ways in which it is useful 2. Limitations on its usefulness 3. Ways in which its usefulness is overestimated. Then think of the valid points you want to make in these three areas and make them briefly. Our answer does not use bullet points, but that would have been an equally valid approach.

- Questions (d) and (e) are on statements of cash flows. Don't waste time digesting the whole of the financial statements. Look at the question to see what information you need to extract and get on with it. A methodical approach is really needed here.

- Question (f) is difficult and requires a good knowledge of IAS 8. If you had trouble with it, do revise this, as it could well come up.

Having hacked your way through Section B, taking no more than 9 minutes per question, you should now be left with 90 minutes to do your Section C questions. These are worth 50 marks and you must aim to secure as many of them as possible. Read the questions **twice** if you need to.

For the Section C Questions you must proceed in a methodical way. Set out your formats and then work through the question requirements, doing neat, readable calculations and fill out the figures. Even if you do not finish, you will get marks for what you have done, so do the easy bits first.

Time allocation

Be disciplined. Allocate your time according to the marks available but never go over the time allocation. The last few marks in a question are the hardest to earn.

Be sure to follow the requirements. If four advantages are required, give four. No extra credit will be given for five. Two advantages will only get you half marks.

Answer all of the question. Having a go at every part of all the Section B questions you are required to do will put you in a better position to pass than, say, only doing five questions. However difficult that sixth question seems at first, there are marks to be earned.

If you have time left at the end of the exam ensure that you have attempted every part of every question. If you have, then scan through and ensure you complete any part of an answer you left earlier. Use the full three hours working towards a pass.

Marking the exam

When you mark your exam, be honest. Don't be too harsh though. Give yourself credit for the things you did well, but don't kid yourself with 'I would have done that in the real exam'. It may be worth your while making two lists; strengths and weaknesses.

Strengths will be areas of the syllabus you are confident with and also good exam technique. (Maybe you produced correct financial statement formats.)

Weaknesses will be holes in your knowledge and poor exam technique (maybe you ran out of time and couldn't answer all the requirements of the last question).

Making this list will help you focus your last days of revision on the areas which require attention whilst reminding you of the areas you excel in.

SECTION A

Question 1

1.1

		$
Taxable profit		100,000
Less: depreciation		10,000
		90,000
Add: tax allowable depreciation		25,000
Accounting profit		115,000

1.2   The correct answer is C.

	$	$
Accounting profit		300,000
Add: depreciation	35,000	
disallowed expenses (entertaining)	5,000	
		40,000
		340,000
Less: non-taxable income	10,000	
tax allowable depreciation	30,000	40,000
Taxable profit		300,000

1.3   The correct answer is B. Supranational tax agreements (eg the EU rules on sales tax) are a source of tax rules. The other options are all sources of accounting rules.

1.4   The correct answer is D.

	$
Output tax (230,000 × 15%)	34,500
Input tax ((113,000 – 10,000)/115 × 15)	13,435
Payable	21,065

1.5   The correct answer is B.

Total tax due is $37,500 ($150,000 × 25%) less double taxation relief of $15,000 (less than $100,000 × 25%), leaves $22,500 to pay.

1.6   D   The subsequent sale provides evidence of the net realisable value of the inventory as at the year end.

1.7   B $(100,000 – 80,000) \times \dfrac{5}{5+4+3+2+1} = \$20,000 \times \dfrac{5}{15}$

$$= \$6,667$$

1.8   B $20,938

	TWDV	*Carrying amount*
	$'000	$'000
01.04.20X0	200	200
Tax dep'n/Dep'n	(100)	(20)
31.03.20X1	100	180
Tax dep'n/Dep'n	(25)	(20)
31.03.20X2	75	160
Tax dep'n/Dep'n	(18.75)	(20)
31.3.20X3	56.25	140

Temporary difference 140,000 – 56,250 = 83,750

Deferred tax balance = 83,750 × 25% = $20,938

	20X2	20X3
	$'000	$'000
Costs to date	2,900	4,600
Costs to complete	6,000	3,900
Estimated total cost	8,900	8,500
Projected profit	1,100	1,500
Contract price	10,000	10,000
Completed	30%	55%
Cumulative profit	330	825
Profit recognised	330	495

1.9   C

1.10 C   Number of shares issued:

$$\frac{2,000,000}{5} = 400,000 \text{ shares}$$

	$
Issue price	2
Nominal value	1
Premium	1

	$
∴ Total premium	400,000
Less issue costs	25,000
Net to share premium	375,000

SECTION B

Question 2

Marking scheme

			Marks
(a)	Tax expense	1	
	Tax payable	1	
	Deferred tax balance	1	
	Notes	1	
	Presentation	1	
			5

	$
Statement of comprehensive income (extract)	
Tax expense (Note 1)	25,000
Statement of financial position (extract)	
Current liabilities	
Tax payable	50,000
Non-current liabilities	
Deferred tax (Note 2)	225,000

Notes to the financial statements

		$
1	*Tax expense*	
	Provision for the current period	50,000
	Decrease in deferred tax provision	(25,000)
		25,000
2	*Deferred tax*	$
	Balance brought forward	250,000
	Decrease in provision	(25,000)
	Balance carried forward	225,000

Marking scheme

		Marks
(b)	1 mark per well-presented point	5

In many sets of financial statements, there **may appear to be little relationship** between the figure reported as the profit before tax and the actual tax charge that appears in the statement of comprehensive income. In a simple tax system, the tax charge would be the reported profit multiplied by the tax rate. However this will not normally be the case in real life, due to the complexities of the tax system and the estimates and subjective decisions that the directors must make in estimating the tax charge for the year.

The purpose of the reconciliation between the actual tax charge and the reported profit multiplied by the standard rate of tax is to highlight to the users of the financial statements these estimates and judgements. This reconciliation should **clarify the effect of adjustments** such as changes in tax rates, estimated tax charges differing from final agreed tax liabilities and other factors that have affected the amount that appears as the tax charge in the statement of comprehensive income. Another factor which may affect the tax charge is deferred tax. The reconciliation will therefore draw attention to factors which may lead to an increased tax charge in the future.

			Marks
(c)	Types of report		1
	Expression of opinion		1
	Compliance with legislation and standards		1
	Cannot be expected to detect fraud		1
	May not uncover going concern issues		1
			5

Types of report

Any potential investor will of course examine a company's latest set of audited accounts and will expect to see an unqualified audit report. If the report is **qualified** she/he will ask further questions. If it is a disclaimer or an adverse report, he will probably decide to invest elsewhere.

Unqualified reports

So, assuming that the report is unqualified, how useful will it be to him? The audit report is the expression of the auditor's **opinion**. The auditor has given his opinion that the accounts present fairly the financial position of the company and comply with the relevant legislation and accounting standards. The report will state that he has sought to obtain 'reasonable assurance' that the accounts are free from 'material misstatement'.

The reason he auditor feels able to give nothing more than 'reasonable assurance' is that he did not prepare the accounts and he will not have had time to examine all of the transactions. The auditor will begin by testing the internal control system. If the internal controls appear to be effective, he will reduce the time spent on substantive testing. If fraud or errors are well-hidden, and the auditor's suspicions have not been aroused, the chances of him stumbling across the discrepancy are not that high.

Other matters

While the auditor will certainly give attention to any going concern issues, the audit report cannot be taken as any guarantee of the future viability of the entity. Nor does it assure the effectiveness or efficiency of management. These are probably the two factors which most interest an investor. The audit report is a **useful addition** to whatever other information the investor is able to obtain, but the above points mean that it cannot be used to frame an investment decision.

			Marks
(d)	Net profit before taxation	½	
	Depreciation	1	
	Profit on disposal	1	
	Finance cost	½	
	Working capital adjustments	1½	
	Cash generated from operations	½	
			5

	$'000
Net profit before taxation	2,200
Depreciation (1,110 + 882)	1,992
Profit on disposal of plant (60 – 35)	(25)
Finance cost	600
Increase in trade receivables (W)	(150)
Increase in inventories (W)	(250)
Decrease in trade payables (W)	(70)
Cash generated from operations	4,297

Working

Inventories, trade receivables and trade payables

	Inventories $'000	Trade receivables $'000	Trade payables $'000
Balance b/d	1,500	900	800
Increase/(decrease) (balancing figure)	250	150	(70)
Balance c/d	1,750	1,050	730

Marking scheme

		Marks
(e)	*Cash flows from investing activities*	
	Purchase of property, plant and equipment	1
	Proceeds from sale of plant	1
		2
	Cash flows from financing activities	
	Proceeds from share issues	1½
	Dividends paid	½
	Borrowings repaid	1
		3
		5

Cash flows from investing activities

	$'000
Purchase of property, plant and equipment (W)	(1,977)
Proceeds from sale of plant	60
Net cash used in investing activities	(1,917)

Cash flows from financing activities

	$'000
Proceeds from issue of share capital (6,000 – 3,000 + 2,500 – 1,000)	4,500
Dividends paid	(500)
Borrowings repaid (7,000 – 2,400)	(4,600)
Net cash used in financing activities	(600)

Working

Property, plant and equipment

	$'000
Balance b/d	15,050
Disposals	(35)
Depreciation (1,110 + 882)	(1,992)
	13,023
Cash paid for additions (balancing figure)	1,977
Balance c/d	15,000

Marking scheme

		Marks
(f)	Accounting policies / accounting estimates distinction	1
	Example of each	2
	Treatment of each	2
		5

Accounting policies

Accounting policies are defined in IAS 8 as the 'specific principles, bases, conventions, rules and practices adopted by an entity in preparing and presenting financial statements'. In practice, accounting policies are formulated by reference to the appropriate IAS or IFRS. They should be applied consistently from one period to the next and for all similar transactions within a period.

An example of an accounting policy would be that non-current assets are held at historical cost and depreciated over their useful lives.

Accounting estimates

In applying an accounting policy, it is often necessary to make estimates. When a non-current asset is purchased, its expected life can only be estimated. An entity may have to estimate the expected level of bad debts, the possibility of some of its inventory becoming obsolescent, the fair value of assets and liabilities.

An example of an accounting estimate would be the method by which an asset was depreciated – this is the means by which the accounting policy of depreciation is applied. So a change from straight-line to reducing balance depreciation would be accounted for as a change of accounting estimate.

Changes

Changes of accounting policy are relatively rare and should be accounted for using **retrospective restatement**. The corresponding figures for previous periods are restated, so that the new policy is applied to transactions and events as if it had always been in use. Changes of accounting estimate are accounted for using **prospective restatement** – the change of estimate is applied to the current period and to future periods if they are affected.

SECTION C

Question 3

> **Text references.** Provisions are dealt with in Chapter 9: *Miscellaneous standards*.
>
> **Top tips.** As with all Section C questions, read the requirements carefully. Notes to the accounts are not required, so you should not have wasted time preparing them. However workings need to be clear and almost a substitute for notes, for example non-current assets.
>
> **Easy marks.** Property, plant and equipment workings are important as they affect both the statement of comprehensive income and statement of financial position, so do these carefully. You may have had trouble with the reorganisation costs and the tax but, once you had handled property, plant and equipment, the rest of the statement of comprehensive income and statement of financial position would give you plenty of easy marks.

Marking scheme

	Marks
Statement of comprehensive income	
Revenue	½
Cost of sales	1
Distribution costs	½
Administrative expenses	2
Overprovision	2
Profit on disposal	1
Investment income	½
Income tax expense	2
Other comprehensive income	2
	11½
Statement of financial position	
Property, plant and equipment	3
Available for sales investments	1½
Receivables	1
Revaluation surplus	1½
Retained earnings	1½
Deferred tax	1
Other provisions	1
Taxation	1
Restructuring accrual	1½
	13
Presentation	½
	25

HI
STATEMENT OF COMPREHENSIVE INCOME FOR THE YEAR ENDED 30 SEPTEMBER 20X3

	$'000
Revenue	9,415
Cost of sales (W2)	(4,410)
Gross profit	5,005
Distribution costs	(314)
Administrative expenses (W3)	(860)
Reorganisation costs overprovision (W4)	45
Profit on disposal of asset (W1)	6
Investment income	37
Profit before tax	3,919
Income tax expense (W5)	(1,205)
Profit for the year	2,714
Other comprehensive income:	
Gain on available-for-sale investments	30
Total comprehensive income for the year	2,744

HI
STATEMENT OF FINANCIAL POSITION AS AT 30 SEPTEMBER 20X3

	$'000	$'000
Assets		
Non current assets		
Property, plant and equipment (W1)		9,856
Available-for-sale investments (W6)		522
		10,378
Current assets		
Inventory	822	
Receivables (852 – 45)	807	
Cash at bank and in hand	1,409	
		3,038
		13,416
Equity and liabilities		
Equity		
Ordinary shares of $1 each	5,000	
Share premium	2,388	
Revaluation surplus (W6)	202	
Retained earnings (1,890 + 2,714 – 800)	3,804	
		11,394
Non current liabilities		
Deferred tax	281	
Other provisions (W3)	100	
		381
Current liabilities		
Trade payables	396	
Taxation	1,180	
Accruals: restructuring (W4)	65	
		1,641
		13,416

Workings

1   *Property, plant and equipment*

		Buildings $'000	Equipment and fixtures $'000	Total $'000
Cost				
Opening balance		11,200	2,625	13,825
Additions		–	–	–
Disposals		–	(210)	(210)
		11,200	2,415	13,615
Accumulated depreciation				
Opening balance		1,404	1,741	3,145
On disposals		–	(205)	(205)
Charge for year				
• $11,200 × 3%		336	–	–
• $2,415 × 20%		–	483	819
Closing balance		1,740	2,019	3,759
Carrying value		9,460	396	9,856

Profit on disposal:

	$'000	$'000
Sale proceeds		11
Carrying value		
Cost	210	
Accumulated depreciation	(205)	
		5
Profit		6

2   *Cost of sales*

	$'000
Per trial balance	3,591
Depreciation (W1)	819
	4,410

3   *Administrative expenses*

	$'000
Per trial balance	715
Bad debt written off (Note 1)	45
Provision for legal claim re faulty product (Note 2)	100
	860

Notes

1   Although the customer went into liquidation after the year end, this provides additional evidence of conditions existing at the year end. It is thus an adjusting event under IAS 10.

2   The obligation is probable, therefore a provision must be made.

4   *Reorganisation costs*

	$'000	$'000
Provision in 20X2 accounts		1,010
Reorganisation expenses	900	
Invoice received after y/e	65	
		965
Provision surplus		45

5   *Taxation*

	$'000	$'000
Income tax payable		1,180
Deferred tax		
Provision b/fwd	256	
Provision required	281	
∴ Increase required		25
Charge to statement of comprehensive income		1,205

6   *Investments and revaluation surplus*

	Investments $'000	Revaluation surplus $'000
Per trial balance	492	172
Revaluation of investments to market value	30	30
	522	202

Question 4

Text references: The consolidated statement of financial position is covered in Chapter 14.

Top tips: There are some tricky parts to this question, including the share for share exchange and the excess depreciation you had to calculate on the fair value adjustments to buildings, however there were easy marks available in other areas. Remember to work methodically through the question and tackle the bits you are confident with first.

Easy marks: There were some easy marks here once you had the formats down correctly. Once you had calculated the unrealised profit, marks were available on receivables, payables and inventory.

Marking scheme

			Marks
(a)	Goodwill on acquisition		5
(b)	*Consolidated statement of financial position*		
	Goodwill	1	
	Land and building	3	
	Plant	½	
	Investment in associate	3	
	Inventory	1½	
	Receivables	1½	
	Bank	2	
	Share capital	2	
	Retained earnings	3½	
	Payables	1½	
	Presentation	½	
			20
			25

(a)   *Calculation of goodwill*

		$'000
Consideration transferred		
Cash (600,000 x $0.25)		150,000
Share exchange (600,000 x ½ x $2.5)		750,000
		900,000
Net assets acquired		
Share capital	600,000	
Retained earnings	150,000	
Fair value adjustment – land	40,000	
Fair value adjustment – buildings	30,000	
		820,000
Goodwill		80,000

(b) HORNET GROUP
CONSOLIDATED STATEMENT OF FINANCIAL POSITION AS AT 31 OCTOBER 20X5

	$'000	$'000
Assets		
Non-current assets		
Goodwill (a)		80,000
Land and buildings (W3)		661,500
Plant		365,000
Investment in associate (W4)		96,000
		1,202,500
Current assets		
Inventory (W2)	597,000	
Receivables (375 + 126 – 25)	476,000	
Bank (208 + 30 – 150 (a))	88,000	
		1,161,000
		2,363,500
Equity and liabilities		
$1 ordinary shares (700 + 300 (a))		1,000,000
Share premium		450,000
Retained earnings (W5)		624,500
		2,074,500
Current liabilities		
Payables (220 + 94 – 25)		289,000
Total equity and liabilities		2,363,500

Workings

1   Group structure

Hornet

100% / \ 30%

Wasp   Ant

2   Inventory

	$m	$m
Hornet		357
Wasp	252	
Less unrealised profit	(12)	
		240
		597

3   Land and Buildings

	$m	$m
Hornet		315.0
Wasp	278.0	
Land revaluation	40.0	
Buildings revaluation	30.0	
Less excess depreciation (30/20)	(1.5)	
		346.5
Total land and buildings		661.5

4   Investment in associate

	$m
Cost of investment	100
Impairment of associate	(10)
Share of post acquisition retained earnings (20 x 30%)	6
	96

5   *Retained earnings*

	Hornet $m	Wasp $m	Ant $m
Per question	580.0	212	80
Less impairment of associate	(10.0)		
Less unrealised profit	(12.0)		
Less excess depreciation	(1.5)		
Pre-acquisition		(150)	(60)
		62	20
Wasp	62.0		
Ant (20 x 30%)	6.0		
	624.5		

CIMA

Financial Pillar

F1 – Financial Operations

Mock Exam 2

Question Paper
You are allowed three hours to answer this question paper.
You are allowed 20 minutes reading time *before the examination begins* during which you should read the question paper and, if you wish, highlight and/or make notes on the question paper.
You are strongly advised to carefully read ALL the question requirements before attempting the question concerned (that is all parts and/or sub-questions).
You should show all working as marks are available for the method you use.
ALL QUESTIONS ARE COMPULSORY
Section A comprises of 10 sub-questions.
Section B comprises of 6 sub-questions.
Section C comprises of 2 questions.
The country 'Tax Regime' for the paper is provided on the next page.

DO NOT OPEN THIS PAPER UNTIL YOU ARE READY TO START UNDER EXAMINATION CONDITIONS

CIMA
Financial Pillar

F1 – Financial Operations

Mock Exam 2

Question Paper

You are allowed three hours to answer this question paper.

You are allowed 20 minutes reading time before the examination begins during which you should read the question paper and, if you wish, highlight and/or make notes on the question paper.

You are strongly advised to carefully read ALL the question requirements before attempting the question concerned (that is all parts and/or sub-questions).

You should show all workings as marks are available for the method you use.

ALL QUESTIONS ARE COMPULSORY

Section A comprises of 10 sub-questions.

Section B comprises of 6 sub-questions.

Section C comprises of 2 questions.

The country 'Tax Regime' for this paper is provided on the next page.

DO NOT OPEN THIS PAPER UNTIL YOU ARE READY TO START UNDER
EXAMINATION CONDITIONS

Country X – Tax regime for use throughout the examination paper

Relevant tax rules

Corporate Profits

Unless otherwise specified, only the following rules for taxation of corporate profits will be relevant, other taxes can be ignored:

(a)   Accounting rules on recognition and measurement are followed for tax purposes.

(b)   All expenses other than depreciation, amortisation, entertaining, taxes paid to other public bodies and donations to political parties are tax deductible.

(c)   Tax depreciation is deductible as follows:

- 50% of additions to Property, Plant and Equipment in the accounting period in which they are recorded

- 25% per year of the written-down value (i.e. cost minus previous allowances) in subsequent accounting periods except that in which the asset is disposed of

- No tax depreciation is allowed on land

(d)   The corporate tax on profits is at a rate of 25%.

Value Added Tax

Country X has a VAT system which allows entities to reclaim input tax paid. In country X the VAT rates are:

Zero rated   0%

Standard rated   15%

SECTION A – 20 marks

Answer ALL sub-questions in this section

Question 1

1.1 Which of the following statements most closely defines double taxation relief?

A   The group is treated as one entity for tax purposes
B   Losses of one group member can be offset against the profits of another.
C   Capital gains tax is deferred until an asset is sold outside the group.
D   Tax paid by a company in one country is offset against the tax due in another country.   **(2 marks)**

1.2 Company T has sales of $230,000, including sales tax, in a period. Its purchases, excluding sales tax, total $180,000, of which $20,000 are zero-rated. What is the sales tax payable for the period?

A $6,000
B $6,522
C $10,500
D $11,022   **(2 marks)**

1.3 Company P makes an accounting loss of $320,000 during the year. This includes non-taxable income of $20,000 and depreciation of $33,000. In addition, $40,000 of the expenses are disallowable for tax purposes. If the tax allowable depreciation totals $45,000, what is the taxable amount?

A $182,000 loss
B $300,000 loss
C $312,000 loss
D $328,000 loss   **(2 marks)**

1.4 An asset has to meet two recognition criteria before being recognised in financial statements. One of these is the probability that future economic benefits will flow to the entity. The other criterion is:

A   The asset has a cost or value that can be measured reliably
B   The future economic benefits will be received within the current accounting period
C   The future economic benefits can be reliably measured
D   The asset has an open market value   **(2 marks)**

1.5 Which of the following are covered by the auditors' report?

1   Statement of cash flows
2   Statement of changes in equity
3   Statement of financial position

A   All three are covered.
B   1 and 2 only
C   2 and 3 only
D   1 and 3 only   **(2 marks)**

1.6 IAS 1 *Presentation of financial statements* defines the classification of liabilities as current or non-current.

Which of the following liabilities should be included within current liabilities?

1   Loan notes issued five years ago, due for repayment within one year, which have been agreed to be refinanced on a long-term basis before the financial statements are approved

2   Trade payables due for settlement more than twelve months after the year end, within the normal course of the operating cycle

3   Trade payables due for settlement within twelve months after the year end, within the normal course of the operating cycle

4   Bank overdrafts

A   All four items
B   1, 3 and 4 only
C   1 and 2 only
D   2, 3 and 4 only   **(2 marks)**

1.7 The following figures apply to a construction contract at the end of the first year:

	$'000
Total contract price	36,000
Costs to date	10,000
Expected costs to completion	20,000
Cash received from customer	24,000

What amounts will be included as attributable profit in the statement of comprehensive income and shown under *amounts due to customers* in the statement of financial position?

	Profit $'000	Amounts due to customers $'000
A	16,000	14,000
B	6,000	14,000
C	2,000	12,000
D	6,000	12,000

(2 marks)

1.8 Which of the following statements about IAS 17 *Leases* are correct?

1   A finance lease is one which transfers substantially all the risks and rewards of the ownership of an asset to a lessee.

2   A leased asset should be depreciated over the shorter of the lease term and the useful life of the asset.

3   All obligations under finance leases will appear in the statement of financial position under the heading of 'Current liabilities'.

4   An asset held on an operating lease should appear in the lessee's statement of financial position as a non-current asset and be depreciated over the term of the lease.

A   1 and 3 only
B   1 and 2 only
C   2 and 4 only
D   All four statements are correct   **(2 marks)**

1.9　An asset with a fair value of $15,400 is acquired under a finance lease on 1 January 20X1 with a deposit on that date of $4,000 and four further annual payments in arrears of $4,000 each. The interest rate implicit in the lease is 15%.

What figure would appear in the statement of financial position at 31 December 20X1 under the heading of current liabilities?

A　$2,634
B　$4,000
C　$6,476
D　$9,110　　　　　　　　　　　　　　　　　　　　　　　　　　　　　　　　　　**(2 marks)**

1.10　Which of the following is a non-adjusting event after the reporting period in accordance with IAS 10 for financial statements prepared to 30 June 20X6 and approved on 3 October 20X6?

A　Final agreement of the price for the sale of a building which had been under contract since 28 June 20X6

B　Receipt of the financial statements for the year ended 31 May 20X6 of an unlisted company in which the business owns 10% of the share capital showing that it is going into liquidation

C　A decision made on 1 July 20X6 to close a division of the business which made significant losses in the year ending 30 June 20X6

D　Information showing that a long-term contract on which profit had been taken in the year ending 30 June 20X6 will in fact not be profitable due a defect in materials used in January 20X6

(2 marks)

(Total for Section A = 20 marks)

SECTION B – 30 marks

Answer ALL six sub-questions

Question 2

(a) Tax rules arise from four main sources. List the sources and describe two of these in detail.

(Total for sub-question (a) = 5 marks)

(b) Discuss briefly the problems encountered in attempting to regulate financial reporting in the absence of a conceptual framework.

(Total for sub-question (b) = 5 marks)

(c) Jedders Co has three long leasehold properties in different parts of the region each of which had an original life of 50 years. As at 1 January 20X0, their original cost, accumulated depreciation to date and carrying (book) values were as follows.

	Cost	Depreciation	Carrying value 1.1.20X0
	$'000	$'000	$'000
Property in North	3,000	1,800	1,200
Property in Central	6,000	1,200	4,800
Property in South	3,750	1,500	2,250

On 1 January an independent surveyor provided valuation information to suggest that the value of the South property was the same as book value, the North property had fallen against carrying value by 20% and the Central property had risen by 40% in value against the carrying value.

The directors wish to show all their properties at a revalued amount in the accounts as at 31 December 20X0.

Required

Calculate the charges to the statement of comprehensive income and the non-current asset extracts in the statement of financial position for all the properties for the year ended 31 December 20X0. You should follow the requirements of IAS 16 *Property, plant and equipment*.

(Total for sub-question (c) = 5 marks)

(d) IAS 10 distinguishes between 'adjusting' and 'non-adjusting' events.

Required

Explain what is meant by 'adjusting events' and 'non-adjusting events' and give three examples of each.

(Total for sub-question (d) = 5 marks)

(e) The International Accounting Standards Committee Foundation (IASCF) oversees a number of other International committees, two of which are the Standards Advisory Council (SAC) and the International Financial Reporting Interpretations Committee (IFRIC).

Required

Explain the role of the SAC and the IFRIC in assisting with developing and implementing International Financial Reporting Standards.

(Total for sub-question (e) = 5 marks)

(f)   GJ commenced business on 1 October 20X5 and, on that date, it acquired property, plant and equipment for $220,000. GJ uses the straight line method of depreciation. The estimated useful life of the assets was five years and the residual value was estimated at $10,000. GJ's accounting year end is 30 September.

On 1 October 20X7, GJ revalued all of its assets; this led to an increase in asset values of $53,000.

Required

Calculate the amount of the deferred tax provision that GJ should include in its statement of financial position at 30 September 20X8, in accordance with IAS 12 *Income Taxes*.

(Total for sub-question (f) = 5 marks)

(Total for Section B = 30 marks)

SECTION C – 50 marks

Answer BOTH of these questions

Question 3

The statements of financial position of YZ are given below:

STATEMENT OF FINANCIAL POSITION AT

	30 September 20X3		30 September 20X2	
	$'000	$'000	$'000	$'000
Assets				
Property, plant and equipment		634		510
Current assets				
Inventory	420		460	
Trade receivables	390		320	
Interest receivable	4		9	
Short term Investments	50		0	
Cash in bank	75		0	
Cash in hand	7		5	
		946		794
Total assets		1,580		1,304
Equity and liabilities				
Equity				
Ordinary shares $0.50 each	363		300	
Share premium account	89		92	
Revaluation surplus	50		0	
Retained earnings(loss)	93		(70)	
		595		322
Non-current liabilities				
10% loan notes	0		40	
5% loan notes	329		349	
		329		389
Current liabilities				
Bank overdraft	0		70	
Trade payables	550		400	
Income tax	100		90	
Accruals	6		33	
		656		593
Total equity and liabilities		1,580		1,304

Additional information

(a)   On 1 October 20X2, YZ issued 60,000 $0.50 ordinary shares at a premium of 100%. The proceeds were used to finance the purchase and cancellation of all its 10% loan notes and some of its 5% loan notes, both at par. A bonus issue of one for ten shares held was made on 1 November 20X2; all shares in issue qualified for the bonus.

(b)   The current asset investment was a 30 day government bond.

(c)   Property, plant and equipment include certain properties which were revalued in the year.

(d)   Property, plant and equipment disposed of in the year had a net book value of $75,000; cash received on disposal was $98,000. The balance on the disposal account has been added to sales revenue.

(e)   Depreciation charged for the year was $87,000.

(f)   The accruals balance is interest payable of $33,000 at 30 September 20X2 and $6,000 at 30 September 20X3.

(g)   Interim dividends paid during the year were $23,000.

(h)   Sales revenue for the year was reported as $2,900,000 and purchases were $1,694,000. Other expenses (not including depreciation) were $775,000. YZ earned investment income of $5,000 and finance costs for the year were $19,000. The tax charge is estimated at $104,000.

Required

Prepare the following for YZ for the year ended 30 September 20X3:

(a)   A statement of comprehensive income   **(10 marks)**
(b)   A statement of cash flows, using the indirect method   **(15 marks)**

(Total 25 marks)

Question 4

The following are the financial statements relating to Straw, a limited liability company, and its subsidiary company Berry.

STATEMENT OF COMPREHENSIVE INCOME
FOR THE YEAR ENDED 31 DECEMBER 20X5

	Straw	Berry
	$'000	$'000
Sales revenue	235,000	85,000
Cost of sales	(140,000)	(52,000)
Gross profit	95,000	33,000
Distribution costs	(12,000)	(5,000)
Administrative expenses	(45,000)	(8,000)
Dividend income from Berry	5,000	–
Profit before tax	43,000	20,000
Tax	(13,250)	(5,000)
Profit for the year	29,750	15,000

STATEMENTS OF FINANCIAL POSITION
AS AT 31 DECEMBER 20X5

	Straw		Berry	
	$'000	$'000	$'000	$'000
Assets				
Non-current assets				
Property, plant and equipment		100,000		40,000
Investments				
30,000,000 $1 ordinary shares in Berry at cost		34,000		–
		134,000		40,000
Current assets				
Inventory, at cost	13,360		3,890	
Trade receivables and dividend receivable	14,640		6,280	
Bank	3,500		2,570	
Total assets		31,500		12,740
		165,500		52,740
Equity and liabilities				
Equity				
$1 Ordinary shares		100,000		30,000
General reserve		9,200		1,000
Retained earnings		27,300		9,280
		136,500		40,280
Current liabilities				
Trade payables	9,000		2,460	
Dividend payable	20,000		10,000	
Total equity and liabilities		29,000		12,460
		165,500		52,740

Additional information

(a) Straw purchased its $1 ordinary shares in Berry on 1 January 20X1. At that date the balance on Berry's general reserve was $0.5 million and the balance of retained earnings was $1.5 million.

(b) At 1 January 20X5 the total goodwill arising from the acquisition of Berry was valued at $960,000. Straw's impairment review of this goodwill at 31 December 20X5 valued it at $800,000.

(c) During the year ended 31 December 20X5 Straw sold goods which originally cost $12 million to Berry. Straw invoiced Berry at cost plus 40%. Berry still has 30% of these goods in inventory at 31 December 20X5.

(d) Berry owed Straw $1.5 million at 31 December 20X5 for some of the goods Straw supplied during the year.

Required

(a) Calculate the goodwill arising on the acquisition of Berry. **(2 marks)**

(b) Prepare the following financial statements for Straw.

    (i) The consolidated statement of comprehensive income for the year ended 31 December 20X5.
    (8 marks)

    (ii) The consolidated statement of financial position as at 31 December 20X5. **(15 marks)**

    Disclosure notes are not required. **(Total = 25 marks)**

(Total for Section C = 50 marks)

Answers

DO NOT TURN THIS PAGE UNTIL YOU HAVE
COMPLETED MOCK EXAM 2

244

Answers

DO NOT TURN THIS PAGE UNTIL YOU HAVE
COMPLETED MOCK EXAM 2

A plan of attack

This is the second mock exam, so you will now have some feel of what you have to get done in the exam.

Your approach

This paper has three sections. All sections, and all questions, are compulsory. The first section contains 20 multiple choice questions. The second has six short questions. The third has one accounts preparation question which carries 30 marks.

Question by question

So lets look at the Section B questions in the paper:

- Question (a) is fairly easy but to score marks you must do exactly as specified in the question – list **four** and describe **two** (not one or three).

- Question (b) looks easy but is not. It is very easy to write off the point in a question like this. So before you start, list out the problems, and then briefly discuss each one.

- Question (c) is more straightforward than it looks, but you must read it carefully so that you know exactly what to do. Then write your answer out methodically.

- Question (d) should have given you no trouble as long as you were clear about what constitutes an 'adjusting event'. You are asked for three examples of each – six altogether – so do exactly that.

- Question (e) is on SAC and IFRIC. You should know enough about these to answer the questions. Don't spend too long on it.

- Question (f) needs to be written out carefully so that you don't miss any steps.

For the Section C Questions you must proceed in a methodical way. Set out your format and then work through the question requirements, doing neat, readable calculations and fill out the figures. Even if you do not finish, you will get marks for what you have done, so do the easy bits first.

Time allocation

Be disciplined. Allocate your time according to the marks available but never go over the time allocation. The last few marks in a question are the hardest to earn.

Be sure to follow the requirements. If four advantages are required, give four. No extra credit will be given for five. Two advantages will only get you half marks.

Answer all of the question. Having a go at every part of all the Section B questions you are required to do will put you in a better position to pass than, say, only doing five questions. However difficult that sixth question seems at first there are marks to be earned.

If you have time left at the end of the exam ensure that you have attempted every part of every question. If you have, then scan through and ensure you complete any part of an answer you left earlier. Use the full three hours working towards a pass.

Marking the exam

Marking the MCQs is not too difficult. You only have 2-4 marks to award. In the longer questions, give yourself credit where you used the correct method, even if your answer was wrong.

Most important, list out all the items you did not know or got wrong, and make sure you revise them.

SECTION A

Question 1

1.1 D Option A is the definition of group relief and options B and C show aspects of group relief.

1.2 A
		$
Output tax $\frac{230,000}{115} \times 15$		30,000
Input tax ((180,000 – 20,000) × 15%)		24,000
Payable		6,000

1.3 C
	$	$
Accounting loss		(320,000)
Add: depreciation	33,000	
disallowed expenses	40,000	
		73,000
		(247,000)
Less: non-taxable income	20,000	
tax allowable depreciation	45,000	
		(65,000)
Taxable loss		(312,000)

1.4 A The cost or value can be measured reliably.

1.5 A An audit report covers all three.

1.6 A Item (1) is now included as a current liability after the revision of IAS 1.

1.7 C
	$'000
Total contract price	36,000
Total expected costs (10,000 + 20,000)	30,000
Total expected profit	6,000
Profit to date = 6,000,000 × 10/30	2,000
Due to customer:	
Progress billings	24,000
Costs to date	(10,000)
Profit to date	(2,000)
Balance due to customer	12,000

1.8 B 3 Obligations under finance leases due after twelve months will be shown under *non-current* liabilities.

4 An asset held under an operating lease is *not* capitalised by the lessee.

1.9 A

FINANCE LEASE ACCOUNT

	$m		$m
20X1 1 Jan deposit	4,000	Non-current assets	15,400
31 Dec – instalment	4,000	Interest 15% × $11,400	1,710
Balance c/d	9,110		
	17,110		17,110
		Balance b/d	9,110
20X2 31 Dec – instalment	4,000	Interest 15% × 9,110	1,366

31 December 20X1

Current liabilities = 4,000 – 1,366
= $2,634

1.10   C

> <u>Theory underlying answer</u>
>
> The decision to close the division was taken after the year end and therefore does not affect the accounts for the year to 30 June 20X6 even though the division was loss-making. Option A confirms the final price of a transaction entered into before the year end and is therefore an adjusting event. Option B provides evidence of a diminution in value of an investment held at the year end and is therefore an adjusting event. Option D provides evidence that the previous estimate of accrued profit was inaccurate and therefore an adjustment should be made.

SECTION B

Question 2

Marking scheme

		Marks
(a)	4 main sources - ½ mark each	2
	Describe 2 in detail - 1½ marks each	3
		5

The four main sources are as follows.

- Domestic tax legislation and court rulings
- Domestic tax authority practice
- Supranational bodies
- International tax treaties

Domestic tax legislation and court rulings

The main source of tax rules arises from the domestic tax legislation of the country, eg in the UK, the annual Finance Act. Although the legislators try to think of all possible situations, business is always changing and so the law may have to be interpreted by the courts. This gives rise to court rulings that have the force of law.

Domestic tax authority practice

Every tax authority develops its own practice on how the law is applied. For example, UK tax law states that employees should be taxed on all 'benefits' supplied by the employer. However, in practice, certain benefits are exempted from the rules because it would be too time consuming and yield little in the way of tax.

Alternative answers. You could have chosen to explain any of the four main sources and so would have gained credit for the following.

Supranational bodies

Supranational bodies, such as the European Union (EU), can affect tax rules. The EU has a number of rules on value added or sales tax, which have to be applied by all members of the EU.

International tax treaties

Some businesses trade in many different countries of the world, so called 'multi-national' companies. This means that their profits will be subject to tax in the local countries they trade in, as well as the country where the company has its headquarters. This could mean that the company pays tax on certain profits twice. In order to avoid this 'double tax', countries enter into tax treaties which set out which country taxes the profits. These treaties also allow relief for local taxes paid, for example withholding taxes.

Marking scheme

		Marks
(b)	Define conceptual framework	1
	Problems – 1 mark for each well-explained point – max 4	4
		5

A conceptual framework provides the theoretical basis upon which financial reporting can be regulated. It establishes generally agreed-upon principles and accounting standards can be developed in accordance with this. Lack of a conceptual framework can lead to the following problems:

(i) Standards being developed in a **firefighting fashion**, in response to problems or abuses as they arise. Standards developed in this way are unlikely to be well thought-out and may need further revision as more problems are identified.

(ii) Because standards are not being developed as part of a consistent whole, there may be **conflicts** and **inconsistencies** between different standards. Also issues may be addressed in more than one standard, leading to duplication of effort and confusion.

(iii) If there is no overall framework to which reference can be made, standard setters will feel the need to cover every eventuality. This can lead to standards becoming very detailed and **prescriptive**. This has already been observed in the USA with the FASB standards.

(iv) A conceptual framework provides some sort of **protection from political pressure** from vested interests. A new standard developed as part of a conceptual framework cannot be amended in a way which will bring it into conflict with the conceptual framework.

Marking scheme

		Marks
(c)	Depreciation charges	2
	Revaluation loss	1
	Property, plant and equipment	2
		5

STATEMENT OF COMPREHENSIVE INCOME (EXTRACTS)

	$'000
Depreciation charge	
North (($1.2m × 80%)/20 years)	48
Central (($4.8m × 140%)/40 years)	168
South ($2.25m/30 years)	75
	291
Loss on revaluation of North property (20% × $1.2m)*	240
Other comprehensive income	
Gain on revaluation of Central property ($4.8m × 40%)	1,920

STATEMENT OF FINANCIAL POSITION (EXTRACTS)

	Cost/ revaluation $'000	Depreciation $'000	Carrying value $'000
North	960	48	912
Central	6,720	168	6,552
South	2,250	75	2,175
	9,930	291	9,639

It is assumed that the properties are depreciated on a straight-line basis. At 1 January 20X0 the accumulated depreciation of the Central property is $1.2m, which represents 10 years' worth of depreciation, leaving 40 years remaining life. For the South and North properties, the respective lives in these calculations are 30 and 20 years.

* It is assumed that there is no previous revaluation surplus on the North property, so the loss in the current year is classed as an impairment, and is taken to profit or loss.

Marking scheme

		Marks
(d)	Definition adjusting / non adjusting event	2
	Examples adjusting event – ½ mark each	1½
	Examples non-adjusting event – ½ mark each	1½
		5

Adjusting events are events that provide further evidence of conditions that existed at the reporting date.

Examples of adjusting events include:

(i)   The subsequent determination of the purchase price or of the proceeds of sale of non-current assets purchased or sold before the year-end

(ii)   The renegotiation of amounts owing by customers or the insolvency of a customer

(iii)   Amounts received or receivable in respect of insurance claims which were in the course of negotiation at the year end

Non-adjusting events are indicative of conditions that arose subsequent to the end of the reporting period.

Examples of non-adjusting events might be:

(i)   Losses of non-current assets or inventories as a result of a catastrophe such as fire or flood

(ii)   Closing a significant part of the trading activities if this was not begun before the year-end

(iii)   The value of an investment falls between the year end and the date the accounts are authorised

Marking scheme

		Marks
(e)	1 mark per well-presented point	5

Standards Advisory Council (SAC)

The SAC provides a forum for groups and individuals to give advice to the International Accounting Standards Board (IASB), the board responsible for setting IFRS. The committee members are from diverse geographical and functional backgrounds to allow them to gather opinions from a wide range of representatives.

The committee meets three times a year and advises the IASB on its agenda and priorities for setting new IFRS. Consultation with the SAC continues throughout the development of an IFRS. In particular, the SAC advises the IASB on issues related to the practical application and implementation of new IFRS. It also advises on the advantages and disadvantages of different proposals.

International Financial Reporting Interpretations Committee (IFRIC)

The IFRIC provides timely guidance on the application and interpretation of IFRS. It normally deals with complex accounting issues that could give rise to a diversity of accounting treatments. In this way it assists the IASB in setting and improving IFRS.

IFRIC produces interpretations which, once finalised, are ratified and issued by the IASB. The IASB may choose to add an item to its own agenda if an interpretation is not ratified.

Marking scheme

		Marks
(f)	Tax WDV	1½
	Accounting carrying value	1½
	Deferred tax provision	2
		5

Deferred tax provision = $16,865

Tax written down value:

	$
1.10.20X5 cost	220,000
2006 tax allowance 50% × 220,000	(110,000)
30.09.20X6 tax written down value	110,000
2007 tax allowance 25% × 110,000	(27,500)
30.09.20X7 tax written down value	82,500
20X8 tax allowance 25% × 82,500	(20,625)
30.09.20X8 tax written down value	61,875

Accounting carrying value:

	$
Cost	220,000
Depreciation 2 × (220,000-10,000)/5	(84,000)
30.09.20X7 accounting carrying value	136,000
	53,000
Revaluation	189,000
Depreciation $(189 – 10)/3	(59,667)
30.09.20X8 carrying value	129,333

	$
Accounting net book value	129,333
Tax written down value	(61,875)
Temporary difference	67,458
Deferred tax @ 25%	16,865

SECTION C

Question 3

Text references. Statements of cash flows are covered in Chapter 8: *IAS 7 Statement of cash flows* .

Top tips. This is fairly straightforward, especially the statement of comprehensive income, although the bonus issue may have confused you. If so, leave the more difficult calculation to the end and concentrate on those areas you can do confidently. Be methodical and don't get bogged down in one part of the question. Write out for yourself a reconciliation of the movement on share capital and share premium and you will see that the only cash flow is $60,000 from the share issue.

Easy marks Start with the statement of comprehensive income and then the cash flow proforma and get cash flows from operating activities done. You can get easy marks on all of this. You will need to do a working for property, plant and equipment, but you have done a statement of comprehensive income, so the rest of the statement of cash flows is relatively easy. If you have worked out property, plant and equipment, you will also get the marks on investing activities.

Marking scheme

		Marks
Statement of comprehensive income		
Sales revenue	1	
Cost of sales	1	
Other income	1	
Other expenses	1	
Investment income	1	
Finance cost	1	
Income tax expense	1	
Other comprehensive income	2	
Presentation	1	
		10
Statement of cash flows		
Cash flows from operating activities		
Profit before tax	1	
Finance cost	1	
Depreciation	1	
Profit on disposal	1	
Working capital adjustments - ½ each	1½	
Interest paid	1	
Income taxes paid	1	
		7½
Cash flows from investing activities		
Purchase of PPE	1½	
Proceeds of sale of PPE	1	
Interest received	1	
		3½
Cash flows from financing activities		
Proceeds from issue of share capital	1½	
Purchase of loan notes	1	
Dividends paid	1	3½
Cash and cash equivalents		½
		15
Total		25

(a) YZ
STATEMENT OF COMPREHENSIVE INCOME FOR THE YEAR TO 30 SEPTEMBER 20X3

	$'000	$'000
Sales revenue (2,900 – 23)		2,877
Cost of sales (460 + 1,694 – 420)		(1,734)
Gross profit		1,143
Other income – profit on disposal (W2)		23
Other expenses (775 + 87 (W2))		(862)
		304
Investment income (W5)	5	
Finance cost	(19)	(14)
Profit before tax		290
Income tax expense (W4)		(104)
Profit for the year		186
Other comprehensive income:		
Gain on revaluation of properties		50
Total comprehensive income for the year		236

(b) YZ
STATEMENT OF CASH FLOWS
FOR THE YEAR ENDED 30 SEPTEMBER 20X3

	$'000	$'000
Cash flows from operating activities		
Profit before tax	290	
Adjustments for		
Finance cost	14	
Depreciation	87	
Profit on disposal (W2)	(23)	
Operating profit before working capital changes	368	
Decrease in inventory (W1)	40	
Increase in receivables (W1)	(70)	
Increase in payables (W1)	150	
Cash generated from operations	488	
Interest paid (W3)	(46)	
Income taxes paid (W4)	(94)	
Net cash from operating activities		348
Cash flows from investing activities		
Purchase of property, plant and equipment (W2)	(236)	
Proceeds from sale of property, plant and equipment	98	
Interest received (W5)	10	
Net cash used in investing activities		(128)
Cash flows from financing activities		
Proceeds from issuance of share capital (W6)	60	
Repurchase of loan notes	(60)	
Dividends paid	(23)	
Net cash used in financing activities		(23)
Net increase in cash and cash equivalents		197
Cash and cash equivalents at beginning of period		(65)
Cash and cash equivalents at end of period		132

Workings

1   *Inventories, trade receivables and trade payables*

	Inventories	Trade receivables	Trade payables
	$'000	$'000	$'000
Balance b/d	460	320	400
Increase/(decrease) (balancing figure)	(40)	70	150
Balance c/d	420	390	550

2 *Property, plant and equipment*

	$'000
Balance b/d	510
Revaluation	50
Disposals	(75)
Depreciation	(87)
	398
Cash paid for additions (balancing figure)	236
Balance c/d	634

Disposals

	$'000
Proceeds	98
PPE disposed	(75)
Profit on sale	23

3 *Interest paid*

	$'000
Balance b/d	33
Finance costs	19
	52
Cash paid (balancing figure)	(46)
Balance c/d	6

4 *Income taxes paid*

	$'000
Balance b/d	90
Income tax charge	104
	194
Cash paid (balancing figure)	(94)
Balance c/d	100

5 *Interest received*

	$'000
Balance b/d	9
Interest received in statement of comprehensive income	5
	14
Cash received (balancing figure)	(10)
Balance c/d	4

6 *Share capital issue*

	Share capital	Share premium
	$'000	$'000
Bal b/f	300	92
Share issue for cash	30	30
Bonus issue ($\frac{1}{10} \times 330$)	33	(33)
	363	89

Question 4

Marking scheme

			Marks
(a)	Goodwill calculation		2
(b)	**Consolidated statement of comprehensive income**		
	Revenue	1½	
	Cost of sales	2	
	Distribution costs	1	
	Administrative expenses	1½	
	Tax	1	
	Profit for the year	1	
			8
(c)	**Consolidated statement of financial position**		
	Goodwill	1	
	Property, plant and equipment	1	
	Inventory	1½	
	Trade receivables	1½	
	Bank	1	
	Share capital	1	
	Retained earnings	2½	
	General revenue	1½	
	Trade payables	1½	
	Dividend payable	1½	
	Presentation	1	
			15
	Total		25

(a) Calculation of goodwill

	$	$
Consideration transferred		34,000
Net assets acquired		
Share capital	30,000	
Share premium	500	
Retained earnings	1,500	
		32,000
Goodwill		2,000

(b) (i) STRAW GROUP
CONSOLIDATED STATEMENT OF COMPREHENSIVE INCOME
FOR THE YEAR ENDED 31 OCTOBER 20X5

	$'000
Revenue (235 + 85 – 16.8 (W1))	303,200
Cost of sales (140 + 52 – 16.8 + 1.44 (W1))	(176,640)
Gross profit	126,560
Distribution costs (12 + 5)	(17,000)
Administrative expenses (W2)	(53,160)
Profit before tax	56,400
Tax (13,250 + 5,000)	(18,250)
Profit for the year	38,150

(ii)   STRAW GROUP
CONSOLIDATED STATEMENT OF FINANCIAL POSITION AS AT 31 OCTOBER 20X5

	$'000	$'000
Assets		
Goodwill	800	
Property, plant and equipment (100 + 40)	140,000	
		140,800
Current assets		
Inventory (W4)	15,810	
Trade receivables (W5)	9,420	
Bank (3,500 + 2,570)	6,070	
		31,300
Total assets		172,100
Equity and liabilities		
Share capital	100,000	
Retained earnings (W8)	32,440	
General reserve (W7)	9,700	
		142,140
Current liabilities		
Trade payables (W6)	9,960	
Dividends	20,000	
		29,960
Total equity and liabilities		172,100

Workings

1   *Intragroup sale*

Sale price to be eliminated from consolidated revenue:

	$'000
Cost to Straw	12,000
40% mark up	4,800
Cost to Berry	16,800

Unrealised profit in inventory: $4,800,000 × 30% = $1,440,000

Gross profit   = $95,000,000 + $33,000,000 – $1,440,000
                        = $126,560,000

2   *Administrative expenses*

	$'000
Straw	45,000
Berry	8,000
Impairment of goodwill (W3)	160
	53,160

3   *Impairment of goodwill*

	$'000
Impairment at 1.11.20X4 (2,000 – 960)	1,040
Impairment during year (bal. fig.)	160
Impairment at 31.12.X5 (2,000 – 800)	1,200

4   *Inventory*

	$'000
Straw	13,360
Berry	3,890
Less unrealised profit (W1)	(1,440)
	15,810

5   *Trade receivables*

		$'000	$'000
Straw		14,640	
Less dividend receivable		(10,000)	
			4,640
Berry			6,280
Less intragroup			(1,500)
			9,420

6   *Trade payables*

	$'000
Straw	9,000
Berry	2,460
Less intragroup	(1,500)
	9,960

7   *General reserve*

	Straw	Berry
	$'000	$'000
Per question	9,200	1,000
Less pre-acquisition		(500)
		500
Share of Berry 500 × 100%	500	
	9,700	

8   *Retained earnings*

	Straw	Berry
	$'000	$'000
Per question	27,300	9,280
Less PUP	(1,440)	
	25,860	
Less pre-acqn.		(1,500)
		7,780
Share of Berry: 100%	7,780	
Impairment of goodwill (2,000 − 800)	(1,200)	
	32,440	

CIMA

Financial Pillar

F1 – Financial Operations

Mock Exam 3

Question Paper
You are allowed three hours to answer this question paper.
You are allowed 20 minutes reading time *before the examination begins* during which you should read the question paper and, if you wish, highlight and/or make notes on the question paper.
You are strongly advised to carefully read ALL the question requirements before attempting the question concerned (that is all parts and/or sub-questions).
You should show all working as marks are available for the method you use.
ALL QUESTIONS ARE COMPULSORY
Section A comprises of 10 sub-questions.
Section B comprises of 6 sub-questions.
Section C comprises of 2 questions.
The country 'Tax Regime' for the paper is provided on the next page.

DO NOT OPEN THIS PAPER UNTIL YOU ARE READY TO START UNDER EXAMINATION CONDITIONS

Country X – Tax regime for use throughout the examination paper

Relevant tax rules for years ended 30 April 20X7 to 20Y0

Corporate Profits

Unless otherwise specified, only the following rules for taxation of corporate profits will be relevant, other taxes can be ignored:

(a) Accounting rules on recognition and measurement are followed for tax purposes.

(b) All expenses other than depreciation, amortisation, entertaining, taxes paid to other public bodies and donations to political parties are tax deductible.

(c) Tax depreciation is deductible as follows:

- 50% of additions to property, plant and equipment in the accounting period in which they are recorded

- 25% per year of the written-down value (ie cost minus previous allowances) in subsequent accounting periods except that in which the asset is disposed of

- No tax depreciation is allowed on land

(d) The corporate tax on profits is at a rate of 25%.

Value Added Tax

Country X has a VAT system which allows entities to reclaim input tax paid. In country X the VAT rates are:

Zero rated	0%
Standard rated	15%

SECTION A – 20 MARKS

[Note: The indicative time for answering this section is 36 minutes]

ANSWER *ALL* TEN SUB-QUESTIONS IN THIS SECTION

Instructions for answering Section A:

The answers to the ten sub-questions in Section A should ALL be written in your answer book.

Your answers should be clearly numbered with the sub-question number and ruled off, so that the markers know which sub-question you are answering. **For multiple choice questions, you need only write the sub-question number and the letter of the answer option you have chosen**. You do not need to start a new page for each sub-question.

1.1 CR is resident in Country X. CR makes a taxable profit of $750,000 and pays an equity dividend of $350,000.

Equity shareholders pay tax on their dividend income at a rate of 30%.

If CR and its equity shareholders pay a total of $205,000 tax between them, what method of corporate income tax is being used in Country X?

A   The classical system
B   The imputation system
C   The partial imputation system
D   The split rate system   **(2 marks)**

1.2 Which ONE of the following is NOT a benefit of pay-as-you-earn (PAYE) method of tax collection?

A   It makes payment of tax easier for the tax payer as it is in instalments.
B   It makes it easier for governments to forecast tax revenues.
C   It benefits the tax payer as it reduces the tax payable.
D   It improves governments cash flow as cash is received earlier.   **(2 marks)**

1.3 In relation to a Value Added Tax (VAT) system, which ONE of the following would be classified as the formal incidence of VAT?

A   The entity submitting a VAT return and making payment to the tax authorities.

B   The date the tax is actually paid.

C   The person that pays a retail entity for the goods plus VAT.

D   A retail entity paying a wholesale entity for goods plus VAT.   **(2 marks)**

1.4 Which ONE of the following is NOT a reason for governments to set deadlines for filing tax returns and payment of taxes?

A   To enable governments to enforce penalties for late payments.

B   To ensure tax deducted at source by employers is paid over promptly.

C   To ensure tax payers know when they have to make payment.

D   To ensure that the correct amount of tax revenue is paid.   **(2 marks)**

1.5   UF manufactures clothing and operates in Country X. UF and ZF are both registered for VAT.

UF manufactures a batch of clothing and pays expenses (taxable inputs at standard rate) of $1,000 plus VAT. UF sells the batch of clothing to a retailer ZF for $2,875 including VAT at standard rate. ZF sells the clothing items separately to various customers for a total of $6,900 including VAT at standard rate.

Calculate how much VAT UF and ZF **each** has to pay in respect of the above transactions?   **(2 marks)**

1.6   An external auditor has completed an audit and is satisfied that proper records have been maintained and that the financial statements reflect those transactions. However the auditor has one disagreement with the management of the entity. The disagreement involves the treatment of one large item of expenditure that has been classified by management as an increase in non-current assets. The auditor is of the opinion that the item should have been classified as maintenance and charged as an expense to the statement of comprehensive income. The amount is material in the context of the reported profit for the year.

Assuming that the management refuse to change their approach, which ONE of the following modified audit reports should the auditor use?

    A   Emphasis of matter
    B   "Except for" qualification
    C   Adverse opinion
    D   Disclaimer of opinion   **(2 marks)**

1.7   TS purchased 100,000 of its own equity shares in the market and classified them as treasury shares. At the end of the accounting period TS still held the treasury shares.

Which ONE of the following is the correct presentation of the treasury shares in TS's closing statement of financial position in accordance with IAS 32 *Financial Instruments: Presentation*?

    A   As a current asset investment
    B   As a non-current liability
    C   As a non-current asset
    D   As a deduction from equity   **(2 marks)**

1.8   Which ONE of the following is NOT a topic included in the International Accounting Standards Board's (IASB) *Framework for the Preparation and Presentation of Financial Statements (Framework)*?

    A   The objective of financial statements
    B   Concepts of capital maintenance
    C   Regulatory bodies governing financial statements
    D   Measurement of the elements of financial statements   **(2 marks)**

1.9   Which ONE of the following would be regarded as a related party of Z in accordance with IAS 24 *Related Party Disclosures*?

    A   FG is Z's banker and has provided an extensive overdraft facility on favourable terms.
    B   JK is Z's principal customer, accounting for 60% of its revenue.
    C   MN is Z's marketing director who holds 20% of Z's equity shares.
    D   QR is Z's main supplier, supplying nearly 50% of Z's purchases by value.   **(2 marks)**

1.10   (Which ONE of the following is NOT included in the definition of an operating segment in accordance with IFRS 8 *Operating Segments*?

     A   A component of an entity that earns the majority of its revenue from sales to external customers.

     B   A component of an entity that engages in business activities from which it may earn revenues and incur expenses.

     C   A component of an entity whose operating results are regularly reviewed by the entity's chief operating decision maker, to make decisions about resource allocations and assess performance.

     D   A component of an entity for which discrete financial information is available.   **(2 marks)**

(Total for Section A = 20 marks)

Reminder

All answers to Section A must be written in your answer book.

Answers or notes to Section A written on the question paper will **not** be submitted for marking.

End of Section A
Section B starts on the next page

SECTION B – 30 MARKS

[You are advised to spend no longer than 9 minutes on each sub-question in this section.]

ANSWER *ALL* SIX SUB-QUESTIONS IN THIS SECTION – 5 MARKS EACH

Question Two

(a)   ZK is part of a group of entities and has traded profitably for a number of years. During the year to 31 August 20X9, ZK made a tax adjusted trading loss of $30,000 and a capital gain of $5,000. In the following year to 31 August 20Y0, ZK made a taxable trading profit of $10,000. ZK expects to increase taxable trading profits to $50,000 for the year to 31 August 20Y1. ZK does not expect any capital gains or losses in the year to 31 August 20Y1.

Required:

Explain FOUR methods that a Country can allow to relieve trading losses of an entity and **illustrate** the effect of each method on ZK for the years ended 31 August 20X9 to 20Y1.

(Total for sub-question (a) = 5 marks)

(b)   HW, an entity resident in Country X, owns 40% of the equity shares in SV, an entity resident in a foreign country, Country Y. For the year to 31 March 20Y0 SV had taxable profits of $12,500,000 and paid corporate income tax of $1,875,000. On 31 October 20Y0 HW received a dividend of $3,375,000 from SV, the amount received is net of tax of 10%.

Country X has a double taxation treaty with Country Y. The treaty provides for a group of entities to only be taxed once on each entity's profits. Credit is given for withholding tax and underlying tax paid in other countries, but no refunds are available if a higher rate of tax has been paid.

Required:

(i)   **Explain** the meaning of "withholding tax" and provide an explanation as to why countries levy "withholding" taxes.   *(2 marks)*

(ii)   **Calculate** the amount due to be paid by HW on receipt of this dividend in Country X. Show all workings.   *(3 marks)*

(Total for sub-question (b) = 5 marks)

(c)

Required:

Explain the FOUR qualitative characteristics of financial information specified in the IASB's *Framework*.

(Total for sub-question (c) = 5 marks)

(d)   HB paid $2.50 per share to acquire 100% of PN's equity shares on 1 September 20X9. At that date PN's statement of financial position showed the following balances with equity:

	$'000
Equity shares of $1 each	180
Share premium	60
Retained earnings	40

PN's net asset values were the same as their book values, except for land which was valued at $70,000 more than its book value.

HB directors estimate that any goodwill arising on the acquisition will have a useful life of 10 years.

Required:

(i)   **Calculate** goodwill arising on the acquisition of PN.   *(2 marks)*

(ii)   **Explain** how HB should record the goodwill in its group financial statements for the year ended 31 August 20Y0, in accordance with IFRS 3 *Business Combinations*.   *(3 marks)*

(Total for sub-question (d) = 5 marks)

(e)   HI, a parent entity, is planning to acquire a shareholding in ABC. The following alternative investment strategies are being considered:

(i)   HI can purchase 80,000 preferred shares in ABC

(ii)   HI can purchase 40,000 equity shares and 50,000 preferred shares in ABC

(iii)   HI can purchase 70,000 equity shares in ABC and no preferred shares

ABC has the following issued share capital:

	$
$1 Equity shares	100,000
$1 10% Preferred Shares	100,000

Holders of preferred shares do not have any votes at annual general meetings.

Required:

Identify with **reasons** how HI would classify its investment in ABC in its consolidated financial statements for each of the alternative investment strategies.

(Total for sub-question (e) = 5 marks)

(f)   MN obtained a licence free of charge from the government to dig and operate a gold mine.

MN spent $6 million digging and preparing the mine for operation and erecting buildings on site. The mine commenced operations on 1 September 20X9.

The licence requires that at the end of the mine's useful life of 20 years, the site must be reinstated, all buildings and equipment must be removed and the site landscaped. At 31 August 20Y0 MN estimated that the cost in 19 years' time of the removal and landscaping will be $5 million and its present value is $3 million.

On the 31 October 20Y0 there was a massive earthquake in the area and MN's mine shaft was badly damaged. It is estimated that the mine will be closed for at least six months and will cost $1 million to repair.

Required:

(i)   **Explain** how MN should record the cost of the site reinstatement as at 31 August 20Y0 in accordance with IAS 37 *Provisions, Contingent Liabilities and Contingent Assets.*   *(2 marks)*

(ii)   **Explain** how MN should treat the effects of the earthquake in its financial statements for the year ended 31 August 20Y0 in accordance with IAS 10 *Events after the Reporting Period.*

(3 marks)

(Total for sub-question (f) = 5 marks)

(Total for Section B = 30 marks)

End of Section B

SECTION C – 50 MARKS

[You are advised to spend no longer than 45 minutes on each question in this section.]

ANSWER *BOTH* QUESTIONS IN THIS SECTION – 25 MARKS EACH

Question Three

XB's trial balance at 31 October 20Y0 is shown below:

	Notes	$000	$000
Administrative expenses		185	
Cash and cash equivalents		216	
Cost of sales		237	
Distribution costs		62	
Donations to political party		5	
Entertaining expenses		12	
Equity dividend paid	(i)	50	
Interest paid	(ii)	3	
Inventory at 31 October 20Y0		18	
Land at cost – 31 October 20X9	(iii)	730	
Long term borrowings	(ii)		200
Ordinary Shares $1 each, fully paid at 31 October 20Y0	(iv)		630
Property, plant and equipment – at cost 31 October 20X9	(iii)	320	
Provision for deferred tax at 31 October 20X9			10
Provision for property, plant and equipment depreciation at 31 October 20X9	(v)		192
Purchase of property, plant and equipment during the year	(v)	110	
Retained earnings at 31 October 20X9			168
Revenue			690
Share premium at 31 October 20Y0	(iv)		99
Suspense	(vi)	3	
Taxation	(vii)	6	
Trade payables			77
Trade receivables		109	
		2,066	2,066

Additional information provided:

(i)   The final dividend for the year to 31 October 20X9 of $50,000 was paid on 31 March 20Y0.

(ii)   Long-term borrowings consist of a loan taken out on 1 May 20X9 at 3% interest per year. Six months loan interest has been paid in the year to 31 October 20Y0.

(iii)   At 31 October 20X9 the tax written down value of XB's assets was $90,000. None of these assets were fully depreciated at this date.

(iv)   XB issued 330,000 equity shares on 30 June 20Y0 at a premium of 30%.

(v)   Property, plant and equipment is depreciated at 20% per annum using the straight line method. Depreciation of property, plant and equipment is considered to be part of cost of sales. XB's policy is to charge a full year's depreciation in the year of acquisition and no depreciation in the year of disposal.

(vi)   Purchased goods, invoiced at $3,000 received in September 20Y0 were returned to the supplier in October. At 31 October 20Y0 the supplier had not issued a credit note. XB had correctly deducted the amount from purchases with the corresponding double entry posted to the suspense account.

(vii)   The balance on the taxation account is the income tax underestimated in the previous year's financial statements.

Required:

(a)   **Prepare** XB's statement of comprehensive income for the year to 31 October 20Y0, including a **calculation** of income tax expense.

(Note there are up to 8 marks available for the taxation computation)   *(14 marks)*

(b)   **Prepare** XB's statement of changes in equity for the year to 31 October 20Y0 **and** a statement of financial position at that date.   *(11 marks)*

All statements should be in a form suitable for presentation to the shareholders and in accordance with the requirements of International Financial Reporting Standards.

Notes to the financial statements are not required, but all workings must be clearly shown. Do not prepare a statement of accounting policies.

Note: Your answer should be to the nearest $000.

(Total for Question Three = 25 marks)

Question Four

The financial statements of YG are given below.

STATEMENT OF FINANCIAL POSITION AS AT:

	31 OCTOBER 20Y0		31 OCTOBER 20X9	
	$000	$000	$000	$000
Non-current Assets				
Property, plant and equipment	4,676		4,248	
Development expenditure	417		494	
		5,093		4,742
Current Assets				
Inventory	606		509	
Trade receivables	456		372	
Cash and cash equivalents	1,989		205	
		3,051		1,086
Total Assets		8,144		5,828
Equity and Liabilities				
Equity shares of $1 each		3,780		2,180
Share premium		1,420		620
Revaluation surplus		560		260
Retained earnings		1,314		1,250
		7,074		4,310
Non-current liabilities				
Long term borrowings	360		715	
Deferred tax	210		170	
		570		885
Current liabilities				
Trade payables	425		310	
Current tax	70		170	
Accrued interest	5		3	
Provision for redundancy costs	0		150	
		500		633
Total Equity and Liabilities		8,144		5,828

STATEMENT OF COMPREHENSIVE INCOME FOR THE YEAR ENDED 31 OCTOBER 20Y0

	$'000
Revenue	6,640
Cost of sales	(3,530)
	3,110
Administrative expenses	(2,040)
Distribution costs	(788)
	282
Finance cost	(16)
	266
Income tax expense	(120)
Profit for the year	146
Other comprehensive income:	
Gain on revaluation of property, plant and equipment	300
Total comprehensive income for the year	446

Additional information:

(i)   On 1 November 20X9, YG issued 1,600,000 $1 ordinary shares at a premium of 50%. No other finance was raised during the year.

(ii)   YG paid a dividend during the year.

(iii) Plant and equipment disposed of in the year had a net book value of $70,000; cash received on disposal was $66,000. Any gain or loss on disposal has been included under cost of sales.

(iv)   Cost of sales includes $145,000 for development expenditure amortised during the year.

(v) Depreciation charged for the year was $250,000.

(vi) The income tax expense for the year to 31 October 20Y0 is made up as follows:

	$'000
Corporate income tax	80
Deferred tax	40
	120

(vii) During the year to 31 October 20X9 YG set up a provision for redundancy costs arising from the closure of one of its activities. During the year to 31 October 20Y0, YG spent $177,000 on redundancy costs, the additional cost being charged to administrative expenses.

Required:

(a) **Prepare** a statement of cash flows, using the indirect method, for YG for the year ended 31 October 20Y0, in accordance with IAS 7 Statement of Cash Flows. *(20 marks)*

(b) Someone you have known for many years has heard that you work for YG, a well known international entity. There are rumours in the press that YG's latest share issue was to raise cash to enable it to launch a takeover bid for another entity. Your friend wants to treat you to dinner at an expensive local restaurant, so that you can give him details of the proposed takeover before it is made public.

Explain how you would respond to your friend. Your answer should include reference to CIMA's Code of Ethics for Professional Accountants. *(5 marks)*

(Total for Question Four = 25 marks)

End of question paper

Answers

**DO NOT TURN THIS PAGE UNTIL YOU HAVE
COMPLETED MOCK EXAM 3**

274

A plan of attack

This is the third mock exam, so you should now have a really good idea of what to expect in the real thing.

Your approach

As before, this paper has three sections. All sections, and all questions, are compulsory.

Question by question

Lets look at the Section B questions in the paper:

- Question (a) might have tripped you up a bit as trading losses don't often get examined. There was a lot to get down to answer this question fully, however you should make sure that you stick to timings, you only have 9 minutes to answer this question. Get down all the four methods of giving relief onto your paper, with lots of space after each one, then work on the illustrations. Remember that tax is 25% of your syllabus at F1 and will be thoroughly examined!

- Question (b) again is examining tax – this time international tax. The definition in part (i) should have been easy. For part (ii), even if you weren't sure how to work out the double tax relief, you should have been able to work out the underlying tax and the withholding tax. If not, go back and revise this topic.

- Question (c) is a pure knowledge test and you should have no problems scoring highly here.

- Question (d) was on goodwill, one of the two group accounts questions on the paper. The calculation of goodwill was fairly standard, but don't forget that fair value adjustment. If you did miss it out, you will have still picked some marks for the rest of your calculation. Don't be mislead by the 'useful life' of the goodwill in part (ii), IFRS 3 does not permit the amortisation of goodwill.

- Question (e) is the only other question on group accounts in the paper. At first the question may have appeared easy, however you may have found it tricky to work out the accounting treatment of each investment when you got into the detail. Remember the definitions of associate and subsidiary, and that shares need votes in order to count.

- Question (f) covers both provisions and events after the reporting period. For part (i), don't forget to use all the detail in the question, the present value is there for a reason and should jog your memory for the required accounting. For part (ii), you need to justify your answer using IAS 10 requirements for adjusting or non-adjusting events, as well as explain the treatment in the accounts.

For the section C questions, have a look at the top tips in the suggested solutions for how to tackle the question, what the easy traps to fall into were and where to pick up easy marks.

Marking the exam

Marking the MCQs is not too difficult. You only have 2 marks to award. In the longer questions, give yourself credit where you used the correct method, even if your answer was wrong.

Most important, list out all the items you did not know or got wrong, and **make sure you revise them**.

Remember

Always **allocate your time** according to the marks for the question in total and then according to the parts of the question. And **always, always follow the requirements** exactly.

You've got spare time at the end of the exam ... ?

If you have allocated your time properly then you **shouldn't have time on your hands** at the end of the exam. But if you find yourself with five or ten minutes to spare, **go back to the questions** that you couldn't do or to **any parts of questions that you didn't finish** because you ran out of time.

Forget about it!

And don't worry if you found the paper difficult. More than likely other candidates will too. If this were the real thing you would need to **forget** the exam the minute you leave the exam hall and **think about the next one**. Or, if it's the last one, **celebrate**!

SECTION A

Question 1

1.1   B   The imputation system

	Classical $	Imputation $
Tax on profits (25% x 750)	187,500	187,500
Shareholder:		
Dividend received		350,000
Tax at 30%	105,000	105,000
Less tax credit (350 x 25%)		(87,500)
Tax on dividend (30%)		17,500
Total tax due	292,500	205,000

1.2   C   The tax payable is the same if it is collected by PAYE or in one lump sum.

1.3   A   The **formal incidence** of a tax is on the person or organisation who has direct contact with the tax authorities.

1.4   D   A deadline will not help ensure the correct amount of tax is paid.

1.5   Net VAT due = output VAT – input VAT

	UF $	ZF $
Output VAT		
Standard rate		
($2,875 × 15/115)/($6,900 × 15/115)	375	900
Input VAT		
Purchases		
($1,000 × 15 %)/($2,875 × 15/115)	(150)	(375)
VAT due	225	525

1.6   B   The auditor should issue an audit report with a qualified opinion on the basis that the misstatement identified is material, but not pervasive to the financial statements. The audit opinion should be modified to include the phrase "In our opinion, **except for** the effects of the matter described in the Basis for Qualified Opinion paragraph, the financial statements present fairly, in all material respects ...."

1.7   D   Treasury shares are shown in the statement of financial position as a deduction from equity.

1.8   C   Regulatory bodies is not a topic discussed by the *Framework*.

1.9   C   MN is a related party of Z as MN is a member of the key management personnel of Z (marketing director), and also owns 20% of the equity of Z which is presumed to give MN significant influence over Z.

Note that IAS 24 states that the following are not necessarily related parties: a customer, supplier, franchisor, distributor or general agent with whom the entity transacts a significant volume of business, merely by virtue of the resulting economic dependence.

1.10 A   External revenue is only considered when determining **reportable** operating segments as at least 75% of total external revenue must be reported by operating segments.

SECTION B

Question 2

Marking scheme

		Marks
(a)	1½ marks available for each method plus illustration, up to a maximum of	<u>5</u>

Four methods for relieving **trading losses** are:

1   *Carry the loss forward against future trading profits*

	31.08.X9	31.08.Y0	31.08.Y1
	$	$	$
Trading profit/(loss)	(30,000)	10,000	50,000
Offset previous trading loss	–	(10,000)	(20,000)
Capital gain/(loss)	5,000	–	–
Taxable profit	5,000	–	30,000
Tax at 25%	1,250	–	7,500
Trading loss carried fwd	(30,000)	(20,000)	–

2   *Offset the loss against other income or capital gains of the same period*

The trading losses can be offset against the capital gains made by ZK in 20X9. In the illustration below, the trading losses remaining in 20X9 have also been carried forward to be offset against the trading profits of the following years. Some countries may not allow the remaining losses to be carried forward.

	31.08.X9	31.08.Y0	31.08.Y1
	$		$
Trading profit/(loss)	(30,000)	10,000	50,000
Capital gain/(loss)	5,000	–	–
Offset trading loss against capital gain/trading profit	(5,000)	(10,000)	(15,000)
Taxable profit	–	–	35,000
Tax at 25%	–	–	8,750
Trading loss carried fwd	(25,000)	(15,000)	–

3   *Carry the loss back against profits of previous periods*

Some countries, including the UK, allow trading losses to be carried back against the taxable profits of previous periods. If we assume that ZK made a taxable profit of $40,000 in 20X8, we can illustrate this method of relief as follows.

	31.08.X8	31.08.X9	31.08.Y0	31.08.Y1
	$	$	$	$
Trading profit/(loss)	40,000	(30,000)	10,000	50,000
Capital gain/(loss)	–	5,000	–	–
Carry back trading loss against profits	(30,000)	–	–	–
Taxable profit	10,000	5,000	10,000	50,000
Tax at 25%	2,500	1,250	2,500	17,500

4   *Offset the loss against the profits of another group company ('group loss relief')*

If ZK is part of a group of companies, then the trading loss made by ZK in 20X9 could be transferred to another company in that group and offset against the taxable profits of that company instead. For example, assume that ZK is the parent of ZL and ZL makes a trading profit of $40,000 in 20X9, the trading loss made by ZK could be offset as follows.

	ZK 31.08.X9 $	ZL 31.08.X9 $
Trading profit/(loss)	(30,000)	40,000
Transfer trading loss	–	(30,000)
Capital gain/(loss)	5,000	–
Taxable profit	5,000	10,000
Tax at 25%	1,250	2,500
Trading loss carried fwd	–	–

Marking scheme

				Marks
(b)	(i)	Explaining the meaning of withholding tax		1
		Explanation of why countries levy withholding tax		1
				2
	(ii)	Calculation – underlying tax		1
		Calculation – withholding tax		1
		Calculation – tax due		1
				3
		Total		5

(i)   A withholding tax is a tax levied on payments, such as interest payments, dividends and royalties, made by a company to another company or individual resident in another country.

Withholding taxes are levied because countries have no power to tax non-resident companies, so they charge withholding tax to ensure that they gain some income from the payments made by non-resident companies with operations in their country to overseas companies or individuals.

(ii)   Tax paid by SV on dividend

	$'000
Net dividend received	3,375
Withholding tax (3,375 × 10/90)	375
Gross dividend	3,750
Underlying tax (3,750 ×1,875/(12,500 – 1,875)	662
Total tax paid by SV on dividend	1,037

Tax due by HW

	$'000
Dividend received	3,375
Tax paid in Country Y	1,037
Gross dividend	4,412
Tax due in Country X (4,412 x 25%)	1,103
Double tax relief (restricted to $1,103)	(1,037)
Tax payable in Country X	66

Tutorial note: Underlying tax is calculated as follows:

$$\text{Underlying tax} = \text{gross dividend} \times \frac{\text{tax actually paid by foreign company}}{\text{foreign company's profit after tax}}$$

Marking scheme

		Marks
(c)	1½ marks available for each explanation, up to a maximum of	<u>5</u>

The four principal qualitative characteristics of financial information are as follows.

Relevance

Information is said to be relevant when it influences the economic decisions of users by helping them to evaluate past, present and future events or by confirming, or correcting their past evaluations. So relevant information has both a predictive and confirmatory role. The relevance of information is affected by its nature and materiality. Information should be released on a timely basis to be relevant to users.

Reliability

Information is reliable when it is free from material error and bias, and can be depended upon by users to represent faithfully that which it either purports to represent or could reasonably be expected to represent. Faithful representation of a transaction is only possible if it is accounted for according to its substance and economic reality, not with its legal form. The information should also be complete.

Comparability

The importance of comparability is that users must be able to compare the financial statements of an entity over time and to compare the financial statements of different entities. For this to be possible users must be informed of the accounting policies employed in the preparation of the financial statements and any changes in those policies and their effects. The financial statements must also show corresponding amounts for the previous period.

Understandability

The financial statement information should be readily understandable to users. For this purpose users are assumed to have a reasonable knowledge of business and economic activities and accounting and a willingness to study the information with reasonable diligence. A complex matter should not be left out of financial statements simply due to its difficulty if it is relevant information.

Marking scheme

			Marks
(d)	(i)	Goodwill calculation	2
	(ii)	Explanation of how goodwill is recorded, including IFRS 3 treatment	3
			<u>5</u>

(i) Goodwill arising on acquisition of PN

	$'000	$'000
Consideration transferred (2.5 x 180)		450
Share of net assets acquired		
Share capital	180	
Share premium	60	
Retained earnings	40	
Fair value adjustment	70	
		350
Goodwill		<u>100</u>

(ii) Treatment of goodwill in HB's group financial statements at 31 August 20Y0

- HB should record the goodwill in its consolidated statement of financial position under the caption 'Intangible non-current assets: goodwill arising on consolidation'.

- The goodwill should be initially recognised as the difference between the fair value of the purchase consideration and the fair value of the identifiable assets and liabilities, as calculated above.

- IFRS 3 does not permit amortisation of goodwill. Instead it should be tested for impairment at least annually. After initial recognition, goodwill is measured at the original amount less any accumulated impairment losses.

- Assuming there is no impairment at 31 August 20Y0, the goodwill should be included in the statement of financial position at the original amount calculated on acquisition of £100,000.

Marking scheme

		Marks
(e)	½ mark per valid point, up to a maximum of	5

(i) *80,000 preferred shares in ABC*

The preference shares in ABC do not have any voting rights attached to them so if HI purchased these shares, it would not have the power to control or exercise significant influence over the financial and operating policies of ABC. The investment should be classified as a simple non-current asset investment in the consolidated financial statements and should be accounted for in accordance with IAS 39.

(ii) *40,000 equity shares and 50,000 preference shares in ABC*

An investment in 40,000 equity shares would give HI a shareholding of 40%. As this is more than 20% of the voting power of ABC, it should be assumed that HI will have significant influence over ABC. ABC should be classified as an associate of HI and accounted for using the equity method in the consolidated financial statements of HI. The preference shares should be accounted for as a simple investment as per (i) above.

(iii) *70,000 equity shares*

An investment in 70,000 equity shares would give HI a shareholding of 70%, as this is more than 50% of the voting power of ABC, it should be assumed that HI will have the power to control ABC unless it can be clearly shown otherwise, however this is rare. ABC should be classified as a subsidiary of HI and consolidated on a line by line basis in the consolidated financial statements of HI.

Marking scheme

				Marks
(f)	(i)	Site reinstatement	– explanation of why provision required	1
			– inclusion of provision present value	$\frac{1}{2}$
				$\overline{\overline{2}}$
	(ii)	Earthquake	– explanation of why non-adjusting event	$1\frac{1}{2}$
			– treatment in financial statements	$1\frac{1}{2}$
				$\overline{3}$
		Total		$\overline{\overline{5}}$

(i)   *Site reinstatement*

IAS 37 requires that a provision for the costs of reinstating this site is set up immediately when the licence is obtained. This is because a legal obligation exists to reinstate the site at the date the licence is obtained. The provision should be the present value of the estimated costs to reinstate the site, so at 31 August 20Y0 this is $3m. The income statement should also include the unwinding of the discount on the fair value of the provision when it was first recorded in the accounts at 1 September 20X9 to 31 August 20Y0.

The costs of reinstating the site should be capitalised along with the costs of the buildings and equipment used in the mine.

(ii)   *Earthquake*

Assuming that the financial statements have not yet been authorised for issue, the earthquake is a non-adjusting event in accordance with IAS 10. This is because it is indicative of conditions that arose after the end of the reporting period.

No adjustments should be made to the financial statements at 31 August 20Y0 for this event and no provision for the repair costs should be included in the accounts at this date. The closure of the mine for six months and the repair costs of $1m means that the earthquake is likely to be a material event and as such should be disclosed in a note to the accounts at 31 August 20Y0.

SECTION C

Question 3

Text references. Preparation of single company financial accounts is covered in Chapters 4 to 12. Calculation of income tax on company profits is covered in Chapter 18 and deferred tax is covered in Chapter 19.

Top tips. The question specified that 8 marks out of 14 were available for the tax calculations, so this should have highlighted to you that tax was a major issue in part (a). Don't let this put you off though, you should still lay out your statement of comprehensive income proforma and work through the TB and the adjustments plugging in the figures to your proforma. This will give you the accounting profit figure required to then work out the income tax charge. Part (b) was a pretty straightforward preparation of a statement of financial position and a statement of changes in equity.

These errors were easy to make:

- Charging all tax depreciation at 25% instead of 50% for the new additions and 25% for the remaining balance

- Not recording the accrued interest payable on the long term loan in both the SOCI and the SOFP

- Incorrectly including the underprovision of tax in the tax payable balance in the SOFP or forgetting to include it in the SOCI tax charge

Easy marks. There were plenty of easy marks to be gained in this question by inserting all the numbers that didn't require calculation into the proformas, particularly in part (b). The time pressure may have got to you in this question though as there was a lot to do.

Marking scheme

		Marks
Statement of comprehensive income		
Sales revenue	½	
Cost of sales	1	
Distribution costs	½	
Administration expenses	½	
Other costs	½	
Finance cost	1	
Income tax expense	1½	
Presentation	½	
		6
Tax computation		
Accounting profit	½	
Add back: entertaining expenses	1	
political donation	1	
accounting depreciation	1½	
Less: tax depreciation	2	
Deferred tax	2	
		8
Total		14

Statement of financial position

Property, plant and equipment	½
Land	½
Current assets	1½
Share capital	½
Share premium	½
Retained earnings	½
Deferred tax	½
Long-term borrowings	½
Trade payables	½
Tax payable	1
Interest payable	1
Maximum of	7

Statement of changes in equity

Share capital	1
Share premium	1
Retained earnings	1½
Maximum of	3
Presentation	1
	11

Total marks for question	25

(a) XB STATEMENT OF COMPREHENSIVE INCOME FOR THE YEAR ENDING 31 OCTOBER 20Y0

	$'000
Revenue	690
Cost of sales (237 + 86 (W))	(323)
Gross profit	367
Distribution costs	(62)
Administrative expenses (86 + 125)	(185)
Other costs (12 + 5)	(17)
Profit from operations	103
Finance cost (3 + 3% × 200 × 6/12)	(6)
Profit before tax	97
Income tax expense (31(W) - 2(W) + 6)	(35)
Profit for the year	62
Total comprehensive income for the year	62

Working

Taxation

	$'000	$'000
Accounting profit		97
Add back: entertaining expenses	5	
political donation	12	
accounting depreciation (W2)	86	
		103
Less: tax depreciation (W2)		(78)
Taxable profit		122
Tax charge @ 25%		31

	Carrying value $'000	Tax base $'000
Cost	320	–
Depreciation 25%	(192)	–
Balance 31.10.X9	128	90
Additions	110	110
	238	200
Depreciation (20% x (320 + 110))	(86)	–
Tax depreciation ((110 x 50%) + (90 x 25%))	–	(78)
Balance 31.10.Y0	152	122

*Deferred tax at 31.10.Y0 = (152 – 122) × 25% = $7,500, round to **$8,000***

Decrease in deferred tax balance = $8,000 - $10,000 = $2,000

Note. The question specifies working to the nearest $'000.

(b)   XB STATEMENT OF FINANCIAL POSITION AS AT 31 OCTOBER 20Y0

	$'000	$'000
Assets		
Non-current assets		
Land	730	
Property, plant and equipment (a)	152	
		882
Current assets		
Inventory	18	
Trade receivables	109	
Cash and cash equivalents	216	
		343
Total assets		1,225
Equity and liabilities		
Equity		
Share capital	630	
Share premium	99	
Retained earnings	180	
		909
Non-current liabilities		
Long-term borrowings		200
Deferred tax (a)		8
Current liabilities		
Trade payables (77 – 3)	74	
Tax payable (a)	31	
Interest payable (3% x 200 x 6/12)	3	
		108
Total liabilities and equity		1,225

XB STATEMENT OF CHANGES IN EQUITY FOR THE YEAR ENDING 31 OCTOBER 20Y0

	Share capital $'000	Share premium $'000	Retained earnings $'000	Total $'000
Balance at 1.09.X9	300 (bal.fig)	0 (bal.fig)	168	468
Issue of share capital	330	99	–	429
Dividends	–	–	(50)	(50)
Total comprehensive income for the year	–	–	62	62
Balance at 31.10.Y0	630	99	180	909

Question 4

Marking scheme

			Marks
(a)	**Statement of cash flows**		
	Cash flows from operating activities		
	Profit before tax	1	
	Finance cost	1	
	Depreciation	1	
	Loss on disposal	1	
	Working capital adjustments - 1 each	3	
	Interest paid	1	
	Income taxes paid	1	
			9
	Cash flows from investing activities		
	Purchase of PPE	2	
	Proceeds of sale of PPE	1	
	Development expenditure	2	
			5
	Cash flows from financing activities		
	Proceeds from issue of share capital	1½	
	Repayment of borrowings	1	
	Dividends paid	1½	4
	Cash and cash equivalents		1
	Presentation		1
	Total		20
	Cash flows from operating activities		
(b)	½ mark per valid point for each strategy, up to a maximum of		5
	Total marks for question		25

Text references. Statements of cash flows are covered in Chapter 9. Ethics is covered in Chapter 3.

Top tips. This is question is very time pressured and you will probably have struggled to get all the figures into the statement of cash flows in the time allowed. However remember that you need to leave some time to address part (b) as you can pick up an easy 5 marks there. You must be logical in your approach to answering part (a) – set up the proforma, and insert the numbers that don't require adjustment first. Most of the adjustments (PPE, interest, tax, development) were pretty straightforward if you had practiced a few SOCF questions. The redundancy provision was a bit unusual, but if you keep in mind that you are showing cash movements, it wasn't too tricky to work out the extra amount to include in cash from operating activities.

Easy errors to make were:

- Getting the signs mixed up on the working capital adjustments
- Incorrect treatment of the redundancy provision
- Missing out the dividend paid
- Not including the revaluation of PPE in the PPE working

Easy marks. The question gave you amortisation, depreciation and cash received on disposal of PPE, you should have inserted these straight into your proforma to get some quick easy marks. Writing sensible comments in part (b) would get you 5 easy marks.

(a)   YG STATEMENT OF CASH FLOWS FOR THE YEAR ENDED 31 OCTOBER 20Y0

	$'000	$'000
Cash flows from operating activities		
Profit before taxation	266	
Finance cost	16	
Depreciation	250	
Loss on disposal of PPE (66 - 70)	4	
Amortisation of capitalised development expenditure	145	
Decrease in redundancy provision	(150)	
Operating profit before working capital changes	531	
Increase in inventory (W1)	(97)	
Increase in receivables (W1)	(84)	
Increase in payables (W1)	115	
Cash generated from operations	465	
Interest paid (W2)	(14)	
Income taxes paid (W3)	(180)	
Net cash from operating activities		271
Cash flows from investing activities		
Purchase of property, plant and equipment (W4)	(448)	
Proceeds of sale of property, plant and equipment	66	
Development expenditure (W5)	(68)	
Net cash used in investing activities		(450)
Cash flows from financing activities		
Dividend paid (W6)	(82)	
Repayment of long term borrowings (715 – 360)	(355)	
Proceeds from issue of shares (1,600 + 800)	2,400	
Net cash from financing activities		1,963
Net decrease in cash and cash equivalents (1,200 – 150)		(1,784)
Cash and cash equivalents at 31 October 20X9		205
Cash and cash equivalents at 31 October 20Y1		1,989

Workings

1   *Inventories, trade receivables and trade payables*

	Inventories	Trade receivables	Trade payables
	$'000	$'000	$'000
Balance b/d	509	372	310
Increase (balancing figure)	97	84	115
Balance c/d	606	456	425

2   *Interest paid*

	$'000
Balance b/d	3
Finance costs	16
	19
Cash paid (balancing figure)	(14)
Balance c/d	5

3   *Income tax payable*

	$'000
Balance b/d – current tax	170
Income tax charge	80
	250
Cash paid (balancing figure)	(180)
Balance c/d – current tax	70

4   *Property, plant and equipment*

	$'000
Balance b/d	4,248
Revaluation	300
Disposals	(70)
Depreciation	(250)
	4,228
Cash paid for additions (balancing figure)	448
Balance c/d	4,676

5   *Development expenditure*

	$'000
Balance b/d	494
Amortisation	(145)
	349
Cash paid (balancing figure)	68
Balance c/d	417

6   *Retained earnings*

	$'000
Balance b/d	1,250
Profit for the year	146
	1,396
Dividend paid (balancing figure)	(82)
Balance c/d	1,314

(b)   *Ethical issues*

I should not accept the dinner invitation as this may cause me issues with **objectivity** as I will feel pressure to reveal information that I should not disclose about the proposed takeover.

Revealing information about the proposed takeover before it is made public would be unethical. It would give my friend 'insider information' about the proposed takeover, which he could then use to his advantage to make money on buying or selling shares in either entity, which is illegal.

Giving this information to my friend would breach the fundamental principle of **confidentiality** in the CIMA Code of Ethics. The information I have obtained in my role as a professional accountant at YG should not be shared with third parties unless there is a legal or professional right or duty to disclose, there is neither in this case. The information I have obtained should also not be used for the personal advantage of myself or third parties, there is a risk it might be in this case.

If my friend used this 'insider information' to make a personal gain, which is illegal, this would breach the fundamental principle of **professional behaviour** in the CIMA Code of Ethics which requires that a professional accountant should comply with the law.

MATHEMATICAL TABLES

290

PRESENT VALUE TABLE

Present value of $1 ie $(1+r)^{-n}$ where r = interest rate, n = number of periods until payment or receipt.

Periods (n)					Interest rates (r)					
	1%	**2%**	**3%**	**4%**	**5%**	**6%**	**7%**	**8%**	**9%**	**10%**
1	0.990	0.980	0.971	0.962	0.952	0.943	0.935	0.926	0.917	0.909
2	0.980	0.961	0.943	0.925	0.907	0.890	0.873	0.857	0.842	0.826
3	0.971	0.942	0.915	0.889	0.864	0.840	0.816	0.794	0.772	0.751
4	0.961	0.924	0.888	0.855	0.823	0.792	0.763	0.735	0.708	0.683
5	0.951	0.906	0.863	0.822	0.784	0.747	0.713	0.681	0.650	0.621
6	0.942	0.888	0.837	0.790	0.746	0.705	0.666	0.630	0.596	0.564
7	0.933	0.871	0.813	0.760	0.711	0.665	0.623	0.583	0.547	0.513
8	0.923	0.853	0.789	0.731	0.677	0.627	0.582	0.540	0.502	0.467
9	0.914	0.837	0.766	0.703	0.645	0.592	0.544	0.500	0.460	0.424
10	0.905	0.820	0.744	0.676	0.614	0.558	0.508	0.463	0.422	0.386
11	0.896	0.804	0.722	0.650	0.585	0.527	0.475	0.429	0.388	0.350
12	0.887	0.788	0.701	0.625	0.557	0.497	0.444	0.397	0.356	0.319
13	0.879	0.773	0.681	0.601	0.530	0.469	0.415	0.368	0.326	0.290
14	0.870	0.758	0.661	0.577	0.505	0.442	0.388	0.340	0.299	0.263
15	0.861	0.743	0.642	0.555	0.481	0.417	0.362	0.315	0.275	0.239
16	0.853	0.728	0.623	0.534	0.458	0.394	0.339	0.292	0.252	0.218
17	0.844	0.714	0.605	0.513	0.436	0.371	0.317	0.270	0.231	0.198
18	0.836	0.700	0.587	0.494	0.416	0.350	0.296	0.250	0.212	0.180
19	0.828	0.686	0.570	0.475	0.396	0.331	0.277	0.232	0.194	0.164
20	0.820	0.673	0.554	0.456	0.377	0.312	0.258	0.215	0.178	0.149

Periods (n)					Interest rates (r)					
	11%	**12%**	**13%**	**14%**	**15%**	**16%**	**17%**	**18%**	**19%**	**20%**
1	0.901	0.893	0.885	0.877	0.870	0.862	0.855	0.847	0.840	0.833
2	0.812	0.797	0.783	0.769	0.756	0.743	0.731	0.718	0.706	0.694
3	0.731	0.712	0.693	0.675	0.658	0.641	0.624	0.609	0.593	0.579
4	0.659	0.636	0.613	0.592	0.572	0.552	0.534	0.516	0.499	0.482
5	0.593	0.567	0.543	0.519	0.497	0.476	0.456	0.437	0.419	0.402
6	0.535	0.507	0.480	0.456	0.432	0.410	0.390	0.370	0.352	0.335
7	0.482	0.452	0.425	0.400	0.376	0.354	0.333	0.314	0.296	0.279
8	0.434	0.404	0.376	0.351	0.327	0.305	0.285	0.266	0.249	0.233
9	0.391	0.361	0.333	0.308	0.284	0.263	0.243	0.225	0.209	0.194
10	0.352	0.322	0.295	0.270	0.247	0.227	0.208	0.191	0.176	0.162
11	0.317	0.287	0.261	0.237	0.215	0.195	0.178	0.162	0.148	0.135
12	0.286	0.257	0.231	0.208	0.187	0.168	0.152	0.137	0.124	0.112
13	0.258	0.229	0.204	0.182	0.163	0.145	0.130	0.116	0.104	0.093
14	0.232	0.205	0.181	0.160	0.141	0.125	0.111	0.099	0.088	0.078
15	0.209	0.183	0.160	0.140	0.123	0.108	0.095	0.084	0.074	0.065
16	0.188	0.163	0.141	0.123	0.107	0.093	0.081	0.071	0.062	0.054
17	0.170	0.146	0.125	0.108	0.093	0.080	0.069	0.060	0.052	0.045
18	0.153	0.130	0.111	0.095	0.081	0.069	0.059	0.051	0.044	0.038
19	0.138	0.116	0.098	0.083	0.070	0.060	0.051	0.043	0.037	0.031
20	0.124	0.104	0.087	0.073	0.061	0.051	0.043	0.037	0.031	0.026

CUMULATIVE PRESENT VALUE TABLE

This table shows the present value of $1 per annum, receivable or payable at the end of each year for n years

$$\frac{1-(1+r)^{-n}}{r}.$$

Periods (n)	1%	2%	3%	4%	Interest rates (r) 5%	6%	7%	8%	9%	10%
1	0.990	0.980	0.971	0.962	0.952	0.943	0.935	0.926	0.917	0.909
2	1.970	1.942	1.913	1.886	1.859	1.833	1.808	1.783	1.759	1.736
3	2.941	2.884	2.829	2.775	2.723	2.673	2.624	2.577	2.531	2.487
4	3.902	3.808	3.717	3.630	3.546	3.465	3.387	3.312	3.240	3.170
5	4.853	4.713	4.580	4.452	4.329	4.212	4.100	3.993	3.890	3.791
6	5.795	5.601	5.417	5.242	5.076	4.917	4.767	4.623	4.486	4.355
7	6.728	6.472	6.230	6.002	5.786	5.582	5.389	5.206	5.033	4.868
8	7.652	7.325	7.020	6.733	6.463	6.210	5.971	5.747	5.535	5.335
9	8.566	8.162	7.786	7.435	7.108	6.802	6.515	6.247	5.995	5.759
10	9.471	8.983	8.530	8.111	7.722	7.360	7.024	6.710	6.418	6.145
11	10.368	9.787	9.253	8.760	8.306	7.887	7.499	7.139	6.805	6.495
12	11.255	10.575	9.954	9.385	8.863	8.384	7.943	7.536	7.161	6.814
13	12.134	11.348	10.635	9.986	9.394	8.853	8.358	7.904	7.487	7.103
14	13.004	12.106	11.296	10.563	9.899	9.295	8.745	8.244	7.786	7.367
15	13.865	12.849	11.938	11.118	10.380	9.712	9.108	8.559	8.061	7.606
16	14.718	13.578	12.561	11.652	10.838	10.106	9.447	8.851	8.313	7.824
17	15.562	14.292	13.166	12.166	11.274	10.477	9.763	9.122	8.544	8.022
18	16.398	14.992	13.754	12.659	11.690	10.828	10.059	9.372	8.756	8.201
19	17.226	15.679	14.324	13.134	12.085	11.158	10.336	9.604	8.950	8.365
20	18.046	16.351	14.878	13.590	12.462	11.470	10.594	9.818	9.129	8.514

Periods (n)	11%	12%	13%	14%	Interest rates (r) 15%	16%	17%	18%	19%	20%
1	0.901	0.893	0.885	0.877	0.870	0.862	0.855	0.847	0.840	0.833
2	1.713	1.690	1.668	1.647	1.626	1.605	1.585	1.566	1.547	1.528
3	2.444	2.402	2.361	2.322	2.283	2.246	2.210	2.174	2.140	2.106
4	3.102	3.037	2.974	2.914	2.855	2.798	2.743	2.690	2.639	2.589
5	3.696	3.605	3.517	3.433	3.352	3.274	3.199	3.127	3.058	2.991
6	4.231	4.111	3.998	3.889	3.784	3.685	3.589	3.498	3.410	3.326
7	4.712	4.564	4.423	4.288	4.160	4.039	3.922	3.812	3.706	3.605
8	5.146	4.968	4.799	4.639	4.487	4.344	4.207	4.078	3.954	3.837
9	5.537	5.328	5.132	4.946	4.772	4.607	4.451	4.303	4.163	4.031
10	5.889	5.650	5.426	5.216	5.019	4.833	4.659	4.494	4.339	4.192
11	6.207	5.938	5.687	5.453	5.234	5.029	4.836	4.656	4.486	4.327
12	6.492	6.194	5.918	5.660	5.421	5.197	4.988	4.793	4.611	4.439
13	6.750	6.424	6.122	5.842	5.583	5.342	5.118	4.910	4.715	4.533
14	6.982	6.628	6.302	6.002	5.724	5.468	5.229	5.008	4.802	4.611
15	7.191	6.811	6.462	6.142	5.847	5.575	5.324	5.092	4.876	4.675
16	7.379	6.974	6.604	6.265	5.954	5.668	5.405	5.162	4.938	4.730
17	7.549	7.120	6.729	6.373	6.047	5.749	5.475	5.222	4.990	4.775
18	7.702	7.250	6.840	6.467	6.128	5.818	5.534	5.273	5.033	4.812
19	7.839	7.366	6.938	6.550	6.198	5.877	5.584	5.316	5.070	4.843
20	7.963	7.469	7.025	6.623	6.259	5.929	5.628	5.353	5.101	4.870

Notes

Notes

Notes